W9-BXT-270

STEALING

HOME

Stealing Home

ISRAEL
BOUND AND
REBOUND

HAIM
CHERTOK

FORDHAM
UNIVERSITY
PRESS
NEW YORK

For My Mother and My Father

The life in us is like the water in the river. It may rise this year higher than man has ever known it, and flood the parched uplands; even this may be the eventful year, which will drown out all our muskrats. It was not always dry land where we dwell.

Henry David Thoreau

Each man is obligated to give life to his own being by modeling his personality upon the image of the prophet; he must carry through his own self-creation until he actualizes the idea of prophecy—until he is worthy and fit to receive the divine overflow.

Rabbi Joseph B. Soloveitchik

CONTENTS

ACKNOWLEDGMENTS

Most of *Stealing Home* first appeared as separate articles in various journals. Quite apart from the vagaries of the Israeli postal system, it always seemed to me a small miracle when weeks or sometimes months after submission would arrive at my small Negev home either an acceptance or the returned manuscript, the latter usually accompanied by words of thoughtful response. Naturally, I preferred the acceptances, but without the check and flow of professional criticism, I would not have continued and this book would not have been. I wish to acknowledge my debt to all those editors at the other end of the post who almost unfailingly have been generous with their advice and measured praise.

My particular thanks to Alex Berlyne, Joel Carmichael, Mitchell Cohen, Helen Davis, Leonard Fein, J. J. Goldberg, Dr. Robert Gordis, Amnon Hadary, Aron Hirt-Manheimer, Marion Magid, Mordecai Newman, Reginald T. Roberts, Hanan Sher, Zelda Shluker, Marc Silver, Alan M. Tigay, Yehudit Wade, Dr. Ruth B. Waxman, Asher Weill, Joy Weinberg, and Trude Weiss-Rosmarin.

In somewhat different versions, then, you may have already encountered portions of *Stealing Home* in *Commentary, Forum, Growing Without Schooling, Hadassah, Israel Scene, Jewish Frontier, The Jerusalem Post, Manasseh, Midstream, Moment,* and *Sh'ma.*

I must reserve my most profound appreciation for two persons whose help has been powerfully sustaining: George Fletcher at Fordham University Press with whom it has been a delight to work, and my wife, Marcia, who has lived it all twice.

INTRODUCTION
TEN YEARS
AFTER ALIYA
The Risky Longshot and

The Dying Certainty

What sustained us in our bitter exile was the thought of the Land. When we forgot about settling in the Land, we ourselves were forgotten like the dead. Hearts stopped yearning for the Land, imagining that they had found a new Land of Israel and a new Jerusalem. They completely forgot that they were in exile, and they mixed with the people among whom they lived and learned their ways, finally assimilating into them.

Rabbi Yaacov Emden (1697–1776)

A commonplace: when over 20 years ago my wife and I named our first child Jennifer, we suffered from no notion that we were expressing anything more than our parental prerogative: we liked the name. Yes, following Jewish custom, we coyly struck the J-note of Joseph, the name of my father's father who had died five years earlier, but we did not dally long over the burden that the name carried forward the theme of some vital tradition any more than we long reflected on its Hollywooden lilt. We just liked the name; we were incurious *why*.

Five years later in California, Jennifer encountered a bevy of other Jennifers in her kindergarten class. Not even Tracy could rival our J-tag for popularity, was more trendy, was more "American." At first, I was merely bemused at this curiosity. Later, I can recall that I felt a vague uneasiness, an inner distress I was scarcely able, at the time, to identify. In short order, however, it passed.

In our mid-30s, disguised to ourselves as tourists, we first touched down in Israel. It was early in the winter of 1974. Not long contemplated, the excursion was to all appearances adventitious, the sheerest of fortunate flukes. At the time, one of Fresno's two congressmen happened to be a lawyer named Krebs, till then the only Israeli-born representative ever to serve in Washington. Since we lived in a rural part of Fresno County, he was not actually *our* congressman, but, naturally enough, we maintained a keen interest in his doings.

One Krebsian doing in particular came to affect the very course of our lives. Bypassing the usual bureaucratic channels of the Sister City Program, Krebs, it seems, had arranged directly with the Israeli Consul in San Francisco for agribusiness capital Fresno to serve as adoptive sister city to Afula, a much smaller municipality that is, nonetheless, the agricultural marketing center of the Galilee. A secondary link: both locales are probably best known as mid-way, stopover points between other destinations: Los Angeles and San Francisco, Tel Aviv and the Sea of Galilee. The better to inaugurate the new connection, an official 8-day trip to Israel for Fresno dignitaries was scheduled for shortly after Thanksgiving.

As the time of the sororial expedition approached, an embarrassment as thick as the San Joaquin Valley winter fog settled over the Fresno Jewish community. Among others, the traveling party would embrace Fresno's dapper Mayor Wills (together with Mrs. Wills), a liberal city councilwoman (and her mother), and a conservative newspaper publisher. It seemed, however, that all the more likely participants from the Jewish community—the big givers, the mainstays of the businessworld—would not commit themselves to accompany the Mayor. With the onset of the Christmas shopping season, the timing was, well, inopportune. In fact, as I learned one morning after teaching a Sunday School class at Fresno's Temple Beth Israel, though the trip would be highly subsidized—a real bargain—not one person among the 2,000 or so Jews of Fresno had indicated a readiness to go.

No one!

Neither Marcia nor I had ever before visited Israel. We decided that it was an opportunity not lightly to be dismissed. We had, of course, not the faintest suspicion that the ensuing weeks would result in the derailment of our most deeply-held American certainties, that within 20 months we and our two children would be snaffled into a one-and-a-half–room dormitory-apartment at an immigrant absorption center (*mercaz klita*) in Beersheba and rolling our tongues over daily classes in Hebrew.

All that was not merely unpredictable. It was inconceivable. I was shortly to become English Department Chairman at my college; Marcia was halfway through her term as a member of our local school board. We had already contacted the authorities about adopting a child to join our nuclear family of four. Surely we were content and involved in our California lives, were we not?

Yet, reflecting backward from the present, the matter seems virtually transparent, the pattern bold. Had we not for years been carrying on a flirtation, at stretches a lively dalliance, with Shabbat and *kashrut*? Yet at the same time, there was the paradoxical counter-pattern. Had I not chosen a Jesuit university at which to matriculate, a (non-practicing) Methodist to wed, the Anti-War Movement as my closest community, Thoreau and Melville as my daily professions, and a nearly *judenrein* California town as my last-stand, longest-run American home?

For nearly 20 years of his adulthood, I can perceive a familiar figure fleeing with distaste from the "vulgarity" and "shallowness" he came to anticipate from repeated encounters with organized Jewish life, yet, almost perversely, incapable of writing it all off as a bad debt. The course of this extended affair was devious, contradictory, and mostly subterranean. In time, however, something had to give. That center would not firm up indefinitely.

It now seems to me likely that the footing of perhaps most American Jews of my generation has been tentative indeed. My intuition is that slippage for most has now passed beyond the point of retrieval. I am aware, of course, that not all observers of the American Jewish scene concur in that judgment. A good many commentators and "professional Jews," in recent years most notably men such as Rabbi Jacob Neusner and Charles E. Silberman, never seem to flag in trumpeting the resilience of contemporary American Judaism. Indeed, its very Renaissance!

This harsh lullaby is no harmless puffery. It is a self-induced croon that lulls our very instinct to survive. One wonders what the hundreds of undergraduate Jewish Studies courses dealing with Jewish history conclude about the earlier Diaspora apparitions of "revitalized interest in Judaism"? Was not, say, the Buber and Rosenzweig flourish in pre-war Germany, a late bloom, inflated in impact well beyond its true proportions and played out against a communal background of indifference and Jewish deanimation? Can we not distinguish grim reality from blips and epiphenomena, deviations from the longest-running black comedy in Western history—*Galut*?

Of course "America is different," but at its most salient point of departure from Spain, Germany, Poland, South Africa, and the dozen other temporarily commodious homelands it is most lethal. America bears for its Jews a guilelessly insidious, truly remarkable gift of absorptivity. No other host culture has ever made it quite so easeful for us to jettison our Jewishness; no other has posed such a disingenuous but genuine threat to our inner viability. Indeed, America is not generally perceived by its Jews as a host culture at all. It is of us, hide and bone.

To be sure, an exaggerated counterflow has propelled small numbers of American Jews, many of whom like myself could easily have tipped into Jewish ghostliness, in the direction of self-renewal. For only a trickle, however, has the recoil embraced the sticky logic of *aliya*, and only a fraction of these few have felt the contrapuntal beat of both enhanced religious observance and *aliya*. In short, much as this light tide is welcome, its minuscule proportions warrant the clearest iteration.

In 1983 I made a first (and last) trip from Israel to the United States as an "emissary." My mission was to attract Jewish college students to study for full credit at a small, experimental college in my Negev town. My expectations were hopeful but modest. A mere ten recruits would have made my trip worth the while. Disregard the merits or shortcomings of that particular program; accept that, at the least, it offered "an experience" that could fairly rival backpacking in Anatolia or guruhopping in Nepal. Grant as well that, after 20 years of learning and teaching at various American campuses, I was no neophyte. This was my scene. Moreover, prior to my departure, hundreds of letters were sent to old friends, colleagues, useful contacts, and Hillel rabbis. The path was greased.

I went to Queens, I went to Brown; I spoke at Ann Arbor, I spoke at Berkeley; I visited U.C.L.A., I visited the University of Arizona. For three non-stop weeks I kept at it daily. Despite the burgeoning of Jewish Studies Programs, on campuses containing upwards of 5,000 Jewish students, Hillel Foundation rolls generally counted between 200 and 300, at the most 25 of whom were "activists." Had I teaching positions in Israel to offer, three times could I have hired despairing Hillel rabbis!

There were no bright spots. And who, despite the self-congratulatory asseverations to the contrary, is not already aware of this real situation? As Rabbi Arthur Hertzberg, one of the most acutely honest observers of our American Jewish "condition," has frequently noted, young Jews have long since found their parents out. They have acted accordingly. The overwhelming majority of them are not likely to attain even this generation's degree of Jewish insensateness. Such, it seems to me, is the shape and texture of the Jewish future in America.

But still, American life is so comfortable and beguiling. During our Israeli pleasure jaunt, what striking occurrence took place to alter our lives so dramatically? Just this: five days into our swing through museums, restaurants, archaeological sites, and hotels, in the lobby of Jerusalem's Diplomat Hotel, I stopped to buy some picture postcards. To my amused consternation, except for the two great mosques of the Old City, every last card I could find displayed Christian holy places. It seems that the hotel was hosting a convention of Evangelicals; indeed, we had met several of them from Oklahoma and Missouri the evening before. I chose a few cards, but I then asked the elderly clerk, a Jew in his late 60s, whether he did not have some "Jewish postcards" as well.

He glanced at me briefly, reached behind his counter to retrieve some cards depicting Jewish sites in Jerusalem, then fixed me with his eye.

"You are a Jew. [I nodded.] You live in America, yes? [A second nod, followed by a lengthy pause as if he measured the depths of his presumption before proceeding in an unclerkmanlike manner.] Excuse my asking, young man, but please, I really would like to know what it is that you do in America that is so important to keep you from returning home to Israel to live? I truly do not understand. We are still too few. It is good that you visit, but we badly need more Jews living here in Israel. It is so very, very important."

I stood in silence a lengthy minute and finally offered a foolish smile. I did not have to answer his *chutzpah* with anything, of course. Was this his business? Still, nothing I could think to respond did not sound hopelessly fatuous to my own ears. Should I explain that I taught American and English literature; that I was an explicator of poems; that I assigned, read, and corrected the papers of semestrial waves of students: that this too was a life?

I said nothing. It was all so hopelessly besides the old clerk's mark. Who could deny that creating and maintaining a reborn Israel was the most vital Jewish enterprise of this age or of any age for two millennia? What, then, *were* Jews doing elsewhere? It was suddenly transparent that the Californian life I would shortly be returning to meant in reality distancing myself from what is indisputedly most central to being Jewish in our times, to being a spectator and a critic rather than participant and creator. How could I justify that decision to myself?

Indeed, is not almost all that is touched by organized Jewish life in the United States already so richly Americanized that, no matter what is offered up—or pretended to be delivered—what is covertly lived, is, in reality, *just an alternative path to assimilation?* My private landscape is littered with Jewish assimilationship debris: old classmates, former activists and friends, family. Denizens of Boston and Ann Arbor, Seattle and Manhattan, California and Chicago, many fine, humane, creative persons. Successful scholars, doctors, artists, musicians, mystics—only as Jews are they shipwrecks. Typically, they never prepare notes for insertion in bottles for us other survivors (stragglers?) to ponder. There is, in reality, no need. The stories would be repetitious, boring; it is all implicit in the basic American bargain.

It is not pleasant to contemplate the wondrous perversity of over 99% of the major post-Holocaust remnant of the world's Jews choosing *not* to dwell in the Jewish State. Orchestrating the fanfare in aging, fatigued, zero-pop replenishment American Jewish community is none other than Maestro Thanatos.

As for Israel, it has been for ten years both my home and the idea of home. Despite the wearying, grinding minutiae of its day-to-day, in spite of its emotional toll, for me it remains History's, Destiny's, God's proposal for reconciliation and an extenuation for roundups, mockery, mute degradation, and the screaming white curl of chimney smoke. Israel is, to be sure, a World Almanac reality: a functioning democratic state with a substantial complement of non-Jews within its borders. At the same time it is an emendation of history. The conceptions vie, but both are served.

The generous bags we brought to our Levant homeland were packed with premises that I sense will always set us apart. Yes, I complained of having reclined into American crannies, but here—an immigrant—I will never quite fit at all. Hebrew will always prickle my tongue. To a sensibility contoured elsewhere, this new homeland often seems irremediably quirky, intrusive, and ofttimes illiberal. Unexpectedly, my personal price for sharper transcendent focus has turned out to be, both politically and even culturally, residency on the sidelines—on the margins—more than was the case in America!

I had prepared myself in 1976 to spend the rest of my life, as I did my first three months in the country, loading chickens into trucks and professing the mysteries of greenhouse tomatoes and flowers. Such was not to be. Looking back over the decade, however, I have produced more that pleases me than I could contrive over the previous 15 years in America. I am convinced that a parallel case would prevail for many other American Jews who feel for themselves that their losses would be too great. Our losses, personal and communal, creative and Jewish, have been egregious and irreplaceable.

In Thoreau's idiom, these, then, are my decade's accounts. It should be amply clear, I think, that my quarrel with America was never that it could not or would not accommodate me as an individual. On the contrary, America is delectably hospitable—practically porous. No, for us Jews the problem posed by American Materio-Individualism—that sweetest idolatry—is neither prejudice nor even mild resistance. It is that America ineluctably presses its thumb on the scales against our specifically Jewish survival. Not as lawyers or consumers but only as Jews does America bury us alive. It issues no challenge to our legitimacy. There is no need. The issue in America has been our perdurability in such an easeful climate. The tendency of some observers to confound the former for the latter seems to me a grievous, perhaps a fatal error.

For the main current, American Jewry is inexorably winding down. Those who perceive this and who can get untracked from suicidal self-indulgence have an honorable, indeed, an urgent option. That prescription of classical Zionism—"either liquidate the Diaspora or the Diaspora will liquidate you"— has not been outmoded by some spurious New World dispensation. On the contrary, though Israel remains even now a risky enough longshot, for its Jews America offers a gentling, narcotic certainty. Sure as death.

Our two younger children, born-in-Israel Yishai and Miriam, are now nine and seven. Jennifer and Ted, who ten years ago accompanied us on this adventure, are now 21 and 19. Jennifer studies engineering at Ben-Gurion University in Beersheba. Our removal to Israel has restored to "Jennifer" that unacknowledged hint of panache that originally we must have intended in her naming. Ted is a *hesdernik*, a *yeshiva* student–soldier. I anticipate they will surpass most of my own immigrant devilments.

Some things, however, remain constant: Yishai and Miriam each has several classmates who answer to the same name. This time around, we are neither surprised nor dismayed.

PART ONE.

AMERICA'S
CHARIOT
WINGING AT
MY BACK

Then all the realtors,
Pickpockets, salesmen, and the actors performing
Official scenarios,
Turned a deaf ear, for they had contracted
American dreams.

Louis Simpson
(from "Walt Whitman at Bear Mountain")

Beyond! Beyond! Beyond was "the city," connected only by
interminable subway lines and some old Brooklyn–
Manhattan trolley car rattling across Manhattan Bridge. . . .
Beyond was anything old and American—the name Fraunces
Tavern repeated to us on a school excursion. . . . Beyond! It
was the clean white bread in the A&P that Passover week I
could not eat matzoh, and going home, hid the soft squunchy
loaf of Ward's bread under my coat so that the neighbors
would not see.

Alfred Kazin
(A Walker in the City)

*J*ewish America rolls over me on the airwaves, via airmail, and, during their limited ground time, in the person of Stateside visitors to Israel. It is, of course, indelibly implanted in me as well. I never have tried out a sabra impersonation here in Israel. What a comic failure it would be! If once I thought that by leaving the actual scene I could surpass acerbity, I was mistaken. Distanced, however, America is easier to control, less virulent, and sometimes even subject to imaginative transformation. Physical departure and perspective are my primary vehicles in this process; ruminating in prose, especially, strategically isolated from "Anglo-Saxon" Israel, in *English* prose, has been genuinely helpful. With it all, America, far more than it endears, remains for me a mine field that endures. I enter her compulsively but with the greatest care.

SECRET

FAULTS

The 7:00 o'clock news report in English that spills forth from Kol Yisrael every morning is heralded by a brassy fanfare, a *hora* that conjures up disparate images of *kibbutz halutzim* encircling an evening campfire and latterday tourists in odd caps cavorting like the natives. Too often that musical measure sounds the brightest riff of the ensuing quarter-hour. Still, like virtually everyone here in Israel—sixth generation Jerusalemite and born-again newcomer alike—Marcia and I are addicted to our twice daily news fix. It was different ten years ago when we lived fortified in the ranch-style world of California's San Joaquin Valley. In those days the most appalling news would spot the horizon, perhaps tentatively shadow our lives, but always touch down somewhere else. We could with equanimity miss the news, for it could be depended upon to return the favor.

The hour is poor for concentration. Latest dispatches surface amidst the ceaseless chatter of our two schoolage children: inflationary percentages, political infighting, a bomb blast or casuality. A wry look or exclamation must suffice for commentary between us, the rest deferred—but not on the morning of May 3, 1983. By 7:01 we were immediately aware that far more for us than for any other Israelis, the lead item was exploding with shocking force.

Our perfunctory shushing of the kids grew loud and urgent. Even the outbreak of war could not have dazed us more. A major earthquake had struck Central California. We abandoned breakfast and hovered over our radio like disoriented morning moths. The locale hardest hit was Coalinga, a mapdot of 6,000 some 60 miles southwest of Marcia's hometown of Fresno. Hundreds of houses were reported damaged; the brick buildings of "downtown" were in shambles; dozens of fires raged; scores of townsfolk were injured.

Our eyes sought each incredulously. *Coalinga!*

Remote, bucolic Coalinga, the America our two teenagers best recall, for nearly seven years our last home in America, *Coalinga* was the epicenter of the day's headline fury. Had we been tantalized with a report of Begin and Arafat secretly convening in Nepal or of the Messiah revealing himself in New Zealand our amazement could not have been more profound. All day we could not really fathom it, but there it raged that evening on television, a lengthy filmclip from one of the American networks: buildings razed, neighbors in tents, the Red Cross, a sea of distraught faces. How we peered into that little gray screen for a flick of the familiar; how raveled our twisted skein of fear and sense.

We had first arrived in Coalinga in 1969 at the end of our three-year, ever-narrowing tunnel of counter-educational, antiwar activism in New York City where I co-directed Bensalem, an experimental college fathered by Fordham University. Exhilaration, despair, and constant embattlement had exhausted us both, and teaching English at a small college pocketed in the California foothills not far from hometown Fresno seemed the remedy for burnout. A year earlier we had vaguely toyed with the idea of cutting out for Israel, with *aliya*—that exotic new word—but it had not been, we were aware, a genuinely serious notion. No, our focus would shift to raising our two preschoolers, tomatoes, chard, and our spent spirits. Emerson repeatedly offers an apt tidal metaphor for the longer phases of our lives: we were ebbing out. But after a 3,000-mile journey into the sun, we felt refreshed and ready to wade into our new lives in classic American fashion.

Coalinga is Gothic American-Western. It saddles a low plateau above the first range of hills of California's great central valley—the San Joaquin. Undulating hills to the north, east, and south are leased by Shell, Standard, and Texaco (locally, formerly Getty)—a field producing diminishing returns of oil and revenue to support the local schools, hospital, and other services. The problem has been chronic for some decades, but still hundreds of grasshopper-type oil rigs—some gaudily Disneyed up as kangaroos and rabbits—jigger back and forth in an endless, purgatorial dance marathon. The "oil people" constitute one of the important social groupings who run the town.

Twelve miles to the east, where the highway rises to cross the ribbon of Sacramento–to–L.A. interstate, the vast Harris feedlot hosts about 50,000 head of cattle, well more than can be numbered in all of Israel. With their thousands of acres and livestock, the ranches of the American West overstimulate and overwhelm the popular Israeli imagination for whom *Dallas* still reigns as a supreme appetitive metaphor. Whereas most ranchhands are housed on the nearby ranches, some of the owners have family homes in Coalinga; several, in fact, were our immediate, Yale Avenue neighbors. They are a small but mightily influential segment of "Old Coalinga" stock.

In addition to these there are the Fifth Street business and real-estate people, the Anglo working folks (many of whom have family ties, take summer trips, to Oklahoma or Tennessee), the college people, other teachers, retirees, and the 10% or so Chicanos. Most outlying Valley towns are predominantly Chicano, but Coalinga has always been mainline Anglo, its origins and fortunes fueled by energy rather than grapes and melons. The various groups interact largely among themselves, save for some commingling at the Catholic and outreach churches (especially the Mormon), civic extravaganzas like Horned Toad Derby Day and the weekly or bi-weekly conclaves of men and lady Moose, Elks, Rotarians, and Lions. Though we over the years discovered that more former Jews and Jewish descendants could be found within the town's churches than we had any notion of initially, with one exception none of Coalinga's four Jewish families in this period was active or affiliated in any of these organizations.

Depending upon the sophistication of the observer, we "real" Jews were pegged somewhere along a scale between heathen intellectuals and variant Seventh Day Adventists. In actuality, together with our erstwhile brethren and sustren, we four families struck not merely a vertical slice of Coalinga's middle-class possibilities but, it seems to me in retrospect, a

reasonably just representation of the generality of Jewish fulfillment in America at large. We make, I think, for an instructive if melancholy panorama.

From Chicago, a couple two decades our senior I'll call the
Gersteins had landed in Coalinga a few years before us. A talented violinist (and chess player), Sol taught music at the
college but felt himself greatly undervalued by the town's provincial, tone-deaf yahoos. Their son, married to a British non-
Jew, is an expatriate who lives in London and communicates
infrequently. During our second year in town their daughter, a
promising artist, returned ill from Europe and, at the age of
30, tragically, unexpectedly died, leaving in her wake a permanent residue of sadness.

The Gersteins' attitude toward their Jewishness was a compound of bitterness and pride. More than once Sol described
the puerility of his childhood religious education, of how
when once he asked his rabbi-*melamed* what this *mizbaiach*
was that he kept referring to, the old man paused, stared,
squared off an imaginary artifact with his hands, and finally
spluttered: "A *mizbaiach* is . . . uh . . . a *mizbaiach.*" Gerstein never did inquire further into the question, and to that
day did not know what a *mizbaiach* was. They did not attend
either synagogue in Fresno; nor did Sam absent himself from
college classes on Rosh Hashanah and Yom Kippur. After
some years of noting that I as a matter of course excused myself
from teaching on these holy days, he similarly requested the
administration to be excused. When hit by some flak, he complained bitterly of anti-Semitism.

Often, especially in our last years in Coalinga, the nearby
Gerstein home would be the object of our Shabbat afternoon
walk. A taciturn Eleanor served tea. I lost a game or two of
chess, and Sol would talk about their daughter (whose paintings hung on the walls and whose poetry I was helping to edit),
the idiot college administration, and, with increasing frequency, his puzzlement and disquiet with Judaism. Our mani-
festly accelerating commitment to Jewish observances posed
for him an implicit challenge but at the same time provided a
queer sort of comfort. He could not believe in the God Who
permitted the tragic death of his daughter, but neither would

he put aside his grievance against this God in Whom he disbelieved. My inevitable tack, which proposed putting aside matters of "belief" or "faith" and underscored that Judaism made few, if any, demands in that line, was persistent but maladroit. Along with a sprinkling of other college "intellectuals" and some musical companions in Fresno, we were among their closest friends.

The family I'll label the Zenders were "oil people" with a daughter and son slightly older than our own. An engineer specializing in pipelines, Stan is a refugee from Germany (via Shanghai) who speaks with an accent that must have sounded remarkable to the ex-Arkies and Oakies with whom he worked. Myrtle, a diminutive but forceful woman, came from Connecticut. She made no pretense of enjoying a life in the sticks. The couple seemed as heavily committed to psycho-emotional self-improvement disciplines as to Judaism; making major claims for both procedures, they transcendentally meditated and family-retreated. For much of our time in Coalinga, their children and ours attended Sunday School together, first at Fresno's conservative synagogue, later (when its Sunday School was terminated) at Fresno's reform temple. Generally, we and the Zenders took turns driving round-trip on alternate Sundays. Unlike our social encounters with the Gersteins, we rarely discussed Judaism with Stan and Myrtle.

For most of these seven Coalinga years, the Chertoks, the Gersteins, and the Zenders gathered together annually for a Passover seder, during Hanukkah, and even occasionally during Sukkot. Since the Gersteins and Zenders tended to quarrel with each other, and the Chertoks became increasingly fussy about *kashrut*, our joint celebrations petered out toward the end. All three families, though for quite different reasons, grew restive with life in Coalinga.

Contemporaries of the Gersteins, the fourth Jewish family—let's call them the Berliners—was "old-time" if not quite mainline Coalinga. Patricians, they kept aloof from the town's "Jewish community." Born and raised in Coalinga, Al Berliner operated the town's largest clothing store; it had been established by his grandfather. This merchandising Jewish element in the smalltown American South and West is now fading but was not uncommon. Once in Tombstone, Arizona on a drive through the Southwest we were astonished by the number of Cohens and Levys marked on a building map of the business district as it was in the 1880s that hangs on the wall of a local museum. But the story is just as true of San Francisco. At least in the West, Jews were numbered among the first of the first families.

Berliner's wife was, like Myrtle Zender, an import from the East. Always amiable, almost courtly in their store, the Berliners never once either extended or accepted an invitation from any of the other Jewish families in Coalinga. We heard rumors that they celebrated Passover with out-of-town relatives, also that one of their sons had spent some time in Israel, but in reality knew little about them for certain. Berliner attended Rotary but not either Fresno synagogue.

Such was the minuscule, stable, visible Jewish community of Coalinga of the 1970s. During the seven years we served as its mainstay and hub, Marcia and I felt the continual tug of contrary forces which ultimately proved sworn antagonists. While we were acutely conscious of them both, we did not at the time appreciate how much the kick of one was virtually a function of the bite of the other.

One motion drew us centripetally: variously viewed, we were digging in, settling down, or selling out. During the summer of 1970, our first Coalinga vacation, we had traveled to "alternative communities" from Tolstoy Farm in southeast Washington State to a women's commune in Lake County, California. By midway through seven years, though we still would spend a long weekend at a War Resisters' League gathering on the Monterey Peninsula and journey to San Francisco to join antiwar demonstrations in Golden Gate Park, our serious involvement in Counter-America had plummeted. A fair measure of this may be gathered by noting that one summer vacation included a writing teachers workshop in Maine, another an educational workshop in Arizona, occasions I earlier (and later!) would have disdained. But they went with the territory we were staking out.

Slowly gathering momentum all the while, however, was a counter-spiral motion powered by an intensifying assertion of latent Jewishness. I am now certain that we would never have moved so precipitously, when move we did, in this direction had not the temptations posed by Coalingahood been so profound. The strains had been quiescent during our three-year stay in New York that preceded Coalinga, but then New York never did exercise on us any serious attraction. No, only in Coalinga did these counter-movements, like the subterranean plates that undergird our earth's seemingly solid surface, grind for a sustained period past each other. When in the event our lives were jolted—and we jilted Coalinga—it startled us nearly as much as anyone.

Our natural element in Coalinga was reformist. After paying my dues sufficient to attain tenure, I headed, in turn, the Faculty Senate, the English Division, and the teachers union chapter where the good fight was waged against the Administration dragons. Outside of college, I chaired (to my present chagrin) the area's McGovern Election Committee, and Marcia and I sparkplugged an independent Citizens Action Committee that initiated the coalition between area liberals and Chicanos. We also organized the Central Valley's first chapter of Amnesty International and a citizens clean-environment group. All this activity led to Marcia's successful bid for election to the local school board. In short, we had secured a mildly eccentric (if scarcely radical) niche in the town's civic life, in the process, of course, buoying our social lives.

We spent hundreds of pleasantly satisfying hours gardening, painting, and puttering in order to transform our house into our own image. We were neighborly. A room was added. We took the children for extensive camping trips to British Columbia and New Mexico. They joined scouts. We bought a vacation house on the Morro Bay coast. Our children were in good schools. Indeed, Coalinga, America had delivered the goods. It provided precisely the safe, stable, attractive fresh beginning we had sought when in 1969 our VW bug had nosed west out of New York City. We were settling snugly into the golden landscape. Almost . . .

What the devil was wrong? It was *us*. It was only as Jews that we felt restive, and increasingly so as our kids moved along in their schooling. We joined and after a time abandoned each of

Fresno's Jewish congregations. We grew so dissatisfied that one year we had resort for the High Holidays to a small synagogue in San Luis Obispo 90 miles away! When during our final two years in Coalinga Fresno's conservative congregation hired a more learned rabbi, we rejoined, but in order that our children would encounter *some* Jewish playmates, we continued, despite our misgivings, taking them to the Reform Sunday School. By then we no longer drove our car on Shabbat, so synagogue affiliation or even attendance was strictly speaking academic anyway. Jewishly, our situation was unsatisfactory.

Looking back, our gradual accretion of *mitzvot* in the fastness of California's coastal foothills seems a small miracle of perversity. In our seasonal jaunts 200 miles north to the Bay Area, our fixed poles were the Berkeley bookshops and the Oakland kosher butcher. Returning, the hood of our Volkswagen would be stocked with a 3-month hoard of frosty chickens, roasts, and paperbacks. We disengaged our phone each Friday afternoon, an act of subscriber disloyalty in which the phone company never acquiesced, and we fashioned each week our separate world of Shabbat. Friends came to know that we were out of bounds, and after a day of intensive involvement with the children, ironically much the greater because of our Jewish isolation than occurs here in Israel, Jennifer, Ted, and I would search the dusky sky for the three stars which signaled *havdalah*, TV, telephone, and Coalinga-time.

There was another, more private, manifestation. Once a month Marcia and I made a mysterious excursion to a secluded turnout in the narrow highway ten miles west of town where a mountain brook's cold, cold waters pooled darkly into a serviceable *mikveh*. My final step, as well I recall, was the "beanie" I began sporting to teach my literature classes. Not since my self-conscious beanie-wearing days as a college freshman in 1954 did headcovering assume such weighty significance. But my timing was fortunate: just then the black athletes had taken to wearing their own version of piquant headgear. My *kippa* was, well, fashionable!

What an odd family on the Coalinga scene were the Chertoks! True, we *were* distressed by ". . . Born is the King of Isra-el" caroled by our children in the elementary schools. True, our Jewish observance *was* increasingly separating us from the usual round of social intercourse. But we thoroughly enjoyed so much about our heart-of-the-country life that I suspect we ultimately could have navigated over the social difficulties and sustained all the obvious tensions past the critical point of psychic retreat had we not been joltingly confronted by mounting evidence, both quick and dead, of its deep-seated insupportability.

Coalinga then had three lawyers. We had some early dealings with two, but only encountered the third, whom I'll call Jeff Franklin, after some years. Franklin, I was informed, was a Jew who had married an Episcopalian. His wife, his children, and he himself were now communicants at the local church. Friendly, quiet, "nice," he seemed openly interested in meeting socially. We invited the Franklin family to our home for Friday night dinner. It was a sad blunder. Their daughter blurted a few questions about our strange doings with the candles and wine. Our response elicited giggles. Mrs. Franklin was stony. Franklin had apparently negotiated his separate peace many years before. We embarrassed him. We all ate rapidly. To everyone's relief, they left early.

Somehow the dismay this teapot fiasco stirred in me was all out of proportion to the banality of such an ordinary occurrence on the American scene. Well, what, after all, had I expected? There we were, far from the center ring, performing the high-wire act of sustaining ourselves as Jews in America— and we had long since determined that only the observance of *mitzvot* actively enhanced *our* Jewish well-being—and suddenly it was all too clear: the odds on one or another of us slipping were inordinate. If not in this generation, then in the next, or the next. And our specifically Jewish current would flow and merge into larger and wider channels of the receptive American sea until it disappeared without a trace. After the Franklins' departure, the cheers from the nearby football field, where "our" team must have scored a Friday night touchdown, crashed against the walls of Shabbat more intrusively than usual.

A few months thereafter we were taken aback by an item in *The Fresno Bee*. Fresno's retired Rabbi David Greenberg, an apostle of ecumenism who had achieved fame during the 1940s when his radio conversations with a priest and a minister were picked up by the networks and broadcast nationally, had officiated at a funeral in Coalinga. We were puzzled. How could we have known nothing of it? Dead at 91 was a Mrs. Zwang, widow of a major rancher in the area, matriarch of the Zwang family. I had taught what must have been her great or great-great grandson in one of my classes. He was a quiet young man who wore pointy cowboy boots and one prominent jeweled earring. Mrs. Zwang, we discovered, was the last Jew in her immediate family, the last for whom a rabbi would have to journey out to Coalinga to provide a Jewish burial. Her children and their descendants had long since filtered into a variety of local options.

I briefly recalled the Einlands, a prominent family of Fresno converts whose grandfather—formerly Einstein—had in the last century founded Fresno's largest local bank. There were dozens, perhaps hundreds, of others. A wan wayward thought: had we only known of her stubborn existence, we could have asked the old woman to a seder. Would she have come? Late for musings that no longer signified. Now her Jewish bones were laid to rest in the California foothills, and with startling, icy clarity, the deepest meaning of America for us, its Jews, declared itself nakedly: give it up! The rest was window-dressing. Give it up!

Two years later, we were *olim hadashim*, new immigrants in Israel.

Sol and Eleanor Gerstein today live in a more cosmopolitan California center where he successfully conducts the community orchestra. He recently arranged for an exhibition of his daughter's paintings. We occasionally correspond. He used to write about taking a trip to see us in Israel, but that was some time ago. It is now almost surely too late for that. The Zenders have also moved. They visited us in Israel for the first time just last Sukkot. Stan's aunt, a Holocaust survivor who lived half the year in Haifa, the other half in Germany, had died. There was her estate to attend to. The children we used to drive to Sunday school have graduated from college. For reasons other than our own, both the Gersteins and the Zenders were very happy to leave the town made briefly famous by disaster.

A few years ago we were surprised by an unannounced visit from the Berliners. On their first trip to Israel, enthralled with the country, they had persuaded their guide to track us down for a buoyant half-hour break in their busy tourists' schedule. Even before our *aliya*, he had sold his store and retired.

Thanks to a barrage of newspaper clippings that family and friends hit us with, we felt the unsettling rumble of aftershock for months after the quake. Unaware until years later when we learned from the Zenders that the Berliners too had departed from Coalinga, I combed all the clippings and photos for the mention of Al Berliner's name, a glimpse of his face. Nothing. Coalinga was abandoned to the Franklins, the Zwangs, and a number of others of attenuated Jewishness. A chastening thought: perhaps after all it is the Skokies and Teanecks that reflect aberrant, vestigial flashes of false Jewish vitality, like Haim Castorps skiing down an American magic slope, whereas parochial Coalinga—the Gersteins, the Zenders, the Zwangs, the Berliners, and, yes, the Chertoks—defines more acutely the visible range of Jewish response for the overwhelming majority of American Jewish families.

Coalinga's ruined downtown and low morale have, with the help of federal funds, been restored. In the last analysis, it almost surely does not really need any Jews at all.

"ALSO A JEW":
A CLIFFIE IN
BEERSHEBA

Without the self-righteous anger, the righteous passion of those faded years of Vietnam—who could have imagined how soon they would dim into nostalgia?—unhitching from the allure of America would have been inconceivable. As for Israel and *aliya*, they would have remained a dormant, inoperative, romantic twitch. The irony seems to me fine-tuned: whereas my own commitment to Jewish traditional observance flickered never so low as during activist years as an overage Student for a Democratic Society—though we kept and maintained a kosher communal kitchen for that year in City Island, we also more or less "skipped" the High Holidays—a radical delegitimization of mythological America was crucial before I could ever seriously entertain cutting out. Yet at the decade's decline into grim 1969, at the very logical moment when S.D.S. was violently imploding, adangle at our loosest ends, I with my wife and children turned not away but deeper into the clinging interior to the west.

That trip carried us along glittering, parallel tracks. It took us fully five years more to perceive that nowhere over the American rainbow would they converge in a manner which we could satisfactorily live with or justify. And yet *then* the final nudge, that adventitious jaunt in 1974 as the token Jews of Fresno to accompany Mayor Wills and the official party to Israel, stunned me when I fully realized just how primed I had grown to chuck my familiar, complacent American life, which since '69 I had persuaded myself I was accustomed to—indeed, grown reconciled with and even somewhat fond of.

It's unnerving. Though it is true that since moving to Israel we have encountered a few others whose lives have taken a similar path, not a single one of *our* former Jewish acquaintances in the Movement, most of whom are now surely successful professionals, have, as far as we know, ever bothered even to reject *aliya*.

During our final two years in America, I felt obliged periodically to write letters to *WIN*, the monthly publication of the War Resisters League to which for many years we had belonged and subscribed, in the self-appointed role of Israeli apologist. Although *WIN* printed every one of my missives, with the single exception of the time when Daniel Berrigan, s.j., declared himself "betrayed" when "lied to" by Yassir Arafat, apparently I alone of all *WIN*'s readers felt moved to object to a continual spate of anti-Israel, covertly anti-Semitic "evenhanded commentary." By the time of our 1976 departure, it had grown achingly clear that what was left of the Peace Movement had little use for Israel and even less for Judaism. By the very end we had written off as unsustaining and unfruitful communities both it and the body of American Judaism.

We determined that, if for ourselves prosy America was played out, we still had a quixotic, validating option to play. The aim was better to integrate our days with our dreams, to make of our lives a kind of seamless, seemly poem. Israel had made erratic music, but on the whole our intuition was sound. The chief illusion was to imagine that by leaving America I would be leaving her—not to speak of her poets and "progressives"—behind.

Graceless Ben-Gurion University of the Negev in Beersheba is the rawest of Israel's seven major institutions of higher learning, more, as has been frequently noted, than it can afford. Each of the low, sprawling buildings on Ben-Gurion's "New Campus" is a sharp-toothed, concrete pile that bears the names of sundry benefactors from the Diaspora. The purported *raison-d'être* of the entire enterprise is the development of the Negev; its coloration is pragmatic and technological gray.

Nevertheless, Humanities are not banished, and the univer-

sity, like all universities in Israel, suffers *two* Departments of
English. One, predominantly male, is a reasonable facsimile
of counterparts on medium-sized American campuses; the
other, "English as a Second Language," is in the main a female preserve and services a much more extensive corps of students. It was, according to the announcement, the former of
these which in November 1983 had invited Pulitzer Prize—
winning American poet Maxine Kumin "to lecture on poetry
and the creative process and read from her own works" to a
noontime gathering on a Wednesday in mid-November, all
courtesy of the American Cultural Center.

Aside from time to time coming across some poems of hers
in a stray periodical, I was unfamiliar with Kumin's work but
had a vaguely pleasurable impression of her as a writer. Opportunities of this sort do not abound in Beersheba. I decided to
attend.

Whoever made arrangements for her appearance knows his
university. I strolled past cavernous auditoriums and large lecture halls to arrive at a small, ordinary classroom in a remote
new arm of a concrete octopus. Spotting former colleague
Cynthia Codish, I plopped myself down among the 20 other
noontime attendees.

"What drew Kumin down here for her third city instead of
Haifa?" I asked my usually reliable source. According to the
announcement, the lady poet was to be lecturing in Israel for
only three days; in such instances, Beersheba ordinarily plays
the dummy to Israel's more established cultural centers.

"Horses," Cynthia countered. "She's into horses. After she
finishes with us, the p.r. people will be taking her to visit the
Negev Horse Farm."

The Negev Horse Farm! I had never heard of any Negev
Horse Farm, but before I could pursue this unexpected tack, a
trim, attractive woman in her mid-50s outfitted in a stylish
purple suit arose from the back row and strode to the front of
the classroom. The poet—horsewoman herself, she was apparently unfazed by the non-appearance of anyone from either
English Department to welcome and introduce her to the waiting audience. It took no more than a few minutes, however,
for Kumin to establish that she would be an articulate, alert,

even gallant lecturer. No smallish turnout would dampen her delivery, and we few implicitly conspired to compensate for our paltriness with heightened attention. A warm deal had been struck.

A matter of which all visiting lecturers to Israel may be certain—particularly Jewish, first-time visitors—is that whether their specialty is meteorology, poultry, or verse, an Israeli audience will take a lively secondary interest in their initial impressions of the place. Indeed, it *expects* a few reassuring words in that line; the briefest allusion will assuage this need. Kumin held aloft her latest volume of poems (her seventh; there are also five novels) and, though most of us present were American-Israelis and surely did not require it, she immediately launched into a detailed explanation of the aviation reference of her title—*Our Ground Time Here Will Be Brief.* She concluded that "it serves as a metaphor of sorts of the general human condition we all share."

Certain that I anticipated (and could appreciate) her rhetorician's strategy, I wore a cozy smile: that title would also serve the occasion as a rather less than universal metaphor enabling Kumin to proffer some words about the scant three or four days of ground time she had for lecturing and horsing around in the Promised Land. Perhaps something appropriate about the Israeli or Jewish condition—she *was* Jewish, after all, was she not?

I was mistaken. Dead wrong! Deliberately or unawares, this visitor had no intention, or at least not yet, of appeasing that sort of plebeian curiosity.

As though she were confronting freshmen on the first day of class, Kumin passed out four pages of faded mimeo, a long poem with a long title: "Lines Written in the Library of Congress After the Cleanth Brooks Lecture." She had, we knew from the announcement, served for two years as Consultant to the Library of Congress, and she proceeded to comment sardonically on the duties and limitations of that ambiguous role. Then, still before actually reading us the poem, there were allusions to demystify, the mise-en-scène to establish: a WATS-line, Lady Bird, "Cliffies."

"I'm a 'Cliffie,'" she coyly confessed. "Radcliffe was the

woman's counterpart to Harvard, the sister school. The Harvard men were the 'Harvies.' But that's all past now," she explained a bit wistfully. "Radcliffe has been absorbed by Harvard, lost its identity; it's all one university." As for Cleanth Brooks, the courtly literary critic whose "*Well-Wrought Urn* especially / poured a warm stream of wisdom / on my undergraduate past . . ." (as she would shortly read aloud in her poem), on that day of her poem's inspiration, lecturing on the previous 30 years in American literature, he had reached no further than Hemingway. "That wasn't *my* last 30 years in American literature, let me tell you," Kumin interjected with mock ferocity. "The only woman Brooks mentioned at all was Emily Dickinson!"

Brooks's lecture, especially his "three touchstones—history, time, personal identity"—had set her to musing. After six months of intermittent reflection, this poem had issued forth. Amply readied to comprehend, we waited patiently for Kumin to launch at last into what was, in fact, an intelligent, modulated reading of her poem. We followed attentively on our mimeo sheets. "Lines Written . . ." is a far-ranging, dour, heavily-topical rumination that deftly incorporates elements as diffuse as the poet's New Hampshire horse farm, her consultantship to the Library of Congress, public floggings in Pakistan, and nuclear irrationality. Its main unifying threads are disillusion and the development of the poet's sensibility: "When I was eighteen I believed in infinite perfectibility. . . . Now I believe in infinite depravity." She closed powerfully with a Yeatsian image of a world "inching toward Armageddon."

Close to the very end of the poem is embedded a single, passing note boding ethnicity, just one in a poem which muses self-consciously on "personal identity," and it made me start:

> the bomb Mr. Brooks
> in the furious grip
> of the Libyans
> the Iraqis Israelis Argentinians
> the bomb written large
> in the Domesday Book.

The reference sailed past without question or comment. After all, fair is fair. I may not *like* Israelis sandwiched, without even benefit of lettucy commas, between military dictatorships (she wrote before Argentina's turn toward President Alfonsín and democracy), but that Israel has the fixings for the bomb is hardly a secret. A late-arriving *New Yorker* from the summer had led off with "Town Talker's" droll commentary about an odd slippage of mind endemic among residents of Long Island's posh North Shore. Secluded from sight, the nuclear facility at Shoreham is blotted from the mind, its very "thereness" veiled in forgetfulness. But no one in Israel could overlook the import of the news that Syrian missiles based in Lebanon can now reach Dimona. In the Negev some 25 miles southeast of Beersheba, just outside of Dimona is housed the only Shoreham Israel has.

There are scarcely any Israelis who would not wish away the *need* for our Shoreham. Its existence, however, is not only an unsuppressed datum of our national consciousness, but, given our objective situation, produces far greater reassurance than anxiety. "Nukes" can clog thoroughfares in Amsterdam, Tokyo, and San Francisco with protest. But never yet in Tel Aviv! How can we Israelis, indeed how could I, a S.A.N.E. activist way back in the Steve Allen '50s, now be so detached or otherwise preoccupied? Is *that* what so irks Kumin by our "furious grip"?

The first question is easier to pursue. Simply, we *know* that we are safer with the bomb than without it. We are not disinterested; on the contrary, our concern is focused and personal. But whatever else divides Israel, the consensus on nuclear preparedness is certain. The reason is not that we cannot conjure forth an appropriate vision of disaster. It is that so readily we can. For all of its visitors possessing a shadow of sensitivity or curiosity, the Israeli attraction par excellence will always remain Yad Vashem.

Kumin's bracketing of Israel with Lybians and Iraqis is an irritation not merely because it obscures the fundamental truth about differences between our society and theirs; thereby, by the way, subverting one of the clarifying objectives of any good poem. It distresses not only because almost most Israelis would, given the chance, give the lie to the notion that this melancholy, equivocal "grip" on the bomb is more in anger than in sadness. No, it irks particularly because it is so gratuitous issuing from an American, an American Jew, and as an American Jewish poet's preachy selection for her host audience. Why, after all, is that angry hold so decidedly Third Worldly rather than a suavely French, frothily Russian, or pre-eminently American grip? (And yet is not Kumin a "progressive"?) How may one account for the seeming vulnerability of an American Jewish poet of stature to the implicit charge of parochialism had she omitted Israel from her band of irresponsible crazies? And what could one make of the insensitivity of this woman of charm, chic, and intellect drawing blood in a context that virtually debarred rejoinder?

Watching Kumin read, my real attention gradually itself withdrew from the reading and narrowed upon her. A wonderful column by Murray Kempton that I once had snipped and saved but not thought about in years instantaneously provided the focus. It was 1960, and Kempton was evaluating his contemporaries Kennedy and Nixon. As I recall, he hearkened back in the article to the late 1930s when he and all the friends he knew and cared about at New York's City College were passionately involved in round after round of Socialist and anti-Fascist activity. Where, Kempton wondered in 1960, were John F. Kennedy and Richard Nixon, his coevals, in those days of crisis? In London and Chapel Hill—making do, making it, making out. Nothing but circumstance really separated the two men, and no latter-day criteria proved for Kempton more telling. No, I did not *know* where committed Kumin was in the fall of 1967, but I did not recall seeing her face or hearing her voice among the poets and writers at the Pentagon March or anywhere else on the map of the '60s. In the context of her poem, the realization altered the nature of my attention.

As I say, however, the unpleasant reference—the entire poem, for that matter—passed with minimal comment, and Kumin moved on to a fascinating, well-honed explanation of how her dream life sometimes gives vent to her poems. One time she had dreamed about her father wearing a much out-of-character, garish necktie. Only later, in working out a poem, did she suddenly perceive that the polka-dotted tie served as a reverse, subterranean symbol for the understated but strong tie between father and daughter. It was a persuasive, even brilliant illustration, and her reading of the resulting poem was effective; I let slide my earlier annoyance. Anyway, what did I know about her "credentials"? Perhaps she had moved in activist circles outside of my own tight sphere? What perversity to allow a thoughtless, possibly even unintentional allusion to taint my pleasure in Kumin's work or performance!

What about her role as Consultant to the Library of Congress? A private person, she found neither being consulted on matters poetic by legislators nor shepherding fellow poets on public occasions especially congenial. She learned, however, as she related with relish, to make the most of it. In particular there was the coup of persuading her old friend and "another old Cliffie," Adrienne Rich, "America's most prominent Lesbian," to give a reading before the Library of Congress. Rich had turned down five or six earlier invitations on political grounds. She attracted an overflow crowd. (Quickly scanning the vacancies of that Beersheba classroom, I involuntarily winced. Kumin had a trick or two to learn.)

"The custodians of culture," Kumin was explaining with a smile, "were worried what all those women and street people would do in the Library of Congress. They decided to serve them only melted Kool-aid. No food! I insisted later that all future gatherings would be provided with real food to eat and drink." We were warming to her chipper recollection of the scene. "Adrienne, she's the mother of two grown sons, introduced herself by announcing, 'I am here as a poet and as a Lesbian.' That's like me saying, 'I am here as a poet and as a Jew.'" And what indeed could be richer than that?

Perhaps in unconscious emulation of crafty Robert Frost, for much of the ensuing hour she chose to project the persona of Kumin, the horse-fancying, New Hampshire farmer-lady, albeit tempered by Kumin, the lib-rad progressive (yes, she confessed, her thinking and practice had changed: whereas once she used to eschew politics in verse, now her poetry had become overtly "committed"). Nevertheless, surely more than was intended did we pick up hints and shards attesting the at-

tenuated Jewish ties of one Kumin, a daughter of Israel. And it
was on that score that our curiosity was most piqued.

In illustration of the quirks of the creative process, Kumin
chose a poem which had left her stymied half-through for over
three years, only virtually to write itself a resolution when it
was ready to come. She was very fond of this poem, which she
called "Shelling Jacob's Cattle Beans," a type of bean she
claimed to intercrop with corn on her farmstead.

And so she began to read aloud her poem, the opening lines
of which place the poet alone on her New Hampshire farm on
the very day of Rosh Hashanah industriously shelling Jacob's
cattle beans at her kitchen table. Somewhere toward the middle
rang some throwaway line about returning the ticket of her tradition. We listened attentively, carefully taking note of the moment the poet resumed writing after the lapse of three years.
Her point concerning the mysterious workings of the creative
imagination had been artfully made, but then Kumin inquir-
ingly looked toward us and paused.

Did anyone here happen to know the origin of the peculiar
name of the striped beans? For years she had puzzled over why
they were called *Jacob's* cattle beans. It must have *something* to
do with the biblical patriarch.

A heavy, palpable hesitation filled the room. Then, shyly,
one, two, five hands tested the air. We all looked around. At
least a dozen others in the room, I would judge, also were familiar with Kumin's arcane allusion. She pointed toward an
elderly woman who politely suggested that the reference probably was to the Bible story of Jacob officiating over the conception and midwifery of sheep and goats with a striped rod, a
stratagem that God revealed to him so that he would acquire
much of Laban's flock for himself.

"Really?," the poet responded with delight. "I never knew
that. Right there in the Old Testament story!"

One of the young men called out from the side that it happened, by chance, to be recounted in that very week's portion
from the Torah, *Vayetze*.

"That's wonderful. Thank you. Thank you very much," exclaimed the former consultant to the Library of Congress. Her
smile was gracious, void of embarrassment. "I'd looked for that
everywhere."

I thought, "No, it's a put-on, a pedagogic ploy." I searched the expression of the woman in purple for a shadow of deception. There was none. As far as I could tell, she was genuinely grateful for the scrap of Torah. I looked around the room. The audience conspiracy had taken on an unexpected dimension: while Kumin exuded the pleasure of discovery, *we* sat in silent embarrassment for her.

Next to me Cynthia mildly inquired why the poem had begun with the telling fact that it was the very day of Rosh Hashanah. "After all," she noted, "it was also a Tuesday or a Wednesday. It's not just a neutral detail."

Kumin smiled, almost surely disingenuously, almost her only false note of the day. "But it really was Rosh Hashanah morning, and I really did happen to be all alone in my farmhouse."

"Yes," Cynthia pursued (more hotly, she later confided, than she had originally intended), "but you surely must have meant something more as well."

"True," rejoined a momentarily chastened Kumin. "You're right, I suppose. It was also a Tuesday, so I must have meant something more as well. But the main thing," she insisted, "is that it really did happen on that day."

A heavyset young man in a cordial though roundabout manner fashioned the question that was puzzling me (and surely many others): how did Kumin connect her Jewishness to her politics, her poetry, her career? (He skipped the countrywoman business.) It struck me that she could not possibly have been unprepared for a question of that sort.

"Well," Kumin began, "my Jewish consciousness almost usurped my early poetry. Then it disappeared for a long while. Now, in recent years, it has returned more strongly." She paused. "I'm not really in control of things like that."

Polite to a fault, no one pushed the matter any further. During her final forty minutes, Kumin again resumed her theme of the complementary satisfactions of rural life and of teaching at Princeton. She closed with a deft demonstration of how she seeks to teach her students to write passable poetry. "I aim to demystify the process. I'm convinced it is a skill that can be conveyed, at least in part, to any intelligent, willing person."

All things considered, Kumin was roundly appreciated by

our small, attentive circle. When last seen she was being taken in tow by a young woman from public relations to check out the horses of the Negev.

I have, however, since mulled much over some puzzling aspects of poet Maxine Kumin's brief ground time in Beersheba, and a number of questions stand unresolved. Would not it have occurred to patronized, superannuated, goyish Cleanth Brooks to locate the reference to Jacob's cattle beans in his Old Testament? Would that not have seemed an obvious recourse to some of her neighboring New Hampshire farmer neighbors? Surely my wife's grandfather, as well as many of her other rural Kansas kin, could as well as the occupants of that Beersheba classroom have determined how and where to decipher it. I have a hunch that this sharp Cliffie, this former consultant to literary legislators, has access to Proust in French, to Rilke in German. I suspect that a similar allusion in Sanskrit, Gaelic, or Urdu would have sent her as well as any willing, intelligent person scouring through her reference shelf. Is it not bizarre that *this* farmer—and Jew—never, despite her "curiosity," quite mustered the gumption to locate it in *B'reshit*—not to mention Genesis?

How is it that this poet, whose Jewish consciousness virtually usurped her early (less mature?) poetry, cannot quite determine or explain why one of her favorite poems begins with an image of herself, alone but industrious on Rosh Hashanah, shelling beans in her kitchen? Or why she chose to read *that* poem to her Israeli audience?

Perhaps it is true that we Israelis are inured, deaf, mute, blind, and paralyzed to the implications of the Bomb we so apologetically grasp. I think not, but given the limpness of the question here, I will, at least in a measure, grant the possibility. But Ms. Kumin, who is plainly a highly talented, thoroughly nice, feminist, Jewish-American, "committed" poet, is subject to the kind of slippage of mind that seems to me, especially among her fellow intellectuals, all too characteristic of New World shores. Only time will tell which failing proves the more egregious.

But finally something I owe directly to Kumin's mandate that we pay closer attention to our dreams, a discipline I normally scant: an unexpected bonus. Just a week after her lecture-reading I awoke in the morning charged with the following recollection which I put immediately to paper. On entering a French restaurant alone, I was met at the door by a dapper maître-d' who said, "Come in, come in, Monsieur." He seated me with éclat, snapped his fingers in the air, and walked off.

At once he was replaced by an elderly, shambling Jewish waiter of Ratner's classic vintage who hovered over my table. I pointed at the menu. The classic old waiter shook his head from side to side. I insisted. He frowned all the harder, then like a magician he produced his own shabby-looking, much-stained menu from behind his back. Just as he thrust it in my direction, the maître-d' reappeared with a pair of shears and, to my astonishment, sliced the old waiter's menu in half. I instantly arose and, surprising myself, snipped the elegant figure's black tie just below the knot. The old waiter threw me a wink, and I awoke to the sound of my own merry chuckling.

I wish that I could have snatched just a peek at the old man's menu. I don't, however, have to undertake a poem to guess that the *soupe du jour* was bean, or consult with a shrink or disturb a prophet to interpret the dream's significance to my own satisfaction. We may not, as Maxine Kumin suggests, be in complete control of things like that. Neither, however, do I believe us more passive than we really choose to be. Might it not be that Kumin overlooked something vital in Cleanth Brooks's address before the Library of Congress, a talk that began with an indwelling on the themes of time, history, and personal identity?

BRONXHEAD
REVISITED

The Bronx—or, more precisely, The Jewish West Bronx—retains for me something of the poignancy James Agee reserved for Knoxville. Save for reduced, aging pockets and a few scattered co-op enclaves, by all accounts its heart has shriveled. It is a seedless husk. I had not daily pressed the chipped, round 4 to rise in the elevator of the six-story building on Morris Avenue, for 15 years my boyhood home, since 1958, the year I graduated from college. Nor had I visited since 1970, a short while before my parents took off, as most of their friends were taking off, for warmer, whiter climes. The building, the neighborhood, the times they were a-changin'. Upbeat, no-slouch, D-train Jews beat it out. Turtle-dumb in the face of more ominous peril, once sniffing out *this* imminent threat, we Jews can jump jackrabbit-quick.

The Florida coastal span where my parents now live is a transmogrified dream-vision of former Bronx ways and days. Not merely a thinned-out network of cousins and acquaintances from the gin rummy, mah-jongg North, it is, as my mother pleasurably puts it, a whole graying world gone "brown as a berry: Here's the butcher shop that used to be on 167th Street, on the next mall is Ralph, the appetizing man from Tremont Avenue, but wait, right there on the Plaza is the deli from Kingsbridge Road." North Miami Beach, Hallandale, and right on two counties up, the well-heeled, condo coast exudes the wondrous redolence of a Bronx that is no more. It is a velvet fabric of familiarities, confortable and comforting, Byzantium cum sauna, indeed, all of *olam ha-ba* its senior residents—about whose sun-filled lives from my half-a-planet's span I have perceived my satellite thoughts increasingly revolving—need or want.

Such is not, however, at least not frontally, my present theme.

Immured by distance and doggedness from both the valentines and mostly unintentional brushback pitches that flew at us in a warm, engulfing stream of American communiqués, emissaries, and gut telepathy, Marcia, the children, and I were gradually moving beyond apprenticeship to the hard-won ordinariness of our chosen state as new immigrants in Israel. Materially, of course, our lives had narrowed rather drastically. We suffered from no false expectations, however; indeed, one of our readier flippancies—no less the truth for all of its seeming glibness—to explain to incredulous friends our departure from America in the first place was the better to reduce what still appears to us an unseemly standard of consumption to a more acceptable level. We have, I confess, had more than one occasion to gaze long with chagrin at the dimension, the wondrous waywardness of our perverse achievement. Nevertheless, living among those who not by cash alone measure how we and they are "doing" has proved generally sustaining.

In the fall of 1983, seven years after making *aliya*, I returned for my third visit to the States in order to join in my parents' golden wedding anniversary festivities. My excursion was for two weeks only. Our first return trip in 1977 had been primarily to wrap up the shirttails of our California lives. Three years later we had two new sabras grandly to display to grandparents on both coasts. Yishai and Miriam served both as our shield and as our higher justification. For this third journey, however, there were two salient differences. First, I knew that it had been finally and genuinely granted by almost everyone that we *meshugoim* would not in time be returning to our senses and to our "real" lives in the United States, that neither war nor harder times would dislodge us from Israel. Second, I was alone.

Like the priesthood for American Catholics, becoming "Israeli" is nowadays, one painfully learns, increasingly a calling for eccentrics (indeed, for the fraternity of us self-chosen ones, that is one of its off-beat attractions). It of necessity summons forth a peculiar style of mental discipline. Laxity or sloppiness at this acquired craft breeds discontent that usually leads to permanent disaffection. Precisely because I no longer felt so insistently the implicit need *again* to explain myself, exacerbated by separation from Marcia and the children, this third roundtrip ticket served more powerfully as a testing of the Waters of Babylon than I had prepared myself for. Dared I admit how easily I could accustom myself to the temptations of condominium swim, sun, and—yes—sauna?

After a few days I mischievously let slip that I felt the urge to revisit, during my coming week in New York, the decayed scene of my boyhood. Yes it was, I admit, a provocation, but did it not spring from a genuine, if unanticipated, impulse?

My parents threw each other a meaningful glance. "If you go," my mother cautioned her perverse offspring, "don't wear your watch! It's all Welfare now. What do you want to go back there for, anyway?" I lacked an adequate answer, but duty had been served. As had theirs: I'd been forewarned.

A plane ride and several days later I descended the INDependent subway station uptown along Central Park West, at the corner of my sister's Manhattan co-op apartment, and, seating myself automatically in the front car (I'd not forgotten!) of the CC local, I discovered myself growing queerly eager as the numbers mounted from 145th St., on to 161th St. (still "Home of the New York Yankees") and 183rd St. (not for years "Home" of the old Bronx High School of Science) on my northward journey to the past.

I was rolling against the rush hour's main current; the car was mostly empty. Blankness has long yielded to acrylic self-expression on the New York subways, but the time of flowering has passed. We are witnesses to a period of graffiti decadence: name-dropping, name-calling, and plain old Kilroying prevailed. My few fellow passengers, for whom plainly this jouncy trip was an exquisite bore, were half-a-dozen middle-aged Whites, some slouchy Blacks & Browns bearing schoolbooks, and a sprinkling of Orientals—all non-menacing. (My Timex dangled loosely at the end of my wrist: I had forgotten!) Finally, the rubber lips of the doors parted at the Kingsbridge

Road Station, and, together with the youngsters, I was climbing the self-same steps with the worn, rounded rims that I had scaled so many hundreds and hundreds of times so many climbs ago to the sunny surface of the exotic Bronx. Scarcely a tourist, still was I not a visitor on the prowl in a remote land? My senses narrowed; I was uncommonly excited.

Designed for an era when The Bronx spelled moving right along in the world, the six-laned, tree-lined Grand Concourse was a conscious emulation of the grandeur of the Champs Elysées. It is an artery that once pumped with Jewishness from around 161st Street, a neighborhood that must still be dominated by the monumental County Courthouse and overbearing Concourse Plaza Hotel—gone like the Yankees to seed but formerly the only reasonably legitimate hostel the borough's million-plus commuters ever seemed to need. The Jewish stream ran north to its green-fringed summit at 205th Street and coexistence with the Irish at Mosholu Parkway. (Jews pronounced it MOSH-ul-u; the Irish favored Mosh-U-lu.) Block ran after block, taxi-metered mile after mile of six-story apartment buildings, synagogues, and storefronts punctuated every six or eight blocks by broader intersections—the shopping streets or "Roads"—and the stone steps that led beneath the ground that roared. Save for a bend at Tremont Avenue's elegant Medical Professions Building, fed by an endless stream of cars, buses, and taxis—no trucks permitted on the Grand Concourse—it courses through my memory straight as the Lone Ranger's silver bullet.

One year on the afternoon of Yom Kippur (I must have been eight or nine), my father, mother, younger sister, and I actually *walked* from our apartment all the way down the Grand Concourse to my grandparents' apartment tucked in at Walton Avenue near 162nd Street, the place where old photos say that my mother was a girl. Never before—or since—had this monotonous boulevard so impressed me with its formality and compass. It was so warm and so, so long. South of Fordham Road, we must have paused to rest on stoops and park benches every block or two. My mother cajoled us along with silly songs; toward the end my sister had to be carried. Actually to walk the length of the Grand Concourse: what a hegira!

When we victoriously climbed the two flights of 1069, the brown brick building on Walton where my grandmother lived for over 40 years, the sun was setting, but my grandfather was not yet returned from *shul*. (His congregation was famous for punctilious *davening*.) We could not forbear, however, to drink a glass of water before his arrival which would finally mark the official end of our fiercely proud ordeal. The Yom Kippur fast is, I think, the one ritual none of us has ever scanted.

I emerged on the northwest Concourse corner of 196th Street, a spot dominated by the high, metal-fenced and crucifix-topped House of the Holy Comforter, which was for years an edifice of appalling mystery. The house of dread, the bus stop, *everything* at this corner looked exactly the same! A turn and a short block to the drug store at Creston Avenue, then another to Morris Avenue, and what wand or wisp of time dare to distance me from the skinny 12-year-old who used five days a week to return at 3:30 to his milk and Mallomars from Creston Junior High School two subways stops to the south, a wrinkled subway pass in his pocket whose color changed like the leaves with the months? Wondrously alert, I had to bridle my footsteps which threatened every moment to precipitate the vessel of the past to presence and transparency.

Though Creston Drugs was boarded up, not a single edifice appeared to have been added or removed from the scene. Hardly anyone loitered about, certainly no one from whom to guard my wallet. But the dirty, ocher-colored brick walls of several buildings on 196th had succumbed to the artists of spray propellant: JULIO & LINDA (six times) and PUERTO RICO LIBRE!

I turned right at the corner of Morris. The street was blocked off, under repair—County of The Bronx. *Someone* thinks things here are not beyond repair. I knew in advance my first destination: Beth Shraga Institute. Here for two (or was it three?) years I was sent three times a week to study Hebrew until, climactically, I was *bar mitzvah*. Still, I could see with relief from across the street, not (yet) an Evangelical Church or Pentecostal Temple. Yes, Jews still hid out somewhere in these six-story hills.

I had been a rare exception. I *liked* Hebrew School, even our regular teacher, Blossom Kramer. How we chortled over "Blossom" whose chief redeeming quality was that she was a cousin of tennis star Jack Kramer. When upon reaching 13 I "graduated," Rabbi Barras, a kindly man of genuinely blessed memory—though it was properly pronounced Bar-ash, oh, how we kids messed with *his* name!—urged me to attend a high school *yeshiva*. If I had had a clearer idea what a *yeshiva* was, I might even have considered it before rejecting the notion. Compared to Bronx Science, that incarnation of ambition and tangibility, it was merely an exotic, even alien thought.

Rabbi Barras was the only person whom I encountered in all the years of my growing who expressed interest in our family's link to Moshe Sharett, then Foreign Minister, later Prime Minister of Israel. "One day," Barras more than once declared, "one day you should become as great a man as your cousin, Moshe Sharett. Perhaps you might even go to live in Israel." The connection between that bizarre notion and sounding out Hebrew letters in class was in no way apparent. Still, those weeks when I would out-enunciate the other bright kids (the 3 G's)—Ronnie Grudberg or Billy Grossman or Gary Gershman—to attain the classroom height of Rabbi Barras' Number One seat, when I would have a letter certifying my achievement to carry home for my parents' approbation, those were Thursday afternoons of sweet triumph.

During the years I attended, Beth Shraga was a modest, single-story building. Several times a year, it seemed, bazaars and dinners were held to raise funds toward the addition of a second floor. After many years, the red mercury in the thermometer of the building fund placard reached the top. Just about the time when so many of its congregants in the orbit of Morris, Jerome, and Creston were getting itchy feet, the structure I was confronting was completed.

For my bar mitzvah I received a gift of several books from the Beth Shraga Institute Men's Club and Sisterhood which I dutifully packed, moved from place to place, unpacked, and sometimes dusted over the years. One was written by Rabbi Barras. More than 20 years later, almost accidentally, I came to turn the pages of *The Righteous Man and the Just Path*. It is a wise book; after many years of silence, upon reading it I wrote to him from California. To my intense pleasure, he replied and sent along a copy of a later book. Surprisingly Rabbi Barras was, within the elastic limits of *halacha*, a moderate feminist. His book takes every opportunity to argue for a maximal role in Judaism for women.

RABBI HYMAN BARRAS, I noted, is still inscribed on the plaque outside of Morris Avenue's two-story Beth Shraga Institute. The doors, however, were all locked, and I know for a dour certainty that there arise far fewer occasions upon which the Sisterhood has cause to bestow books than in the past.

Morris Avenue tilts to a modest crest, on the saddle of which apartment houses yield briefly to tall, narrow private houses with high-pitched roofs. Nothing had changed. Except for old "Pop" who wore odd caps and lived in an isolated house farther down the street, Jews did not inhabit these alien, shingled, wooden dwellings. Catholic kids in parochial school black shoes (we wore brown) lived in them, but on this stretch of Morris Avenue they were too few to pose a significant threat. And then down the gentle slope of Morris to the stand of four apartment buildings that constituted the fulcrum, the center of gravity of "the block," perhaps 100 yards (I had, of course, never heard of *meters*) of street that arches to the left a full 90 degrees just as it reaches 2830, *my* building, and disappears into the larger north–south channel of Jerome Avenue beneath the I.R.T. el.

Though to this day FOrdham 4-2043 is the first phone number that curls past my tongue whenever someone unexpectedly inquires, it is decades since I have errantly written "2830 Morris Ave" for my return address on an envelope flap. As if absentmindedly, *here it yet endured*: young mothers in front of adjacent 2824 clustered around baby carriages, some elderly men on folding chairs reclining in the sun, a black woman—someone's "girl" or a block resident, I couldn't decide. The street presented a face that now was less homogeneous, "in transition," shoddier I suppose than in my boyhood; but ineradicably this was the very selfsame scene of years of weekday afternoon and Saturday morning punchball triumphs and defeats.

True, the two enormous planters that bordered the entrance

to 2830 had themselves vanished (how many pink "spaldeens"—pink, rubber balls stamped with the emblem E. G. Spaulding Co.—had irretrievably disappeared forever into those floral balltraps?), but the doggy, scrawny trees of the block have been preserved or, rather, stunted at the very height I recall them from the time of our shared prime. I had come in the morning. It might have been quite different had I awaited the arrival of the present post–3 o'clock crew of ballpunchers who now hang out in this hank of my past. But I confess to more self-indulgent goals and preferred peopling the block out of my private reserve.

Here I, Alan Klinger, Michael Karmin, Melvyn Harris, Brucie Lasky, Marty Wiliky, some of the bigger kids like David Amster or Jackie Kushin, and a score more irregulars played stickball, fast pitching, four-box baseball, boxball, king, baby bases (known just over the Morris Avenue rise as stoopball), and, whenever possible, punchball. Prowess was measured in "sewers," i.e., the distance between manhole covers that dotted the center of the street. A really good smash might travel one-and-a-half sewers into the obscurant trees so that it would be tough to catch through the foliage. When cars would loom over the crest of Morris, the game would briefly adjourn. Delays were lengthier when the spaldeen would bounce into Pop's backyard (he had a large black dog of uncertain disposition) or plop down a real sewer from where it had to be fished out by means of a looped metal clothes hanger. I was adept at it.

One particularly blissful Saturday morning, a dab of time I recall as among the most perfect of those years, *all* the good kids were around to play, *three* complete games were played, and those trees one-and-a-half sewers up the block could not by me be *missed*. Three times I smiled on the winning team. What I could not understand for years was why no amount of pre-planning could enable us to reproduce the ideality of that morning. Something always happened.

The brightest aura of boytime on the block, however, envelops the magical winter of '47 when, if I correctly recall, 27 inches of snow fell on The Bronx, one storm chasing another, and it all *stuck*. I had received a new sled at "Xmas," the one and only year of my childhood that my parents succumbed to the pressures of that national holiday. Day after endless day, when not manning our snow forts, we kids trudged the three sewers to the top of slippery Mount Morris and flung ourselves down, down, down on our sleds to the lip of the curving street, steered around the bend, and emerged among the pillars of the roaring Jerome Avenue el. The taste of being nine years old in that white Bronx winter of '47 is my very equivalent of the cub riverboat pilot's dawn over a renascent Mississippi.

Jewish cultural imperialism was triumphant. Save for the "girls" who arrived in the mornings to twice-a-week wash and vacuum these apartments and the basement-dwelling building superintendents, everyone and everything here was tinted Jewish. We of course knew that the Parkers were Catholic, but merely by living in an apartment two floors below us at 2830, blonde Melanie, my sister's closest friend, seemed magically conferred with Jewishness. Joe the candystore man was Italian, but he was married to Jewish Minny and served up authentic eggcreams, so he too was daubed. Even Ginny, our "girl," was nearly Jewish. Only our super, Mr. Holtz, was excluded. The threat that hung over the heads of us kids was never the boogieman; it was *the super* with the funny German accent and the huge dog who, if we weren't good, down in the basement would get us. Nearby supers had muscular kids who were my age—Johnny Benca and Roger Shakazian—but they were always too busy helping their fathers to play any games.

It was much the same story at nearby P.S. 86. Though my six years of teachers there comprised a March 17th cortège of Miss Callaghans and Mrs. Learys, each class contained only three or four Catholic kids (all those not Jewish were automatically Catholic). These got off an hour early on Tuesday afternoons for mysterious "religious instruction," a spooky business but it got them off! The only one we Jewish kids picked on was a blond kid named Adolf—Adolf Reuter. We all abhorred Dewey—the rumor was that he would extend school to Saturday—and dreaded getting sent to see the principal, Mr. Klein. Jowly and bald, he would dolely intone a benediction from the Bible—always some prophet from *our* Testament—at the start of weekly assembly. In the fall till after Thanksgiving we sang "Over the river and through the woods / To Grandmother's house we go . . . ," but at all seasons we apartment-denizens got to intone "Bless This House."

How P.S. 86 functioned with four pupils per teacher on Rosh Hashanah and Yom Kippur I could not imagine. After a few hours with our fathers in *shul*, what occupied us dressed-up Jewish kids in the street—we wouldn't play ball—were marathon competitions of Ghost or Geography. "Xenia" was an acceptable response to "Phoenix," but ultimately "Halifax" left us x-less, and the game would peter to a halt. How we hoarded our famished, grownup status on our day of fast! One year I was struck with amazement to see Mr. Eischorn, from the third floor, walk past across the street from us kids munching an apple and smiling. "Didn't he fast?" incredulously I later besought my father. Eischorn, who felt not merely constrained to eat but to perform the deed in the open air would, I adduced, surely go—whatever it was—to Jewish Hell.

When I reached 14 or so and, in the company of high school brains like Herman Gluck and Fred Katz, sensed deficiencies of intellectual background, I felt moved to spend my $1.50 a week allowance "to broaden my horizons." I joined the Doubleday One Dollar Book Club. The arrival of my first books heralded a new sense of self that was fiercely at odds with afternoons on this block that was my strawberry field. I looked up at my old bedroom window and could almost glimpse a slim figure by my window sitting beneath an iconic wall poster of Adlai—LET US TALK SENSE TO THE AMERICAN PEOPLE—E. Stevenson, intellectuals together, both vastly superior to Brucie or Michael in the street below. The young man's hands cup one of his three free gifts for joining: *Six Short Novels* by John Steinbeck (it sits to this day on my shelf), *Annapurna*, or H. G. Wells' *The Outline of History* (read dutifully to the very end); or later his first real selection, *The Caine Mutiny*. It was Wouk's vividly melodramatic trial-scene reversal, the defense of Captain Queeg, that moved me into a first attempt at writing "not for school."

Unlike library books or the paperbacks my father kept in his room, these belonged to me, were the backbone of my own private collection that was the tangible sign of my own newly chosen, indeed, permanent way of life. There were, however, times of remission and remorse when, though I had bidden goodbye to all that, I yearned to round third base on the afternoon pavement and backslide into home. A kind of nadir passed one lonesome, sunfilled, lachrymose afternoon, when, after ducking low behind the window sill, I anonymously rejoined my old companions for a reprise that signaled "I'm still more or less here!" by pouring out into the street at top volume Johnny Ray's wailing "Cry."

I had fully intended to enter the lobby whose twin French provincial couches were getting ratty long before my parents' departure, to summon the elevator from either "6" or "B" where it was sure to be poised, to glance at the irresistible full-length lobby mirror at my present bearded visage—would it make the connection?—and to ascend to the fourth floor where, upon pressing the buzzer at 4E . . .

But that was the furthest limit my imagination could rehearse. How really vital was it for me to behold the worm's work on the step-down, ornate, wall-to-wall carpeted living room with its ersatz fireplace that held a short-wave radio, portrait of my mother lovely in her 20s with me, about 3, clutching a pink stuffed dog sitting at her side, and the old lithograph of Benjamin Franklin's Reception at the Court of Versailles on the wall? Until the television set's radical appearance, we kids were not even allowed to bring our toys down those two steps onto this formal scene in which, in our adolescence, Benjamin Franklin, Mother, and Lucy Ricardo alone bore witness to Stephanie, Melanie, and me at dubious play at blindman's buff. Was it really essential to note the altered wallpaper in the dining alcove where every Friday night my mother, muttering some special words, had covered her hair with a kerchief, her eyes with her fingers to *bench licht* before we ate the chicken or roast whose leftovers would surely be served for lunch on Saturday, invariably to be succeeded Saturday evening by a "dairy" meal which yet later would likely be drowned by the thick cigar smoke puffed forth by my father and his pals intent upon gin rummy or pinochle?

Should I, theatrically confronting 4E's current occupants with an equivocal presence, have burdened them with polite demands for special rights of entry and inspection? Usurpers, mere tenant-farmers on the homestead of my primal patch of imagination—Ginny? Welfare chiselers? an old, abandoned Jewish couple?—now paid the controlled rent by the fifth of the month, now occupied the room I had shared for years with Stephanie, now mother of three, whom I had left 16 floors high overlooking Central Park an hour before. Would not 3E or 5E or 6 serve the purpose as well? What, indeed, *was* my purpose; what needed I to be shown? Where was the spectral audience demanding that this show must go on?

Disdaining to exorcise my recumbent Jamesian ghost, I did not, in truth, even enter the building. Instead, like a spy at a loss, my password temporarily forgotten, I reconnoitered to the rear to the Jerome Avenue side of 2830 where at Harry's Candy-store I had consumed hundreds of noontime hamburgers and straw-sucked thousands of eggcreams (*prix fixe* combination—32 cents) while absorbed in Batman and Archie at a time when the world's certainties were anchored to Columbus' discovery of America in 1492, the Yankees indisputable hold as world champions, and the United States of America totaling 48, all of whose capitals and largest cities I could—can still!—deliver on demand.

Harry's was now an office storefront for some government agency. I did not approach it closeup, but, one block far-ther along Jerome, Joe's Candystore also seemed transformed. Around the corner on Creston, Leifer's Candystore—defunct! There surely were not fewer people now living here. Why were there fewer calls for eggcreams and Batman? But I knew the answer even before the question was fully formulated, and a train roared south on the el overhead. Why, I wondered, had I not at least checked out whether a *mezuzah* still hung aslant above the door at 4E?

Instead I weaved through the elevated pillars forever in need of paint across the street at Jerome Avenue. "The Lots," a weedy, bypassed square block adjacent to the IRT sub-street-level depot, scene of ring-a-leevio and the gang's crusades against the Jerries and the Japs, was now depluralized into a parking lot for automobiles. It was surrounded by a high, wire fence.

One time, in the course of a run and tag game in the old Lots, instead of home-freeing the mailbox base, I unaccountably set off the adjacent fire alarm box. The sudden ringing blazed a streaky line across the surface of the afternoon. I dashed under the el, across the street, and flew up six flights of stairs to the roof where my mother was sitting with a friend and the drying wash. I was so breathless from fear and dash that at first I could not speak. In a matter of minutes, several red trucks and cars, sirens blaring, screeched to a halt at the corner of The Lots. Still puffing from the climb, I was sure I would be fingered and arrested. The firemen talked to the kids for a while, then departed. Later I heard that Brucie Lasky had told them my name. I wasn't surprised—Brucie the Squealer! But no cop came to get me that night. Until the days of protest and modest S.D.S. notoriety, my slate was to stay unstained.

There on Paul Avenue rises still the Arthurian towers of . . . Lehman College. It was not Lehman in the old days. This was uptown Hunter College, during my boyhood, a Girls Only enclosure that briefly served as an early way-station for the United Nations en route to Lake Success. For one P.S. 86 year, the disappointing object of our annual "field trip" was this too-close-to-home U.N. home. Odd: in my undergraduate years I was to serve as a delegate to the Collegiate Council for the United Nations, to be an active propagandist for this Slough of Unsuccess that for many years has become a world center for propagating, in the guise of anti-Zionism, anti-Semitism. But back in the years we Yanks were creaming the Nazis, and the good guys were easier to distinguish from the stinkers, Hunter College had been requisitioned by the U.S. Navy to train blue-jacketed young women—the Waves. For my gang, this place was always "Over the Waves."

We went "Over the Waves" to play touch ("association") football on wide, almost traffic-free (except for the "crazy learners") Paul Avenue. It remains a broad, though busier thoroughfare that still leads north to the Jerome Park Reservoir, to Harris Field (where the bigger kids who wore shiny, orange jackets with ATOMS emblazoned across the back played hardball), and to the tough, non-neighborhood kids of DeWitt Clinton High School—foreign territory.

I turned south past Walton, the girls' high school that my sister had once attended. Scores of black and brown faces were loitering about. The three or four stores that had girdled the corner of Jerome and 196th Street—the street where until the third grade I used to wait for some nice lady to come along who would cross me over—were now collapsed into a Big Apple Supermarket. I stepped lively past the Paradise Pizzeria, once reputedly the best in The Bronx, and east on Kingsbridge Road, the closest major shopping intersection to my old home. (In the other direction, on University Avenue, had lived my closest pal during junior high and high school. Howie Dubin had an enormous aquarium, but his real treasure was a tape recorder on which he and I improvised parodies of radio commercials and Bob & Ray skits that would pitilessly sink us together with our skits into a sea of giggly discomposure. Howie, now an Ann Arbor physician, has cause to revisit this scene more frequently than I: his parents have never deserted University Avenue.)

There was less carnage on Kingsbridge than I had anticipated. True, the movie theater was long vanished. With startling clarity, however, could I summon up, like a kitschy Mount Rushmore engraving, the angry, stony face of the theater matron. Nameless (she was simply "the matron"), armed with her flashlight, she ranged through the Children's Section on Saturday afternoons futilely flashing for the culprits who embellished Martin & Lewis classics by converting emptied boxes of Goobers and Raisinettes into miniature tubas to make farty sounds during the goopy scenes. But the Jewish bakery was a survivor—yes, more Jews than the Dubins senior had not flown south—and the Star Drugstore, and two kosher butchershops where once there had been at least four. Somewhere along the way I had stopped peering that extra half-second at faces, ceased expecting to hear Marty Wiliky or Michael Karmin calling my name from across the street. I was heading for the Kingsbridge Road entrance to the INDependent subway, which lay embedded deep in the underpass beneath the ceaseless tide of the Grand Concourse.

I made a final turn before my descent for Manhattan and was struck anew by the awesome, neo-Gothic spires of vast, imperious, block-square Kingsbridge Armory. Only once in my life had I entered this enormous, red brick pile, but it was,

I vividly recalled, the very scene of my early adolescent, night-time ur-fantasy.

For more months than I can be sure—perhaps, with variations, for years—when "Gangbusters" or "This Is Your F.B.I.," and all my other programs had dwindled into talk shows, and my father, thinking me asleep, had turned off the radio for the night, I would drift off to sleep only after another replay of the heroic adventures of our Jewish gang of kids (assisted by some nubile girls I'd seen from afar who attended Elizabeth Barrett Browning Junior High) who, after the rest of America had succumbed to a Russian invasion, secretly held out beneath the turrets of the Kingsbridge Armory. Harvey, cousin to Batman, secret sharer unawares to little Woody Allen Konigsberg over in alien Brooklyn, led a band that specialized in daring hit-and-run raids against the dumb, dumbfounded Russians before retreating to the safety of our secret, underground redoubt on Kingsbridge Road.

In 1974, two decades after these marvelous adventures had been submerged and "forgotten," my wife and I, on our first, our tourists' encounter with Israel, climbed Masada. Staring down at the Roman encampment with the Dead Sea as the backdrop, I startlingly, astonishingly reclaimed it all, connected it to the subterranean armory hero of Kingsbridge Road, who at the time, of course, did not know Masada from a doughnut.

An elderly woman with two shopping bags, indeed an elderly *Jewish* woman, stood gaping at me in my crocheted *kippa*; she finally began to speak to me in Yiddish. This is assuredly not a strength, but I was finally able to direct her to where the bus stop most probably still stood. Jews still sat in the early afternoon sunshine across the Concourse on the carved wooden benches of Poe Park. (How many dozen times had I wandered through the incredibly tiny cubicles of the cottage-in-the-park to which strange Edgar Poe had brought his child bride Virginia to live? What could have Poe to do with the old Jews who still haunted his abode?)

I descended. I had no interest in examining the balustrades or parapets of Kingsbridge Armory for day-glo messages. Graffiti, peace emblems, and people-power symbols did streak the walls of the underpass, but no, I had been neither robbed nor accosted in a hostile manner. Nearly all of my encounters had been with phantoms Poe would not have bothered to conjure, shapes who not for years have punched a ball a sewer or more down Morris or stopped in at Harry's for an eggcream and comic break.

On my telephone here in Israel, it only takes just six preliminary digits to dial direct through to The Bronx. The overseas line is clear, clearer than any long-distance line within Israel. I suppose it is still vaguely possible that one chilly Negev midnight—it would be dinnertime there—I could yet succumb to the antic impulse to dial FOrdham 4-2043 just on the off-chance that some erratic wire or errant link would enable me to catch Mom home from the interior-decorating store, Dad between calls on his insurance and mutual-fund clients, or even Harvey, that precocious, secretive kid who (everyone says) has my very voice but whom I can barely recognize from his bar mitzvah and high school graduation photos. There are still some questions that I have, some answers I would like to hear. Like Thoreau's misplaced hound and horse and dove, he is a quarry I have longstanding reasons for tracking down.

But I really don't think it very likely. It was enough. I had got for my subway tokens more even than I had come for, more than I had had reason to expect. It will suffice for a long, long time.

"CALL ME JAIME!"

Save for journeying there to meet with touring friends or visiting family, I enter Tel Aviv's Rehov Hayarkon, a strip that parallels the sea, only to renew my American passport. It is one of Israel's most schizoid streets, a very incarnation of Boardwalk nuzzling Mediterranean Avenue: the tariff in the sleazier stretch south of the American Embassy runs in the $2.00 range; the northern reaches—a luxury hotel row—spirals toward $50. When during our ten-day Israeli initiation in 1974 Marcia, I, and the delegation from Fresno were V.I.P.-ed around, we were put up for two nights at the Plaza, a five-star slab up the street on the wave-lapped side of Hayarkon. A parachute concession parked in front of the Plaza's dubious elevator would have done well. But we were not at the time very intent upon seeing critically.

Upon entering the lobby of the Grand Hotel, a scant four-star establishment on the side of Hayarkon which does not front on the white-flecked sea, I was spotted almost at once by a smiling, soft-spoken man in his mid-40s.

"Jaime, it's good to see you again."

The Grand * * * *: subsidies for such junkets must be harder to come by. Pumping my arm was urbane Professor Leobardo Estrada, a demographer from U.C.L.A. whom I had last seen a week before at the start of the quickie excursion he and his party of "Hispanic-American Young Leadership" would be enjoying in Israel. This was now the last full day in Israel for Estrada and the dozen or so other young—i.e., under-45—leaders; their tour, under the auspices of a program dubbed "Project Interchange," was closing out. As for me, I was ambivalently "on assignment" to cover them for an American

Jewish monthly well-known for its dedication to the proposition that American Jewry has entered a revitalized, dynamic phase. Plainly, factotums at Project Interchange had exercised a bit of that dynamic Jewish leverage in this affair: there was no need long to ponder whether the editorial expectation was that I would discover in Project Interchange an endeavor well worth its time and starry expense.

Eight days before, Marcia and I had set out from home for Beersheba so that I could intercept this group on their first full day in Israel at their hotel. We had one prior chore: to visit the branch office of the Americans and Canadians in Israel (A.A.C.I.), which happens to be located in a bomb shelter, to get ourselves registered to vote in the November American elections. (One day in every four years the Embassy sends a representative for this purpose to the Negev.) Good citizenship had availed us nothing in 1980: our ballots arrived two weeks after Election Day. In the shelter we encountered affable Baruch Gold (rabbinic model: Conservative Ortho-prax), an Instructor of Jewish Values at Ben-Gurion University.

"Haim, this morning I spoke to a fabulous group of people at the university—Hispanic-American leaders. Were they sharp! I mentioned that I planned today to register so I could cast my vote for Reagan, that I wanted to make sure the U.S. battleships would make it to the Mediterranean in time in case Israel needed them. Did I get hit with flak! They're really sophisticated. And when I confessed that when I served as a congregational rabbi in Phoenix I had never bothered even once to visit with the Chicano community there, one of them—a judge from Philadelphia—really tore into me. *He* had been concerned enough with Soviet Jewry to have visited Russia on its behalf. How come I hadn't made it across the tracks? Why weren't greater numbers of American Jews supporting Hispanic causes like Affirmative Action and Bilingual Education?

"I had no ready answers, but I did promise to try to see them again. They're staying at the Neot Midbar Hotel. If you have time, you ought to go over and meet with them too. Here, one of them gave me his card."

I took it: Representative Hugo Berlanga, Speaker Pro Tempore, Texas House of Representatives, Corpus Christi, Texas.

Later that afternoon I watched from the lobby as a small tour bus unloaded its American guests at the Neot Midbar. Beersheba's version of the Concourse Plaza, the Hotel Neot Midbar is the city's only "luxury" facility. In fact, it is more like an upscale, kosher Holiday Inn. The Hispanics had just spent several hours at nearby Kibbutz Hatzerim. I had few doubts that in their time in Israel they would see and hear more than they reasonably could absorb: Israeli tour guides are practiced professionals with such groups. It struck me, however, that many, probably most of the *Americans* they would encounter would, like my friend, ingenuously volunteer that they too intended voting for Reagan; that in New York, Miami, or San Diego they had probably displayed the same burning uninterest in Puerto Rican, Cuban, or Chicano priority concerns as he.

At no other juncture in Israel were these Hispanic-Americans likely to encounter a person who once upon a time had picketed Purity Supermarkets and Lucky Stores that sold head lettuce or who had organized a picket line of college students to head off the Teamsters from unloading sweetheart contract table grapes in Stockton. In Israel's perpetual war of *hasbarah*, was I not uniquely well-situated, the improbable man in the sensitive place? Tentative, I was now not only charged with my assignment from Boston but tinged with an uneasy sense of mission, my Israeli civic obligation to do my bit to counteract what was likely to be the Hispanics' problematic impression of American Jews living in Israel. It was a big day for dual-citizenry civics. That my quarry was likely as well to be "a fabulous group of people" was . . . well . . . a nice bonus.

While the tour participants were washing kibbutz dust out of their hair, I received my enthusiastic briefing from the former actress, exuberant, blonde mother of four who dreamed up Project Interchange while studying in Israel in 1981. She later sold the idea to its sponsoring body, the prestigious American-Israel Friendship League. "I almost never take 'no' for an answer," she explained. In addition to this second contingent of young Hispanic leadership, she had already chaperoned several groups of congressional aides, up-and-coming state legislators, and mainline young Christian leadership. Black state legislators were scheduled to follow. Not your everyday tourists, each group was treated to a special program which was arranged at each phase of its itinerary by an Israeli university. "This," my interlocutor gushed, "is an in-depth experience, a hands-on happening, not propaganda or entertainment." It was soon clear that the details I was noting down would interest all too few; nevertheless, I politely absorbed my hour's briefing on the background and inner workings of Project Interchange. Armed at last with an agenda and roster of names and affiliations of the Hispanic-Americans that I copied from her typed list, I left my hostess to her bath and descended to the lobby.

Early evening in the lounge I joined Lourdes Miranda, President of the National Association of American Businesswomen, and Guarione Diaz, Executive Director of the Cuban National Planning Council. Before I could properly begin, however, my scenario started to misfire. First, Rabbi Gold appeared to take up where he had dropped his skein that morning. He took and held the floor. Instead of an antidote to Reagan boosterism, I was able to project little more than the occasional interference of some offshore transmitter.

Moreover, a Mondale ballot or two out of the Negev would hardly have cut much ice anyway. For it was soon clear that I was grievously out of touch, had not given serious thought for years to the Bakke Decision or bilingualism in American education or any of the other issues that preoccupied these visitors. These were such distant, such foreign affairs, were they not? (I read their minds in hi-fi: How come this gringo had never made it across the tracks when they could make it halfway around the world to Israel?) Worse, when I slipped in some salient parallels between American and Israeli experience, I discovered myself dangerously out of phase with the platitudes of American democratic pluralism. Gold, the Conservative Jew with a deep personal stake in ideological pluralism, was closer to home base than Chertok, the former S.D.S. activist!

The hottest encounter came with Samuel Betances, a sociology professor who hosts a Spanish-language TV talk show in Chicago. "How can you possibly justify maintaining your

American citizenship when you live permanently in Israel? Don't Israelis see you as fair-weather friends who might just leave when things got hot? Is it fair for you to vote in American elections when the interests of a foreign country determine for whom you vote?"

For neither Amerisraelis nor sabras a burning issue, our dual citizenship strangely rankled these Hispanics. What really lay behind this barrage was soon manifest. As Raul Yzaguirre, President of the National Council for La Raza, put it, "We don't dare even mention Mexico or Cuba. If we did we'd get shot down for being unpatriotic. So how do you get away with it? Why should Israel be a special case? What's the difference?" And the collateral question: Why should Hispanic-Americans support billions of dollars in aid for Israel—one participant had it at $9,000,000,000 annually, an exaggeration I was sure others in the party recognized but none supported me in pointing out—when in their own community of 26 million Hispanics, less than 3% completed college? Indeed, Israel was just a leaky rowboat adrift in the frigid waters that these days seemed to separate Hispanic-American from American Jewish perceptions of their community's self-interest.

Finally Leobardo Estrada posed a sticky question I thought I could score with: "Are the Arabs within Israel a sub-community that is roughly equivalent to the blacks vis-à-vis the whites in America?"

Oh, did I vault into a quick sketch of an incident that had occurred two weeks earlier when a few of us Yeroham "Anglos" had tried to help some local Bedouins against Israel's Green Patrol in a land dispute. Suddenly, the floor and everyone's attention was mine. I plowed ahead into a selective account of my own years of involvement with The Movement: I had been an active supporter of the farm workers' right to organize into a union; my wife had run on a coalition slate with a Chicano candidate in a school board election in a town near Fresno. Everyone attended to Haim's stirring testimony. I was transmitting clear fraternal signals: "Call me Jaime!," I all but blurted.

"Yes," persisted Leobardo after a pause, "but my question is, are Arabs here in Israel, like blacks in America, a permanent sub-class?"

Stumped how to be frankly evasive, evasively frank, out of breath, out of momentum, I was delighted when Rabbi Gold cut in with a well-worn anecdote about the Israeli Jew who, when his son was yet an infant, built his house with his own hands. Ten years later when his son learned of this, he accosted his father with, "I didn't know, Daddy, that when you were young you used to be an Arab."

We all chuckled somewhat nervously. While Gold was recounting his story, I decided against mentioning that the person who daily swept the street in front of my house in Yeroham just happened to be a Detroit-born member of a cult of American-born, black "Hebrews" based in Dimona.

"Well," Leobardo patiently asked again. He must, I concluded, strew tar babies around his California classroom. Everyone seemed to wait for my response.

"Unfortunately," I began, "and for the foreseeable future," continued my measured response, "your analogy . . . uh . . . clarifies more of the situation than it distorts." I could not make it to the briar patch. "For most Jews in Israel, the Arabs—the children of Ishmael living among us—are our very own blacks. Many of us," I quickly added, "are not pleased with this situation."

Shortly afterward the group left to meet with General Shlomo Gazit, the President of Ben-Gurion University. I was to join them the following morning for their visit to Midreshet Sde Boker, about 20 kilometers south of Yeroham. I had the impression that I had not exactly excelled at generating good *hasbarah*; *mañana*, I vowed to myself, I would hew to observerhood, would keep shut mine mouth.

Israel's Egged bus cooperative provides mostly disservice south from Yeroham, so the next morning I had resort to my thumb for a ride down to Midreshet Sde Boker, an academic preserve a few kilometers south of the better-known Sde Boker, the kibbutz where David Ben-Gurion retired (more than once) from government service. The kibbutz is the site of "Ben-Gurion's Hut": a small cottage ("hut" is a misnomer that oddly has stuck). Midreshet Sde Boker, however, is where B.-G. and his wife Paula are buried and where his archives are housed in a handsome research library. Also located at this complex is the Institute for Desert Research, a facility of Ben-Gurion University where I was to meet my party of visitors at their morning briefing. Traffic was light; cars were filled; I arrived late.

The lecturer, a British-born geographer, was amply witty, but several among the young Hispanic leaders quietly dozed right through his presentation about the Negev. It seemed that the night before, on the return ride to their hotel from the university, their bus driver had turned up the music on the radio. One thing led to another, and before you knew it, the tour participants were enjoying until the wee hours of the morning a hands-on, in-depth experience at a Beersheba disco.

"They were terrific," their blonde cicerone grinned. "Can they dance!"

Some of the less weary began to ask the geographer questions. Again and again they returned to the conflict between the exploitation of the Negev and the preservation of ecological values. Again and yet again the speaker gamely averred that no one exceeded the Institute for Desert Research—"which ranks among the major centers for desert research in the world"—in environmental concern; however, "the very mandate for our inception is the development of the Negev. In this, we and Israel have no real choice."

Here was another impasse, a red-faced instance of *Ein Breira!*—No Alternative!—the vindication for so much that happens in the realm of Israeli realpolitik. Yet was it not so that it is America which is the gaudy exception, a luxury liner stocked with moral choices, pluralism, and multiple options, extraneous baggage that would tip over a precarious craft like Israel? The room for maneuver here was so much narrower, so confined. "American" causes—Zero Population Growth, Nuclear Disarmament, Feminism, Gay Liberation, Ecology, the Military-Industrial Complex, even grayer zones of Civil Liberties—had paltry or at best much-reduced resonance here, where every argument and street led inerrantly to the pre-eminent Jewish concern for survival against the odds, to *ein breira*. Was it not a cul-de-sac? Could these Hispanic-Americans really be expected to comprehend what so many Boston and Berkeley Jews would not?

In spite of my resolve, I had done something gauche. In the bottom drawer of my desk I had uncovered the evening before a small hoard of memento buttons. There, wedged between DR. SPOCK BROUGHT ME UP and MCGOVERN—SHRIVER, was a black, Aztec eagle in a blazing sun-like circle —¡HUELGA! N.F.W.A. The temptation was overwhelming. When again in the course of my life would the opportunity shine by to flash my past support for the National Farm Workers Association? En route to the Ben-Gurion Library, where the agenda declared a historian named Gal was to deliver a lecture on "Values in the Jewish State," the button chipped the ice between me and Raul Yzaguirre and Tony Enriquez (Executive Director of the Unity Council of Oakland). Several of the others, however, seemed to look right through it.

Professor Gal's theme was that democratic values were a cardinal founding principle of both the United States and the State of Israel. The very term "cultural pluralism," he noted, was originated by American-Jewish educator Horace Kallen; Jews and Hispanics in America sit under the same theoretical umbrella. The participants seemed impressed, grew livelier. Then it flashed that many of these people—the Philadelphia judge, Miami banker, perhaps the successful businesswoman—had in the late Sixties probably maintained no little distance between themselves and the likes of Cesar Chavez. (I had read that a decade thereafter Chavez had transformed the N.F.W.A. from a vibrant social-labor movement into something more akin to a mystical, holistic ashram somewhere in the California hills. Had they sniffed him out even before?) It gave me pause. Gal was effectively combating the idea broached by some of the Hispanics that Israel was in some way a theocracy. Rapport was high; there were no dozers.

At several junctures, however, I had to restrain my hand from rising to challenge his point, to remember my place. The professor projected Israel for foreign consumption. At *hasbarah* Gal was first-rate, much better than Jaime the evening before; this was also clearly the Israel that these sharp, fabulous people wanted to believe already existed. Gal's most glaring evasion dealt with the current meaning of Zionism: no one could possibly have guessed from his delivery that at least since 1948 it has been undergoing a prolonged identity crisis.

The group was off to Masada, Jerusalem, the West Bank, the

Technion, the Golan. The strategy that I planned for evaluating the impact of their exposure to Israel: I would intercept them again in Tel Aviv, at the very end of their week of touring. *Hasta luego.* Their bus got smaller, smaller, and disappeared. No other tourists had yet materialized that morning. Before hitchhiking back to Yeroham I slipped behind the library to the pebbly path that led to the gravesite of David Ben-Gurion. For an uninterrupted quarter-of-an-hour I sat alone at that spot which overlooks the drastic canyon-gorge of Nahal Tsin and the stunning mesa that rises beyond to the south.

Soon joining me and Leobardo Estrada were some of the others. It was, however, their last day in the country, a last chance to shop for gifts, to visit the sights of Tel Aviv, to keep an afternoon appointment for a massage. Most had little time to chat. Raul Yzaguirre, Hugo Berlanga, Samuel Betances, and Leobardo must speak for all.

RAUL: We got a really good sense of the whole picture in its four aspects. One: Israel as a State, its secular Zionist roots, its rationale and connection to Yad Vashem. Two: the archaeological, historical, and religious heritage. Three: the development of the land, the Negev, the development of new towns. Four: the culture conflicts—religious versus secular, Arabs versus Jews, Ashkenazim versus Sephardim, West Bankers versus peaceniks.

I was surprised by the impact of Masada, and by the pervasiveness of the Histradrut and the government in almost everything. I'm still not clear how to deal with what one official said, that Israel can't handle 100,000 unemployed. After all, how much support can the U.S. give to ensure that Israelis aren't unemployed? But the trip certainly lived up to expectations, and there's no question that Israel justifies continued American support even if we are only talking about strategic terms. Here, take down my address in Washington.

HUGO: The trip was enlightening and broadened my outlook. To my mind, security is the main thing Israel must be concerned with. Jerusalem was the outstanding experience: obviously it shouldn't be, can't be, divided. We all agreed on that.

SAMUEL: I knew a good deal about the Kotel and about Yad Vashem, but I'd no idea of the importance of Masada as a symbol of resistance to oppression and the determination to be free. It was very moving. My main disappointment could easily be rectified: we had too little free time to visit and experience the Christian holy places in Jerusalem. Some of us had to cut out of a lecture on Arab–Jewish relations at Hebrew University in order to walk on the Via Dolorosa. I definitely intend to work to build better Hispanic-Jewish relations. Without question, this trip was one of the most significant experiences of my life.

LEOBARDO: Yes, I was pleased with what I saw, with the tour as a whole. I'm filled with admiration; if I were Jewish, I would have been inspired. What strikes me most is the amazing diversity of Israel, the heterogeneity of views and people. I was surprised by the emphasis everywhere on the economy. I'd thought I would be hearing most about security, but it was the economy that was on everyone's mind.

In the short term, I'm convinced that the United States should do all it can to ensure Israel's existence and to help with its problems. But in the long run, I'm not so optimistic. As a professional demographer, I see a Jewish population with a high median age and a young, growing Arab sub-society that cannot be assimilated. Separate but equal didn't work in America; it can't, in the long run, work here. So I'm worried for Israel.

When I get home, I plan to talk with Jewish students, rabbis, former Israelis. To tell the truth, I feel better informed than most American Jews.

Inevitably there ran among them a spectrum of impressions; when Hugo was hearing the siren of "security," Leobardo was attuned to "the economy." The abrasive edge that had nicked our initial encounter a week earlier at Beersheba's Hotel Neot Midbar, however, had been appreciably honed, softened. Perhaps profoundly, "Israel, hands-on, in-depth" under the tutelage of Project Interchange had affected these Young Hispanic-American Leaders. One, I believe it was Lourdes Miranda, recalled the busride on one leg of their tour when four of them were debating whether they would, were they Jews, move to

Israel. Two felt that they could not come: Israel was too unstable; Israel was too controlled. The other two thought otherwise. Living among one's own people, with a heightened sense
of history and commitment—that would draw them here.

To my relief, I was satisfied that my account of Project Interchange could be both honest and moderately enthusiastic.
Would, in fact, I thought, that a similar vehicle could be con-
trived for more young American Jews. Was it so unimaginable
that two out of four of them would snap at the same premises
and flow with the same conclusions as two out of four of these
Hispanic-Americans? But, I sharply recalled, similar programs
and opportunities abounded. They are amply publicized on
every major American campus, in many of the periodicals for
which I write, *and still they do not come.*

They! When during my junior undergraduate year I was
studying in Paris, my friend Art Gherdovich surprised me by
deciding on his winter break to visit distant relations in Yugoslavia. Aware all the while that it was out of the question, I
nonetheless entertained the possibility of visiting Cherson, my
father's birthplace in the Crimea. Although I already thought
that I knew the answer, I wrote my father asking whether we
had any remaining family connections in the Soviet Union. I
was sufficiently curious that, had I been able, even in the absence of remaining uncles and cousins I would have jumped
to the Crimea just to nose about. How then came it that I did
not broach the possibility to my parents that they underwrite a
brief trip across the Mediterranean for me to visit Israel where
we *do* have family, and not all that distant at that? I did not
weigh and reject this option. *It had never crossed my mind!*

"Living among one's own people, with a heightened sense
of history and commitment" is such a human, fundamental,
fundamentally fine sentiment, who *except themselves* could
have denied its anodyne satisfactions to the Palestinian Arabs?
Yet have they not, through refusal or incapacity to throw up
leadership willing to compromise, done just that? It is for them
perhaps too late; they can and will, after all, survive as Arabs
amidst the 120,000,000 other Arabs. Though editors in Boston
and Federation Chairmen in New York will differ, for us Jews
much-battered Zionism remains the only seaworthy dream
afloat. We Jews have no other options.

True, Zionism's most grievous injuries have always been self-sustained. True, sorely needed reinforcements are not on the way. True, the danger that Zionism will yet constrict from a national liberation movement to a sort of extended, holyistic Jewish commune is not a remote fantasy. No matter that too frequently it seems as though Zionism's better part may be exhumed in the archives or at a quiet gravesite facing south from Midreshet Sde Boker. *Ein breira* is the bottom line of our brief.

Call *us* Ishmael.

Awkwardly labeled "Fighting a Non-Propaganda War," my approving article made its appearance on schedule. I was content that I had drawn something readable out of the banality of yet another V.I.P. expedition to Zion. The reaction from America was chastening. Important feelings had been ruffled: apparently the Israel-American Friendship League had complained that several details of the workings of the selection process for participants in Project Interchange were inaccurate. ("'O bother!,' thought Pooh.") I checked my notes. As I thought, I had written them up just the way I had received them. Could I not have paid close enough attention to the former actress? From half-a-planet's span, cloutless, I could be nothing but guilty.

"Not only that," the editors rasped, "why the hell couldn't you get the Spanish names right?" What the hell kind of journalist was I, anyway? Abashed, I checked the list I had copied against my carbon. The names were spelled exactly the way I had written them in the article I had submitted. Under advisement, they had changed to "Estrada" the "Estanada" I had copied from the original. Two other names as well. Why, instead of trusting that original list, had I not checked with the participants themselves? I suspected, moreover, that I had not sufficiently purged the piece of its tinge of disbelief in the vitality and long-term viability of the American Jewish community.

I had relearned some American home truths. This was the last article of mine that this particular publication saw fit to publish for over two years.

It must be admitted that we dual citizens of Israel and America, Ishmaels afloat on a bumpy historical wave, are not such fabulous dancers. The terms of our ambiguity call for intricate stepping. We as needfully as the Hispanic-Americans must practice some of the cuter maneuvers, to learn the more graceful moves from the pros of the Jewish-American establishment. Still, like La Raza, so we unreconstructed Zionists hold a final trump: Israel is the very staff of life and pricey spread for those American Jews (at best, a bare majority of the total) still within the smarmy fold of the organized "American Jewish Community," yet they have chosen to breathe the stale, surrogate air of the sidelines. Over the long haul, indications are that it will prove too thin to sustain them.

The future, one must grant, may prove us "duals" comically shortsighted, abysmally wrong—but I think not. On the contrary, it seems painfully, increasingly apparent which is the segment of American Jewry that has apprehended what for our times is the measure of Rabbi Hillel's timeless imperative for us Jews to be at the very least for ourselves, and which the segment that, in order to neutralize what is importunate in Hillel's "And if not now, when?," have conjured for itself a gilt-edged idol.

There will issue no last laugh from the less than one per cent of us American Jews who live here in Israel if and when the time beckons to bear closer witness to the final realization of our blackest, bleakest vision for the vast majority of the 99% of American Jews who have opted to remain there. The fragment attached to Orthodoxy can and will of course endure—Amish-like, even thrive!—but as for that great skeletal frame, that skinned hulk has for so long been habitually anesthetized to its dribbling losses that I foresee that at the last the carcass will succumb to the stillness of waters with neither the respite of a whimper nor the grace of a final sigh.

PART TWO.

FRESH RESERVES:
THUMBS UP
BLUE & WHITE

But then Israel is something else again.

Saul Bellow

Under these historic skies
I am older than Abraham and his stars,
and I am the young father of the children
playing among pink trees.

Gabriel Preil
(from "From Jerusalem: A First Poem")

LOCAL
ARCHAEOLOGY,
SELF-TAUGHT

*I*srael wears a different face to those of us for whom Tel Aviv or Jerusalem is pre-eminently the nice place to visit that we prefer not to inhabit. From my epicenter in Yeroham, it is the Negev—more than 60% of Israel's land mass—that exercises the greater, more immediate attraction, and whose measure, width, and depth are my newfound coextensions: for all my purposes, practical and impractical, Negev is Walden. Forays into it are my social archaeology, my personalist economics, my autodidactic excavations into surrounding, encroaching, clashing versions of Zionism fulfilled. The digs have resulted in a series of impressions from—old Jewish habit—the periphery; hardly disinterested, in the service (at least in part) of self-justification, they are, I think, sufficiently asymmetric to yield some perspectives both valid and new on contemporary Israel that would not easily yield themselves yet for ready, roseate doctoring by some postcard portraitist.

ARAD: A TRANSPARENT ENIGMA

"*A*rad," most any resident will tell you more often than you may really care to hear, "is special. It's just not the same as other development towns."

A midday stroll through Arad's heart tends to substantiate the claim. Central thoroughfares are conceived as boulevards. Streets and walkways are kept clean; bright orange litter receptacles containing dappled orange peels abound. Landscaping and flowers—neat, refreshing, and lively—green the frontage of virtually every apartment block and public building. One needs reminding that he is 50 Negev kilometers east of Beersheba on the approach to the mordant Dead Sea: Jericho's lushness wells up from natural springs, but here neither groundwater nor rainfall accounts for this technological oasis. All of Arad bespeaks tidiness and artifice, patience and know-how. It is difficult to remain unimpressed.

The spacious central shopping center is dominated by five major banks and a large motion picture theater. Shops line not only the main quadrangle but also fringe the several arcades that pool together like feeder streams into an ample reservoir. Since tourism is significant, there are more than a few gift emporiums. A sign of prosperity: I did not come across a single store to let.

In the middle of the plaza stands a massive sculpture of a menorah with eight concrete tines projecting, like a fork waving—or supplicating—into the air. It is Stonehenge-in-the-Negev pitched with irony: whereas the equivalent emblem in the main square of religiously traditional Yeroham is a balancing act abstract, here reputedly the most secularized of Israeli towns has offered up its heart to a menorah. What Tel Aviv joker makes these choices for us provincials, anyway? In early afternoon, scarcely anyone paraded in sight. (Israel is never more "Mediterranean" than between 1:00 and 4:00 P.M.) At an outdoor café sat several young blond tourists (Swedes?, Germans?, Southern Californians?). At one table were a soldier and two American students from W.U.J.S.—the World Union of Jewish Students—which runs a language and Israeli culture institute here in Arad for single, potential *olim* professionals. Under the eye-squinty midday sun, all other establishments were closed.

It *is* hot here at midday, but still a comforting breeze whistled through the nearly abandoned plaza. It is not really unpleasant to be out. Though this technically may be "desert," actually

Arad is noted for its dry, mild, salubrious climate. It is well-known as a haven for asthmatics. When in 1960 town planner Lova Eliav (the same peace-loving Lova on whom I fruitlessly chucked away my ballot in the 1984 national elections) arrived here, he was already much-heralded: it was he who had successfully planned the reclamation of the arid Lachish region of the Northern Negev, the area—including Moshav Masuot Yitzhak—where our first Israeli bags were to be unpacked, for intensive settlement. Here Eliav's operative idea was, while still hewing to the cooler heights, to situate the town as closely as possible to the sharp Dead Sea declivity. And today here indeed, scenically perched 1,000 feet high astraddle a plateau that overlooks the Dead Sea some 40 miles to the east, lounges neat-as-a-pin Arad.

This explicable midday emptiness evokes the paradox of a more mysterious, significant vacancy. Arad was Israel's first truly planned development town. (Its only possible rival would be Carmiel, more to the North.) A Yeroham turned on its head, this city was a technocratic hive of soil analysts, surveyors, and engineers even before the first settler's moving van pulled in to deposit the family before its new threshold in Arad's inaugural year of 1962. Its master plan—every city, town, and hamlet in Israel now hugs to its bosom, like a dowry from a dallying bridegroom prince, its treasured "master plan"—detailed residential areas that could accommodate between 50,000 and 75,000 people. In its inaugural years, more than ten times the number of applicants for residence descended than could be absorbed: only 50 of the first 500 families who wanted to come were, according to a carefully prepared formula, chosen; only 100 of the next group of over 1,000. Yet today, more than two decades later, fewer than 15,000 settlers have materialized!

Explanations for this startling shortfall are readily available; indeed, they are perfectly reasonable. The early deluge of *aliya* is now a dribble; at least since 1967, governmental priorities for national development have been pegged to several elsewheres. The Negev, a political featherweight, has especially since the peace treaty with Egypt been safely taken for granted.

Still, the enigma abides and troubles. Save for the premature abandonment of a distinctive architectural pattern of shade and patio, virtually *every* feature of the original bold conception for Arad has been implemented. Not merely *implemented* but executed with care, intelligence, and éclat: this little city has consistently won national prizes not only for the beauty of its landscaping and environmental quality but also for the efficiency of its municipal administration! And yet this pearl of Israel's new, development towns today can boast barely double the population of my own intractable Yeroham, the very Topsy of settlements. As often occurs in Israel, the mystery of "why don't they come?" both haunts and perplexes those of us who have.

Although I lack serious intimacy with Arad, I am hardly unacquainted with it. My daughter Jennifer attended boarding school here for four high school years. Several close friends from Yeroham have moved here. And for a short period, I traveled once a week to this outpost of civility to teach Israeli literature classes to students at W.U.J.S. This superficial familiarity has bred neither contempt nor (despite the town's surfeit of virtues) much affection. Why, I wonder, does this Léger painting of a place seem so deficient in charm, in waywardness, in human happenstance, and warmth?

Ancient Arad was a major center, a fortified city when the Israelites were first embarked upon the conquest of Canaan; its remains spread over a remarkably large area. Employing an enviable system that trapped the runoff from winter rains in order to irrigate their fields in the spring and summer, once over 10,000 people lived on the trade and agriculture here. Israeli specialists attached to the Desert Research Institute at Avdat, 20 kilometers south of Yeroham, have after many years of experimentation not yet come close to emulating the ancient system's efficiency. (Indeed, a first attempt after World War I at Jewish resettlement in Arad failed precisely for want of water.) Now this triumph of ingenuity and fortitude under the Negev sun is Tel Arad, an archaeological site that is located some 15 kilometers west of its modern, present-day namesake.

More vivid than any impression of my dozens of visits to the modern Arad is the night my family and I passed here in these ruins when encamped under the desert stars at the *tel*. No other campers pulled in. Save for an interlude of helicopter buzzing from Nevatim, a new airbase which is supposed, in time, to alleviate some of the pressure of civilian overseas flights from overcrowded Ben-Gurion Airport, it was an altogether charmed evening. What it would be like here if the planes start landing regularly or (an ungenerous, heretical thought) if the 50,000–75,000 people that fantasist Lova Eliav has fashioned in his well-knit piece of fiction, *The Master Plan of Arad*, were miraculously to materialize, probably calls for as much stomach as imagination.

The outskirts of Yeroham also betray its Ozymandias *tel*. It is virginal. Well, almost: though no money has ever been found to start any professional excavation, there have been some amateurish probes. It has, of course, never occurred to us to spend a night in its precincts.

I sat to talk at length with Michael Copeland ("Copie"), British-born W.U.J.S. Director and on-and-off Arad resident since 1967. Inevitably curious about the town–gown connection, I was also on the trail of narrowing the grounds of my deepening puzzlement about this place. W.U.J.S. (called by everyone "Wujuss") is in significant ways Arad writ small. It seems to be an excellent premise, an ably-administered actualization of a concept. College graduates sign up to come to Israel for a year, the first six months of which are spent at W.U.J.S. studying Hebrew and aspects of Jewish and Israeli culture. According to Copie, about 35% of the 4,000 students who since its inception have studied at W.U.J.S. have actually come on *aliya*. Only a very few, like the Director of Arad's tennis center, have stayed on in this city. Host families, programs for tutoring and volunteering, patient shopkeepers, a helpful City Hall together convey a fair sense of the closeness of the town-and-gown weave.

Plans? Expansion of facilities, more emphasis on drawing students from the "non-Anglo" world. Then came a frown and a pause: "You know, I am for obvious reasons reluctant to say this, but our program is so good that it should be flooded with applications," the Director confessed with some evident consternation. "We're doing all right, mind you, but there are many times when I believe that W.U.J.S. must be the best-kept secret in the Jewish world. I cannot understand it."

His pain and puzzlement struck a painfully familiar chord. Indeed, my personal experience bore out its Director's estimation of the quality of the W.U.J.S. program. When I directed Ramat Hanegev College's Overseas Student Program in Yeroham, its internal kinks were so tangled and insoluble that I was generally surprised when any American students *did* come and stay for the one or two semesters. It was with more relief than despair that I returned in 1984 from a month's *miluim* to discover my program collapsed into a heap of student complaints and departures. The concept, offerings, staff, facilities, housing, location, and administration of W.U.J.S., however, left little room for just complaint. Indeed, were it ever because of low enrollments to be abolished, surely it would have to be reinvented.

Copie's anecdotes of the early days are unconscious echoes of the same theme. There was the time the nearsighted, new student from New York rode right through Arad without being aware that he had been there. And then there was the time when Copie had to wait for a while at Barclay's Bank while the teller went out for some change at a nearby delicatessen. Enjoying his tenure in Arad, justifiably proud of W.U.J.S.'s offerings, Michael Copeland, like Arad's longstanding Mayor Avraham Shohat, must persistently worry about attracting people in sufficient numbers to spell unequivocal success.

I can recall the parallel frustrations of *garin* Mashmia Shalom. A wistful reflection: Were Israel the nation containing not the vast majority of the world's Jews that its founders envisioned but merely most of us, were it a nation of, say, 8–10 million of the world's 13–14 million Jews, such wounding concerns would heal as a matter of course. In actuality, our population of under four million Jews does provide enough of a critical mass for the system to function—but barely. Just barely! When my daughter's high school physics teacher had gone off to *miluim*, there was no available substitute. That for the month ended the study of physics. The country Israel disconcertingly, comically, but also distressingly reminds me of the old New York Knickerbockers of my boyhood Fifties. The Brothers McGuire, Braun, Gallatin, Clifton, Zaslofsky could play so well; on any given day they were a match, or very nearly a match, for those classy Celtics, but the Knicks were

thin, so thin. One injury and the weakness of the bench became decisive.

Our real Jewish bench strength was calamitously struck
down, of course, more than a generation ago. What is left, de-
monstrably reliable and deft for short stretches, will it not
prove in the last analysis too distant, too depleted, too aloof?
All of the endless writhing and mutual accusation and self-
recrimination over enrollments, over numbers, over *aliya*—a
full century of the *yishuv* and national anguish—does it not
reduce itself to this? So much at such cost has been achieved,
and yet, for simple want of Jews, "one injury" and it is all put
at such risk?

Late, cool afternoon. I ambled through the courtyards of
the City Hall complex, crossed two broad streets and arrived at
the handsome Cultural Center. What was doing in Arad? A
bulletin board proclaimed the coming week's arrival of a production of Gilbert & Sullivan's *Iolanthe*, a concert by the
Israel Sinfonietta, and an exhibition of paintings by a Yona
Lui. It is universally agreed that the standard of education, of
recreation, and of culture in Arad is remarkable, far higher
than what would be found, for that matter, in a typical American city twice its size. This is a legacy of the first wave of Arad
settlers, one-third of whom were former kibbutzniks who demanded and got high-quality facilities.

Even casual observation, however, belies Arad's snobby
reputation as an Ashkenazi preserve. In a cavernous supermarket, I saw many housewives who were doubles for their
Yeroham cousins. A group of Bedouin workers were buying
bags of staples to take home after the day's work in an Arad
factory. (Between Arad and Beersheba are concentrated perhaps the largest number of Negev Bedouin; a much smaller
number lives in Arad itself.) New *olim* from Ethiopia surveyed
the shelves with confusion and delight. (Their 10- and 12-
year-old children are already able to help them navigate the
aisles.) Where Arad differs from most other development towns
is that it is not classifiable as a Moroccan or Yemenite or Georgian locale. In fact, its population mix by careful design ap-
proximates that of Israel as a whole. It seems to me a most significant local strength.

What did I purchase in that magically transposed Safeway

that I could not obtain in Yeroham's *souk* or Shekem? A package of rounded toothpicks, a package of bean sprouts, and (delicious irony) *cous cous* in a package mix.

The town's main plaza at 5:30 in the afternoon is very different from the doldrums of 2:00. It is crowded, lively, downright noisy; in essentials, not really all that different from dowdy Yeroham's. A major difference: dozens of well-dressed couples in their 60s and 70s stroll about as if on a luxury cruise. For these seniors, Arad means clean, dry air; it is their asthmatic's haven, their Magic Mountain. (Astonishingly, with the likelihood that for the sake of "Arad's development" a new phosphate plant will be established on its outskirts, all that is now in grave jeopardy.)

I sat down at a café to chat with some accessible W.U.J.S. students. The two young women intended to remain in Israel—but not in Arad. Why? "It's nice and all, but it's too far from Jerusalem. I mean, I am glad that I came to W.U.J.S. first, but living in Arad is like acting out some planner's dream. It's dull." Their plaints have a familiar cast. In fact, whereas a high percentage of that first contingent of eager settlers came here to raise their families and to live out their lives, later comers have been more upwardly-mobile. As soon as they can afford it, most sabra newcomers transplant themselves to the environs of Tel Aviv; the *olim*, of course, to magnetic Jerusalem.

Looking up, I saw bearing down on me two of my former Yeroham neighbors. They, at least, seem content here. Richie: "This place is civilized. The big difference is that everyone in Arad is here because they want to be here." Shira: "Aside from the *nouveaux riches* who let their dobermanns run around without a leash, I have no complaints. In fact, I really like it here. The kids pass nicely tended gardens on their way to school."

With the approach of darkness, I made my way to the nearest synagogue, close by the W.U.J.S. Center. It is recessed from the street; I pushed the heavy, paneled door. Depressingly, the inside of the darkened, spacious building was almost empty. Two old men looked up, then down, when I entered. It was almost past the time to *daven mincha*; evidently, no *minyan* was expected. By the time I had concluded, two more men entered, but I decided not to wait here for a *minyan* to materialize for *ma'ariv*; besides, I had a two-hour, two-bus trip to undergo before I made it back to Yeroham. Why then is this paradise in the Negev growing up at such a petty pace? The day had yielded a provisional remedy for my bafflement. It is not a scientific, objective, dispassionate, or even new answer, but my impression is so distinct and clear that I could eat it for dessert. Arad's special amenities have attracted, by and large, people who want to live as much of "the good life" as they possibly can. The day-to-day tone seems to resemble some impersonal way-station of an American suburb. It is both comfortable and oppressive. People, families are discrete, disconnected; idealism, long *passé*: "We're all right, Yankel."

Naturally, when a good opportunity will present itself—be it Haifa or Johannesburg—many of these bright, young Arad citizens will ride it. The efforts of the old-timers and the true-believers to stem and reverse this outflow by trumpeting Arad's cultural life, tennis center, and good climate seem to me futile. It was not Ben-Gurion's clarion call to settle the Negev that drew them here in the first place. With one eye on the main chance, they will not easily succumb to the transparent lures, no matter how substantial, of hometown boosterism.

I have never seen a dobermann pinscher among the wandering hounds of my funny Yeroham; usually, however, a *minyan* is not very hard to come by. The bus ride home delivered forth in its net, like a silvery fish drawn from the reservoir of the desert night, a quick and slippery trope. I know that hardly any of the many Israel experts would agree with my unprofessional, intuitive evaluation, but it satisfies some pressing need for provisional resolution: Both towns are Israel writ small. Arad runs the slicker operation by far, but over the long, long haul, is it not possible that the extended family networks of Yeroham possess a greater depth and resiliency that will count for more? What I cannot even guess at is whether my two prototypes ultimately are playing intramurally or are, in fact, pulling apart to different ends. Though this resolution matters not at all to Damascus and Riyadh and hardly much more than that to most Jews in Toronto and New York, it will make perhaps all the difference.

DRIPPING WITH
PROSPERITY

*F*our years have passed since the air skittered out of the Tel Aviv Stock Market Exchange with a thrumming burst. For Israel's salaried workers, it has been a gritty-toothed, bullet-biting time. Out in the vulnerable 80% of the country living from month to month on bank overdrafts, there have been stretches when it has been hard to carry on a neighborly confab about much else.

It is true, of course, that since the arrival of the National Unity Government inflation has been dramatically checked. It is the wage-earner, however, who almost exclusively has borne that burden. My wife, for example, working full-time at editorial work, brings home not quite enough to cover our monthly expenses for food alone. People in the public sector never know till the last minute whether their salaries will be paid on time. What, I have these months frequently wondered, can this sort of daily scrambling signify to the privileged 3% among us who inhabit a more insulated Israel, our resident idealists—the kibbutzniks?

I sense my tone betrays an edge of jaundice. It has not always been thus. Indeed, when I co-directed Bensalem, Fordham University's Experimental College in the New York of the late 1960s, Buber's essay on "the experiment that did not fail" served me as a cardinal text. The kibbutz was the most salient model of how to think about and organize aspects of our Sixties ferment-spawned, communal teaching–learning, college live-in. Had I and my family made *aliya* when, after two implosive years, we left Bensalem in 1969, the kibbutz almost surely would have been our first-choice Israeli context. Seven years thereafter, however, aged 38, I had passed the usual upper age-limit for entering kibbutzim; even more pointedly, I felt I had passed a vital inner limit.

Nevertheless, our ten months at Bensalem as "communard activists" at "The Great Panjandrum Himself" on City Island had left a rich if muzzy legacy of experience and memory. The main enterprise of the dozen of us in the tall, gainly house on the anachronistic island oval off the Bronx had been "to raise the consciousness" of its 7,000 ever-suspecting inhabitants. Such was the business that had brought us together. Communalism was a ready means: we ate, worked, shared, fussed, and took our ease together. In innocent '68–'69, we tried to plant ideas—no bombs. As long as it lasted, it worked well, and when we departed for California, it was with relief but also in peace.

When in '76 Marcia and I finally did make our *aliya*, we joined Neot Midbar, a *garin* which planned to live as a communal settlement (*moshav shitufi*) "in the Negev." And when those plans had to be scuttled (malleable Neot Midbarians let themselves get channeled into becoming Gaza Strip artists), we intrepidly organized yet another communal *garin*, dovish Mashmia Shalom, which for a brief time succeeded in establishing itself within the Green Lines in the development town of Yeroham. In short, communalism, ideally embodied by the kibbutz, for many years seemed to me the realizable model of how people should and could disport their lives.

One effect of nine years of living in Yeroham, however, has been to erode to sandpile the penny-bright, Utopia-on-a-hill image of the kibbutz that once I harbored. Our town's connection to nearby Kibbutz Sde Boker is sheerest vacuum—the 20 kilometers could as well be 200. Precisely as depicted in the more vulgar Likud cartoons, Laborites from Negev kibbutzim like Sde Boker, Revivim, Mash'ave Sade really are nonpersons locally save in the signally dubious role of election-day *apparatnichkim*.

A final nudge: for reasons of sentiment, ecology, thrift, and need (Israeli travel agents and funeral homes simply do not flood the land with promotional calendars like their American counterparts), we each year here rummage through our dusty cartons of American memorabilia for a suitable calendar to recycle. All that is necessary is an amiable, old first of January that steps forth on the same day of the week as that of the infant year. At odds of 6 to 1, we have not missed yet. In 1986, our kitchen wall struck gold: a Japan Air Lines glossy gem replete with misty landscapes, gilded silk screens, and pencilled-in reminders of once-critical meetings and yellowing promises-to-keep. The year—1969.

After several Japanese months, the ironies of such disjunctive chronometry were overwhelming. There were matters, both objective and subjective, to be checked out.

K ibbutz Hatzerim is a typical, well-established settlement that sits six kilometers west of Beersheba. Founded in 1946 by 25 young men and 5 young women, it served as an outpost of high strategic importance during the War of Independence. Not only do I pass this kibbutz en route to my home base when I report periodically for reserve duty; I frequently do my service together with one of its *chaverim* who several times had invited me to visit. I had often noted its typically well-tended fields and neat rows of family houses from the road, but never before had I trudged the curving, dusty length of its approach road. After less than a kilometer, I reached an unimposing, oddly ramshackle entrance to the residential area of the kibbutz.

A sprawling, corrugated metal structure first confronts the visitor who enters this gate. This is the headquarters of Netafim, the font and substance of Hatzerim's peculiar prosperity. Kibbutz Hatzerim, which for almost two decades had been a Negev hardship case, has for some time now been doing very well indeed. Controlling the dominant share of Israel's drip irrigation business, Kibbutz Hatzerim, in a Negev dotted with development towns suffering a 30–40% rate of unemployment, is an island dripping with surfeit.

In his functional office sat Natty Barak, in his mid-30s the current manager of Netafim. He had a tale to tell, evidently a set-piece, of Hatzerim's rise to self-sufficiency. The first years had been dispiriting. Season followed disappointing season: crops refused to grow. Not a few members despaired and moved on; by 1959, the remaining members were on the verge of abandoning the Negev. Soil salinity had them licked. Then a personal appeal from Prime Minister Levi Eshkol—who argued that it would be less expensive to install the whole kibbutz in luxury at the Dan Hotel in Tel Aviv than to re-establish it from scratch elsewhere—was followed by a dramatic visit by David Ben-Gurion who pleaded with them to stick it out. They stuck . . . and became big winners!

Everything turned around at the same time. First, their efforts to leech the soil suddenly met success: pomegranates, grapes, later followed by avocados, pears, and other crops flourished. Then Hatzerimites, feeling the need for fresh reinforcements, sent emissaries to Argentina. The first Latin recruits started to arrive in 1965. Today they comprise about 40% of the kibbutz's 260 members. "Their arrival saved us," Barak tersely remarked.

That very year witnessed another signal event in the Algeresque climb of Hatzerim—the founding of Netafim. "We had decided," Barak explained, "that we needed to diversify, to establish an industrial division, so a member was released to work full-time. It took him an entire year. We had, of course, certain criteria: we wanted an enterprise that wouldn't tie up all of our capital or manpower, and we wanted something that would connect to agriculture. Drip irrigation systems seemed ideal. We purchased the patent from the developer, a man named Blass from Tel Aviv. Netafim was a success from the start."

Yes, there had been controversy. Some members objected to the very presence of a factory on the kibbutz; a tiny fraction left. But all that was history. The real story is economics. Current sales run to $10 million annually, 20% of which derives from overseas. Netafim accounts for fully 80% of Hatzerim's total income. The destinies of Kibbutz Hatzerim and Netafim are now inextricably welded together.

Well and good, but how does the kibbutz reconcile its big-business finesse—its capitalist "success"—with its underlying socialist philosophy? Barak admitted that there are problems. "Of course we recognize them, but the governing philosophy within the kibbutz remains 'from each according to his abilities; to each according to his needs.' Yet at the same time we realize that in order successfully to manage a multi-million-dollar enterprise with a world-wide market, we have to be flexible to compete in an open market economy. Our solution has been to seat a person on the Netafim Board of Directors whose specific function is to represent the kibbutz perspective. Further, all major factory decisions are also kibbutz decisions and are discussed at General Meetings. We continue to refuse, for example, to take on hired workers; instead, factory jobs are rotated among all kibbutz members. A new shift comes on every two weeks."

We walked the short distance to Hatzerim's new dining hall, dedicated five years ago. Boasting three large, neatly-appointed sections (one exclusively for non-smokers), replete with special features like an electronically operated front door and a cloth hand-towel dispenser in the washroom, by kibbutz standards it is . . . well . . . lavish. Plainly, Hatzerim is trying to square its circle: to float in upright, egalitarian integrity while splashing about in a gusher of plenty.

The communal line has held fast on private transportation. There is none. The 20 vehicles of Netafim are available for the use of kibbutz members on a signout basis. But have the pinched times affected life on Kibbutz Hatzerim not at all?

"Of course we feel them," Barak responded. "Both here in Israel and abroad, there's much more competition now than formerly in the drip irrigation business. We have to keep looking for new markets, devising systems for new crops and conditions. Netafim systems are operating in South America, Greece, Australia, Yugoslavia—even in Morocco. But since things are tougher just now, the kibbutz has imposed new restrictions on consumption. Except for emergencies and for kibbutz business, trips overseas have been for the present ended."

A temporary curtailment of trips overseas! Was that the full extent of kibbutz pinch in times of national crimp? I recalled that, while thumbing through Netafim's glossy promotional literature an hour earlier, I had noted that Fresno, California would be hosting a major exposition of drip irrigation systems. Would Netafim be sending an exhibit, representatives?

"Of course we'll be there," Barak shot back.

Who would not wonder about incipient tensions within a society where all are "equal," but some push a plow and others traverse the globe? (But Barak would not be the man to ask about this.) More critically, it seemed to me that the seemingly exemplary kibbutz concern for not exploiting hired labor had engendered, indeed encouraged, a barrier of exclusivity and separation between Hatzerim and nearby Negev towns. In fact, rather than expand their enterprise at Hatzerim itself, which would have meant either drastically expanding kibbutz membership or hiring outside workers, the kibbutz had chosen to establish secondary Netafim plants at two distant kibbutzim. (Like a cartel, except that they all "share" the lucrative North American market, the three kibbutzim have divided up the globe so as not to compete with each other for drip irrigation francs and yen.) I challenged this dubious decision. Was not Hatzerim abnegating a responsibility toward its hard-pressed Negev neighbors? Was it not just a shade too expedient that kibbutz sensitivity to non-exploitation translated into a condition wherein all the dollar earnings irrigated the kibbutz's own melon patch?

Obviously pained, Barak passed me along to Gidon Elad at his kibbutz home. About 55, affable Elad is a founding member of Hatzerim and a teacher at the regional high school at Mishmar Hanegev. He has twice served for several years as a *shaliach* to America. Elad was quick to declare that he enjoyed his periodic stints at the Netafim plant. ("It upgrades our involvement in what's going on there.") The very type of a resident kibbutz intellectual, he caught my drift at once.

"You may think us overly concerned about our own good, but in fact among kibbutzim, Hatzerim is a pioneer in implementing a non-elite educational philosophy. Over 200 of our and other Negev kibbutz kids, along with 200 disadvantaged kids from Youth Aliya and 200 other kids from Omer [a well-off Beersheba suburb], now travel to attend the kibbutz regional high school at Mishmar Hanegev. We led the fight ten years ago to accept this arrangement against heavy opposition within our Movement. Now this sort of 'mixed education' has become almost fashionable."

How were Youth Aliya kids helped to manage among their kibbutznik and suburbanite coevals?

"We house them here on the kibbutz as 9th-graders and keep them together for a year, both to get them accustomed to the new surroundings and to try to upgrade them scholastically. From 10th to 12th grades, they merge with the other kids. So far we've had two groups go through successfully. The third group is on its way."

"Is that all?," I pursued facetiously, but Elad smiled and took the bait.

"Oh, there *is* more. Hatzerim sponsors a Youth Village at the site of a failed kibbutz called Kedma. There youngsters between 14 and 18 on the verge of serious trouble with the law go to live and learn. These are kids who otherwise would never be accepted by the army, who would be marked for life. At the Youth Village about 65 of them are boarded. Hatzerim has a representative on the Village's Board of Directors and keeps in close touch with what goes on there. Further, between high school graduation and army induction, the youngsters spend several months living here on the kibbutz. The program is another success story."

There was yet more. Hatzerim was planning to help establish a second Youth Village solely for youngsters from kibbutzim. And more: Hatzerim is the sponsoring settlement for a new kibbutz being established in the Negev.

In spite of myself, I was impressed. Hatzerim's material prosperity seems not to have diluted the zeal of these 260 souls to promote the larger good—as long, of course, as ultimate control over their own enterprise was not in any way jeopardized. Notwithstanding this caveat, the kibbutz still appears to be a self-starting world of its own, its typical youngsters a different breed from many of the kids in Israel's towns and cities who are as adept as their American counterparts at "hanging out."

But had Elad not noticed in the wake of the Lebanese War signs of disaffection with larger Israeli society—say, in a disinclination of Hatzerim youngsters to volunteer for the elite units and leadership roles in the Army?

"True, there has been something of that, but those who point to Lebanon as the cause have it wrong. Lebanon merely exaggerated a tendency toward me-first, a philosophy of personal self-fulfillment as the highest value, which, I believe, is mainly an American import. But things are now improving again. There's a real openness between adults and teenagers here, a lot of genuine listening to each other.

"What's critical to us," he continued, "is that, over the past 15 years, somewhere between 50 and 60% of our own youngsters have opted to stay on as adult members. We need this continuity and stability merely to survive, let alone to take on larger societal tasks. And it is our kibbutz philosophy that we should attempt to solve some of Israel's pressing problems. As I hope you will grant, this is more than a platitude. A full 10% of Hatzerim's annual income goes into our 'Welfare Fund.'" Elad was quick to caution that this was not *tsedaka*. I smiled. "Well," he amended, "we prefer to call it something else." For a mainline Labor kibbutz, Hatzerim is rather ceremonious. Elad noted that candles were lighted on Friday nights and that all the religious holidays were, in a fashion, celebrated.

I was curious to talk with some recent kibbutz recruits from the States, but, surprisingly, there are none. In fact, fewer than a dozen members of Hatzerim (among whom is Elad's British-born wife, one of the rare women to have chosen not to have a stove included among her household furnishings) have made *aliya* from English-speaking countries. In the past three years, the kibbutz has absorbed very few new members from anywhere. Again I showed surprise: with so much unemployment in Israel, I had thought that the economic security afforded by kibbutz life would have attracted more young couples, but such seems not the case.

"We prefer anyway to absorb *garinim* of youngsters from our own kibbutz movement," Elad clarified. "They know what to expect. And singles are much easier for us than families. In general, families from overseas find it very difficult to adjust to life on a kibbutz. Moreover, we differ from some other kibbutzim in that we refuse to depend upon volunteers. The limit here is 20 at a time. We don't want so many that they can form their own subculture on the kibbutz, perhaps negatively influencing our own kids. So far we haven't had drug or similar problems here at Hatzerim."

Prominent among "similar problems," I was aware from several visits watching Rabbi Shmuel Golding at work counseling the confused and the bereft in his Jerusalem office, are Evangelicals and members of fringe cults whose chief incentive for volunteering for a tour on a kibbutz is proximity to its young people. For a variety of reasons, kibbutz youngsters in search of spiritual fulfillment have proved notably vulnerable targets. In fact, the current "in" place for kibbutz youngsters to travel in their traditional post-army year of wander is the Higher Enlightenment Country of the Himalayas. My own kibbutz-raised, *sabrit* second cousin Tal is now somewhere way-out East of Suez.

I left Elad to nose about the kibbutz on my own. Attractive two-story family houses line the road that leads toward the highway from the new dining hall. Peeking in again, I noticed an exhibit of photos and sketches of a variety of entranceways. It was an architect's proposal for a new gate and façade for Hatzerim. Elad had noted that the architect had earlier delivered a closed-circuit television presentation for the *chaverim*.

That very night, after Netafim lights would be dimmed, the chickens fed, and the cowshed darkened, the kibbutz's General Assembly—distant cousin of the *polis* of ancient Athens, the New Hampshire town meeting—would convene, discuss, debate, and fix upon a choice for their settlement's new entrance. Sweat, drips, shekels, and grass roots: this communal life would never suit more than a minute fraction of my fellow Israelis. As for myself, circumstance (inner disposition?) had frayed the once lively cord of affection. Still, even today, could I not grant that Israel was unviable—indeed, inconceivable—without these earnest few?

I entered the cavernous interior of the Netafim plant and trailed along row after row of large bins and tubs filled with different lengths of plastic drip irrigation tubing and valves. Tens of thousands of these black tubelets have raised those comfortable, two-story homes and that snazzy dining hall with its automatic sliding door and individual cloth handcloths. They would soon build for Hatzerim its handsome new façade. The black tubelets of Netafim have enabled this kibbutz to overcome dependence and despondency—to prosper in the Negev. The Negev, however, had in turn amply repaid the kibbutz for its steadfastness: had not the desert and isolation enabled Hatzerim to maintain its élan and a higher degree of purity than could be found on many sister settlements in the North?

Only about a dozen people moved around the factory floor, all joint shareholders in their works and lives together. "To each according to his needs; from each according to his abilities." It would be easy enough to pick further flaws; I had, frankly, expected worse. Even behind its future ostentatious façade, however, it will not be hard to discern much of solid substance. In Israel's Three-Percentland, "To each. . . from each," that tired old clarion-call still has the power to move men and women to lead good lives. (Or, at the least, to want to.)

I rode back to Beersheba in a kibbutz car making its hourly run into the city. My kibbutznik fellow passengers were women going to town to shop for something special. Ordinary people— just your usual, everyday communards with another meeting to attend that evening. I could not decide for certain whether it was more for good or for ill that, no more than their home kibbutz showed excessive concern for the welfare of its nearby development town neighbors, did they seem to care a fig about raising the benighted consciousness of their fellow passenger. In fact, they betrayed not a sign to distinguish them from the other 97% of us, most of whom are these days far more preoccupied than they with trying to make ends meet in a difficult time.

"BUT WHAT DO YOU DO THERE?" A BOOSTER'S RETORT

*I*t was just a routine academic meeting, this time at Bar-Ilan University in Ramat Gan, a suburb of Tel Aviv. I was representing tiny Ramat Hanegev College, the quixotic, anti-establishment institution that the small group of us American *olim*, somewhat at a loss over what to do with ourselves in Israel, founded against odds and smirks a year after we had landed in our small Negev home base of Yeroham. The middle-aged woman's reaction upon hearing the news was unabashed: "Ye-RO-ham! You really live in Yeroham!?" A bit too gauche, she realized at once; she made a nice shot at recovery with a full-blown "*Kol ha-KaVOD* [more power] to you." Over the past decade, I have lost track of all the *kol hakavod*s! Some condescend, others gush: it is long since I have basked in their benign glow.

Nor do I any longer bristle at the alternative thrust: "Ye-ro-HAM! [You must be *meshuge*.] But what do you *do* there?" I have become adept at anticipating and parrying the narrow range of retorts to the delayed revelation of my hometown dazzlepiece. Most are variations, neither feigned nor malicious, on the theme of incredulity. No one, however, can misinterpret their true import: You must be some kind of idiot! The burden of "But what do you *do* there?" is never quite deflected by the offhand "Oh, I write and sometimes teach." Nor does the more aggressive "Much the same, I presume, as you in Ramat Gan (or Haifa or Jerusalem)," because the overt question just barely gloves the real stinger: "*How* can you or anyone *live* there?"

But no, I am not, I think, Prince Myshkin, nor was I meant to be. And "there" is not "Elsewhere, perhaps"; on the contrary, it is one of the State of Israel's least adulterated products. From 1977 my home, since I left boyhood Bronx I have lived "there" longer even than I did in Coalinga, longer than anywhere else I ever thumbtacked down in America. Still, I will grant that more than crass prejudice ("The cultured Moroccans went to France and Quebec; they dumped the Casbah in places like Yeroham") and rank ignorance ("The last time I was there was on *miluim* in 1964: what a dump!") account for this almost universal Israel chorus of awe and pity at the mention of my talismanic Yeroham.

Whereas only one Israeli in thirty lives on a kibbutz, one in *five* inhabits these large and small communities in "development areas." Yet while most people, most notably the Israelis themselves, know a great deal about kibbutz, this darker side of the Israeli moon—the development towns—subsists in shadow. The phrase itself is grossly inconvenient: it deceptively blankets settlements like Arad and Carmiel, which have been planned and laid down with enviable care, with others that have been vegetated like ill-watered weeds, national afterthoughts. The original concept (delineated definitively in Orni & Efrat's standard reference, *Geography of Israel*) was to create new centers that would "draw industry and productive services to hitherto underpopulated regions and to create a closely interlocked rural and urban economy and a more balanced distribution of population over all parts of Israel." For residents of Yeroham, Sderot, Shlomi, and two dozen similar bywaters, that reads like a very flat joke indeed.

Some needful data: This stunted Yeroham of mine is an underdevelopment town of around 6,500 souls who, save for some nearby Bedouin tentdwellers, are every one of them Jews. It hugs the rim of a knoll some 40 kilometers southeast of that would-be metropolis of the Negev, Beersheba. Founded in 1951 as the very first of these new towns in the North Negev, and intended to be the chief center in the area, the "development" tag has proved a pathetic misnomer. Indeed,

the history of the place is a sorry jokebook of planning mis-
calculations. Yeroham foundered and Yerohamites, those who
stuck it out or could not contrive to get themselves unstuck,
floundered without any economic base whatsoever for the first
15 years. Fifteen years! Finally, the first of three good-sized
factories was constructed in the late '60s, but far too late to
forestall Yeroham's only human development worthy of note:
the departure of most residents with initiative and the imposi-
tion of a welfare mentality on those left behind.

How and why all this happened is hardly a secret, but, especially since Israel's recent political impasse hinges upon the
visceral disaffection of the Sephardim in the development
areas from the once-dominant Labor Party, it bears recalling.
At its Independence in May 1948, Israel's Jewish population
totaled 750,000. Within a decade, thanks mostly to the expulsion of Jews from Arabic countries, this figure had more than
doubled. A displaced population equal to itself, mostly penu-
rious, had to be absorbed virtually all at once by an infant nation straining under continual military threat. It was not an
easy situation.

Over 60% of the population of Yeroham are North Africans,
the overwhelming majority from families that were bused
there soon after debarking in Haifa in the early 1950s. Desper-
ately over-burdened Labor Party bureaucrats, virtually all Ashkenazim of course, resorted to duplicity with the reluctant
Sephardi greenhorns from Morocco: first contingents were informed that Yeroham lay "not far from Tel Aviv," and were un-
willingly deposited into tents on the desert site in the middle of
the night. Most felt helpless and abandoned. Even the passage
of one quarter of a century has not assuaged the anger of many
Yerohamites at the memory of their deception. So far, the
Likud, Tami, and Shas Parties have been the major political
beneficiaries of this burden of the sour past.

Another 15–20% of Yerohamites arrived a few years later
from India. An introspective community, they and the more
gregarious Moroccans do not get on especially well. The originally heavy contingent from Rumania looked around at the
uninviting Negev sands and took off for the cities just as soon

as they could, but some elderly Rumanians remain. "Others" include miscellaneous "Israelis," some Iranians and Yemenites, and around 15 households of us "Anglos." Perhaps in all, 10% of the town is Ashkenazi, too few of us to be perceived as a threat to Moroccan hegemony.

It is then understandable and perhaps forgivable that Israel's planners took resort in expediency and bureaucratic fiat to effect provisional "solutions." Less satisfactory has been the obstinate perdurance of the major cause of the social problems that these first steps have entailed. Though the expansion of the development towns has long been held to be a high national priority, Israel's industry, population, and cultural life today remain more concentrated than ever in its central, vulnerable, urban bulge. Policies supposed to disperse the largesse throughout the land to Israel's satellite communities have ever and again received less service than lip.

Yeroham lies only thirteen kilometers south of Dimona—close, much too close. Though founded four years later, Dimona soon eclipsed the older settlement. Why? When laying the new highway from Beersheba to Eilat, the planners jogged east from Dimona to the Dead Sea, *totally bypassing Yeroham.* In consequence, new industry (including the Atomic Energy Development Center) was attracted to Dimona, which soon grew into an independent city of around 25,000. Stymied, Yeroham has stagnated.

Together with their *raison d'être,* many Yerohamites have lost a grip on their self-respect. When we first moved "there" in 1977, one of the more visible emblems of this demoralization was that, despite the existence of a direct road (in need, to be sure, of repair) connecting Yeroham to Beersheba, all public transportation proceeded a long way around, via Dimona. Compounding this inconvenience, intracity Dimona traffic often stretched what should have been a 35-minute Beersheba–Yeroham run into a trip of a full hour. This frustrating situation finally was alleviated only in 1984.

A second sign, however, remains the dozens of Yeroham high schoolers who commute daily to Dimona because they are unable to pursue in the Yeroham schools certain courses of study like electronics. Indeed, being from Yeroham is for many of its residents a purple bruise, a livid stigma, a lively getaway itch.

Marcia and I did not, of course, come on *aliya* in order to live in Yeroham; indeed, we had heard neither of it nor the term "development town" until some time after we had arrived in Israel. During our last year still in California, we had been contacted by a representative of Neot Midbar, a *garin* of 15–20 religious families who were planning to make *aliya* and new lives together on a new, communal rural settlement in the Negev. It was to be a type of modified kibbutz called a *moshav shitufi*. Why not, we reasoned, pick up the communal thread we had dropped in 1969 at The Great Panjandrum Himself on City Island in the land in which, more than any other, this life-mode, far from a seeming aberration or a standing provocation, was both socially sanctioned and officially supported? We had not met most of the other people in this *garin*, but Marcia and I had few doubts that we could find among them people to like and live out our lives with. After all, we reasoned, consider how much the decision to make *aliya* under these communal conditions already seemed to say about their values.

We spent the first three weeks of our new lives in Israel under the comforting auspices of fledgling Garin Neot Midbar at Masuot Yitzhak, a prosperous, attractive rural seat and established *moshav shitufi* near Ashkelon. For weeks I was high on loading Jewish chickens and tending Jewish greenhouse flowers for export to Europe. When after several months, however, the Jewish Agency determined that the parcel of land for our *garin* to settle was a small though coastal stretch between the Arab urban centers of Gaza and Khan Yunis in the Katif region of the Gaza Strip—for us an area on the errant side of the Green Line (as well as being the most densely populated region in all of the country)—we grew despondent. Although we and a few others went through the motions of fruitless protest, we already knew that most of Neot Midbar were fully prepared to go wherever they were told. Katif was so scenic!

We few dissenters—with the support of some families in America who had not yet made *aliya*—then founded a new

garin, Mashmia Shalom, which we based on the fourfold
weighty principles of religious observance, a tradeoff with the
Arabs of land for peace, ecological responsibility, and social
justice. We ran ads, sponsored meetings in Tel Aviv and Jerusalem, spoke on the radio, and attracted considerable interest
(as well as the heavy disapprobation of our former comrades
in Neot Midbar who succeeded in evicting us from Masuot
Yitzhak to an immigrant absorption center in Beersheba). Finally, we achieved official recognition as the peacenik *garin*
showpiece among the National Religious Party settlement
groups. (All other N.R.P. *garinim* tilted toward Gush Emunim
and settlement on the West Bank.) In the years before Camp
David, however, Israel, we were authoritatively assured, had
no plans whatsoever for new, Negev settlements outside of
equivocal Katif.

After half-a-year of meetings (and many broken appoint-
ments) with government and movement officials (at a time that
we should have been devoting to learning Hebrew in our *ulpan*), embattled Mashmia Shalom decided that rather than
dangling in suspense for the five years we were warned it would
take to be awarded some homey hectares of our own, it would
be wiser to accept the generous offer of the City of Yeroham, "a
forlorn development town in the Negev," to move together
there to newly-built, adjacent housing as a *garin*. Whatever
we thought we could achieve by founding a new settlement—
and after all, officials insinuated, was not insisting upon a *new*
settlement a matter more of ego than of ideology?—could we
not do it in a place that was a clearcut challenge, that vitally
needed the infusion of new talent and blood? Fully appreciat-
ing that these disingenuous proposals were largely designed to
appease and to dispose of us, we bought them nonetheless. It
seemed our best shot. Late in 1977 five "Anglo" families—
Mashmia Shalom—moved to Shikun Ben-Gurion, a new
neighborhood of *cottagim*, on the site of the original Yeroham
immigrant campground, the *ma'arbarot* of 1951.

Mashmia Shalom maintained its identity for more than another three years of Saturday night *garin* gatherings. A folder
of typed minutes that sits in a carton near my desk could attest
our initial optimism, our perseverance, our earnestness, our

comic fumbling, our frustration, our gradual loss of heart. Through our *garin*, we five families parented both Ramat Hanegev College and Congregation Afikim Hanegev; both descendants have survived Mashmia Shalom, whose former members work to this day as educators, artists, writers, and social workers in the town. But the *garin* itself, becoming inexorably more our burden than support, though to this day still listed in N.R.P. literature as one of their official *garinim*, finally withered away. Seven further years down the way, even though the official framework has long evaporated, most of us former members remain still in Yeroham as friends, neighbors, and even, from time to time, political comrades-at-arms.

Inexperienced with Israel, we had made a grievous miscalculation. We had thought that Mashmia Shalom could draw to itself—and through us to Yeroham—many of the other religiously observant doves who were floating around Israel. We had gambled that unlikely Yeroham could begin to serve as a counterweight to the right-wing, nationalist settlements, many of them affiliated with Gush Emunim, that were springing up on the West Bank. Week after week we debated new strategy for attracting our scattered ilk to join cause with us. Attractive and inexpensive housing, a communal framework, serious work awaited them. It would be for Marcia and me another round of the activist American Sixties. We were so willing; we were so ready to make our signal contribution to the Israeli body politic.

With the passing weeks, then months, then years, however, the truth slowly asserted itself on us. We were it! Out there, awaiting the word and witnessing our exemplary action, there sat a potential dovish constituency of no more than several dozen! The only "active" religious peace organization in the field, Oz V'Shalom, held a "convention" at our Ramat Hanegev College in 1978. Twenty people appeared, a high percentage of its total membership. Nearly all were established academics who never dreamed of jeopardizing their posts. Six years later Mashmia Shalom's successor organization, Netivot Shalom, held a *kinus* over a Shabbat in Yeroham. It was a great success: around 70 people came, met, debated . . . and departed.

Our quest for an added measure of "higher significance" shortcircuited, what we have salvaged from sunken Mashmia Shalom is a more modest but, all things considered, not lesser vision of ourselves against the background of this dowdy, quaint Yeroham where we have remained out of preference. (After all, we were not dumped here penniless in the middle of the night.) For years regarded with circumspection by the locals—the Rumanians came and went, a group of Russians had come and gone, how long really would these *Americai-im* hang around?—we are now perceived as certified Yeroham fixtures, as a rarified, trifle queer, but highly visible variety of permanent local fauna.

"But what do you *do* there?"

Yes, uncannily, even after a decade, our continued presence here still elicits from some Jerusalemite acquaintances—and even Beershevaites!—the identical *kol ha-kavods*, the same "How do you find it reallys?" that *their very own aliya* evoked from the cousins in Scranton and the friends in Hartford. Understood, if politely unvoiced, is "When are you coming back to your senses?" And just as "American Zionists" have flocked and will continue to flock to Israel, so "Israeli Zionists" have flocked and will continue to flock to these outlying zones where the cultural and economic circulation runs slower, but which everyone grants must, for the nation's health, somehow be flushed with new blood. *In their hearts*, they flock.

And yet . . . and yet, outside of the framework of Mashmia Shalom, of Oz V'Shalom, of Netivot Shalom, our presence *has* been instrumental in attracting other "Anglos" to Yeroham and in the slow growth of a diverse and creative permanent sub-community. Some "stars" have left, but their talented replacements have been more than adequate. Following tradition for ensemble companies, here follows a current cast of characters (partial listing) in alphabetical order: Lucille & Oscar Alexander (a retired engineer, country people hailing from Odessa—i.e., Odessa, Texas!), Shalom Bar-yamin (an engineer from Pittsburgh) and Roni Brown (a children's book writer, both of whom actually preceded us Mashmia Shalomites in Yeroham), Dr. Ruth Borer (an Instructor of Hebrew Literature, living again in Israel after 20 years in the States),

Dr. Moshe Dror (a rabbi—art curator—futurist), Miriam & Dr. Mordecai Gefter (a religious educator holding a doctorate of law, who heads the town's civil defense unit), Chaim Goldberg (a linguist and computer specialist from Yale), Yoheved & Ya'akov Lavon (*haredi* scribe and health food faddist), Alan Rosenberg (a ceramicist), Dr. Tsila Stern (a Professor of Industrial Engineering) & Max Stern (a musician—composer), and Eva & Mota Teumin (a retired aeronautical engineer who in New Jersey set up an underground bazooka assembly works for the Haganah during the War of Independence).

Together with perhaps a dozen others and with us original Mashmia Shalom ideologues, this rather incongruous aggregation comprises the Yeroham "Anglo community." And yet, far more than one would experience or conceive in either suburbanized America or urbanized Israel are we *a community*. Discounting for the moment their "Black Hebrews," bigger Dimona cannot boast anywhere nearly as large an "Anglo" contingent. I find, when I pause to consider, that each of my Yeroham companions is both dear and special. Moreover, more I suspect than is the case most places, cause for pause for such considerations is not all that infrequent.

In general, we "Anglos" interact rather harmoniously with the dominant Moroccan community. Some of us, of course, have integrated more closely than others; four successful local "intermarriages" spring to mind. My psychologist next-door neighbor Moshe Landsman, a former Mashmia Shalomite, who grew up in Gainesville, Florida and who married a *sabrait*, now handles Hebrew better than English, and Chaim Goldberg's Moroccan-flavored Hebrew could fool most anyone. Others of us do not make it in Hebrew much past *boker tov*.

As for myself, I ride an emotional wave in my mental relation to Greater Yeroham. Though lately I have been passive in the role, for some years I served as an elected member of the Yeroham Labor Party Central Committee. And, of course, having young children learn in the local schools, as well as being on the board of Congregation Afikim Hanegev, also serves to keep me humming the same rhythms as my fellow townspeople. Then again, however, I must own up to periods when my most expedient tactic is to distance myself from "the natives," when my most treasured self-image is that of a half-baked literary exile on some Corfu or Cypress of the soul. Overall, Yeroham fulfills certain aspirations that Marcia and I held dear when we left America: a human-scaled place attuned to Jewish rhythms where our kids run freely at all hours; where we grow flowers, grapes, apricots, and plums in front and back yard; where we breathe clean, dry air; where, living modestly, we feel neither poor nor deprived; where we each have found meaningful work to perform. We *like* living out our lives as Jews, Israelis, and Yerohamites, and we positively relish the bonus yield of our perversity: that we *count and may be counted upon*. I cannot be certain, but I strongly suspect that if not Phoenix or Boston, then neither Tel Aviv nor Jerusalem could possibly have served our particular, eccentric needs so well. So, in any event, has been our intuition. Indeed, when I consider the special privations of living in a place like Tel Aviv—*kol hakavod* to all you wonderful Dizengoff *halutzim*—they would not, I warrant, have fetched or possibly kept us in Israel at all.

"But what *do* we do there?" Yes, well perhaps a brief amble from my front door "downtown" would be useful. It is Tuesday; I have an ulterior purpose.

At our corner there stands the neighborhood *makolet*: till the old man died last year, "Aaron's." Now it is "Haim's," the youngest of Aaron's 9 children. I stop by there most days at mid-morning for cheese and a freshly delivered, French loaf. It is usually still warm from the bakery. For observant Jews, bread marks the line of demarcation between what constitutes a repast (and is therefore preceded by formal hand washing and followed by a lengthy grace) and what "occasional food." Given typical American bread (a dubious benefice), that ritual divide seemed gratuitous in the States, but in Israel this crisp particular follows the line of Europe; our daily bread (still heavily subsidized by the government) is a world apart from American sponge. It is, in fact, a scent of Paris that draws me out the front door each morning.

Directly across the street from Haim's, 5th-graders are learning how to stroke the ball squarely. Like most of Yeroham's recent construction, the new tennis courts are a gift of the Jewish community of Montreal, Yeroham's twin under the Project Renewal Program. Montreal was a fortunate draw. The Canadians have over the past seven years contributed not only money but considerable talent and energy to Yeroham. Among the projects they have funded is a splendid new library, a solar-designed old people's center, much-needed high school renovations, refurbishment for some older neighborhoods, and college scholarships. What they have not done is make investments in local industry, so it remains to be seen whether Yeroham's shaky economic base and abnormally high unemployment rate will ultimately render of their efforts a passing thing.

I cross the street that leads off to the high school where, during our first years in Yeroham, I comically strode the part-time boards teaching recalcitrant English. In some ways Yeroham kids are a terrific audience. There were groups of youngsters to whom I could have presented the same lines once a week: the lesson was always as new to them as on opening night. Their lives were at odds with a curriculum which decreed that it was English that shall be compulsory for all. The sad irony is that many of the Moroccan kids grew up in households that spoke French, a natural reservoir for watering language skills that was effectively closed off. Most complete their formal education with scant English and dry-as-a-bone French.

When we first arrived in town, this street had been a winter mudway. After fruitless requests, the parents' organization of the high school refused to send their children any longer to school until the Education Ministry in Jerusalem made a commitment to get the street properly paved: a victory for the politics of tug, pull, and publicity. A similar tactic had succeeded a year earlier in securing the wherewithal for Yeroham to attract several fine young doctors to live and practice in the town. At political finesse, the "natives" can occasionally perform like true sophisticates.

Just ten meters away, next to a playground, sits an inauspicious-looking synagogue—*Bet Knesset* Afikim Hanegev. Yeroham must boast at least 20 additional synagogues—all, of course, "Orthodox." Except for the Indian, the Persian, and the "Rumanian" congregations (the last of which, serving the black-coated *haredi yeshiva* community, is today almost void of Rumanians), all employ a Moroccan Sephardi style of worship. Soon after Mashmia Shalom first appeared in Yeroham, it acquired this small building, then an unused former kindergarten, from the city authorities. We painted it, did some minor repairs, and midwifed yet another Yeroham congregation.

In its employment of *nusach Sfard*, a workable compromise between Ashkenazi and Sephardi traditions that is employed by the *B'nei Akiva* (Zionist) *yeshivot* and by *Tsahal*, Afikim Hanegev is unique in Yeroham. (Only the "Rumanian" synagogue *davens* straight Ashkenazi.) Our mixed congregation of "Anglos," some neighborhood people, and many young, single people from all over town seems to me a singular success. Israel must surely contain other congregations of this sort, but none that I have encountered. Still popularly known among the Moroccans as either "Mashmia Shalom" or "Bet Knesset Americai," Afikim Hanegev retains from its *garin* origins a brief prayer for peace, composed by Rabbi Nachman of Bratslav, which is recited after the reading of the Torah every Shabbat morning. To the best of my knowledge, our congregation is unique in all of Israel in following this particular custom.

Curiously, during Rosh Hashanah and Yom Kippur, occasions when of course the synagogues of the Diaspora attract their maximum patronage, attendance in Afikim Hanegev plummets. That is the season when *nusach* differences between the Sephardi and Ashkenazi traditions become so pronounced that nearly all of the neighborhood Moroccans desert, the young singles withdraw to *daven* elsewhere with their parents, and the *minyan* shrinks to its Anglo-Ashkenazi bareboned inner nucleus. Like most Israeli congregations, we employ no paid functionaries. The leading of prayers and similar duties devolves upon those with appropriate skills—fortunately, a much higher proportion of the congregation than is the American norm—and Rabbi Steve Roth, of the original Garin Mashmia Shalom, performs special liturgical roles with aplomb. Particularly after all our years of dissatisfaction in a variety of American Jewish congregations, little Afikim Hanegev evokes a special strain of affection.

Hovering over the synagogue for the past three years like a bad dream is the superstructure of our "expanded" *bet knesset*, a local embarrassment that a former mayor (since moved away) has bequeathed to us. Funds ran out midway during construction, and there the uncompleted building squats, a monument to overblown ambitions. Worse, until the advent of Oscar Alexander, who has the good old know-how to make repairs, construction work on the larger building had for more than a year actually broken Afikim Hanegev's electric and water lines! In addition, a number of recent fatal accidents to townspeople have, by some of the more superstitiously devout, been laid to the unhinged door of the spectral synagogue. Nevertheless, though the unfinished building casts its ambiguous shadow over our weekly *daven*ing, from Shabbat to Shabbat to Shabbat, small is beautiful.

A short-cut drops me into a *wadi*. Occasionally a thin stream trickles through its channel. Usually, however, it is dry. (Annual rainfall hereabout runs from 6 to 10 inches.) I emerge onto a twisting street that is distinguished by a small Moroccan synagogue and the compound of a gnarled old trashcan scavenger, a Holocaust survivor known to all as "Ben-Gurion." It seems that once while touring here Israel's first prime minister—the very last with a genuine feel for the Negev—noticed in the yard of his Yeroham alter ego a clutter of oil drums, plastic containers, cardboard, and assorted junk: he complimented him for his thrift. Since then "Ben-Gurion" has been Yeroham's primest minister of energy and ecology. His industry has transformed his yard into a loving monument to the squirreling instinct. From time to time local officials persuade him to let the city haul off his trove to a distant site. He then compulsively begins all over again with his recycling labors.

At the turn in the road stands Ramat Hanegev College where I taught and also directed an overseas student program for five years. It consists of two large buildings that back onto the desert. The college is an unlikely cross between an avant-garde school of "Jewish art" and an American junior college. It has struggled against odds, inexperience, local incomprehension, and the ill-disguised machinations of established Ben-Gurion University to quash an upstart from the start. The college grittily carries on, Yeroham's single clearcut edge over rival Dimona and still possibly a harbinger of a different future. Cutting back toward the town center, I enter the main plaza, an unprepossessing open area edged with shops and offices on four sides, but today, a Tuesday, largely empty. The action is not far off. Crossing the center of the square, whose unlikely sculptural focus is a protuberant abstract that rises like a giant panda, thumb extended, I pass and greet two former students and am presented with an invitation to a wedding between a local Moroccan and an American girl volunteer. Gifted Oscar in his CATERPILLAR workcap is leaving the hardware store. It is all quite pedestrian, of course, and that is much the point. I can count on half-a-dozen human, small-talk encounters on any venture down in the town in which I live and work. Car and phone have not undone foot-to-asphalt and face-to-face. I like it here actually flashes through my self-conscious head several times a week. Yeroham is, in short, my Wobegon in the Negev. Neo-romantic, I confess to feeling tight and hickish whenever latterly I have visited the New York City where I was born and raised.

A dusty area just off the town's main center serves as the Tuesday home of the Yeroham once-a-week outdoor market—the *souk*. My adopted home just may be the largest city in Israel that suffers the absence of a supermarket to enhance its "quality of life." I know that farther south down the highway Mitzpe Ramon, a hamlet only half Yeroham's size, boasts a food super-dispensary. Of course, Yeroham does have its smallish Shekem market which, open in larger centers only to military and police personnel, is here open to the general public. But I am aware of no local agitation; the *souk*, the Shekem, the neighborhood groceries seem to be more than adequate. (Indeed, the only item that we must habitually smuggle in from elsewhere is mushrooms.)

There may be a stray exception or three, but in my experience virtually any-local-body may be encountered in the course of a Tuesday wandering among the potatoes, the avocados, the fresh fish, salted olives, linoleum, cap pistols, jeans, coconuts, and light bulbs. It is a community outpouring, a weekly celebration. I admit to prejudice in the matter, but it is my fixed impression that Yeroham's weekly *souk* bears witness to less jockeying for position and impersonal elbowing than the permanent, 6-day-a-week affairs that tourists may encounter in Jerusalem and Beersheba. There is here greater congeniality, better nature, indeed, more innate *grace* than in these affairs which in size dwarf our local efflorescence.

Fresh fruit and vegetables in my cart, after a final errand and chat at the post office, I walk back up the main drag toward my own neighborhood, Shikun Ben-Gurion. The picturesque flowers in the streets of Yeroham are like spring blossoms in the Negev. Elderly Moroccans in gauzy gowns of blue or white shuffle along in slippers out of Sindbad the Sailor. Two Indian matrons in flowing orange saris, each carrying half-a-dozen sacks of rice from Shekem, gossip at the streetcorner. Audibly giving vent to some Muddy Water blues, a Black Hebrew cult member (most are ex-Chicagoans via Dimona) in bright green poncho and purple stocking cap sweeps the trash. And *"Zevelman,"* the wizened Bedouin who, like a parody of a Jewish peddler, hauls his bulging sacks of sheep and camel manure door to door, ambles along, prodding his weary donkey. In less than five minutes I once again pass Haim, our neophyte grocer, and pull my cart of fresh produce up the steps to our home in Shikun Ben-Gurion.

Yeroham could never be convicted of bearing the taint of the drawingboard. It displays, rather, a layered human quality of spontaneity. Its droll, grandiose access road leads onto Rehov Zvi Bornstein, the broad main thoroughfare that knows to run straight for no more than six blocks, then dribbles at either end into twisting, narrow highway. Quirky streets dart out in surprising directions. There is an unexpected abundance of playground and park, a fair amount of it (considering the rainfall and high cost of irrigation) green and floral. Less attractive is the abundant trash. In most areas, four-story apartment buildings, a skyline redolent of Gulliver Bronx, dominate a Coalinga-scale world of Lilliput: *tout court* dating from the '60s, an Israeli-wide blunder of disproportion and shortsightedness in housing North Africans whose families generally run large. The Ben-Gurion and Shaked neighborhoods, around 300 single-family "cottagim," "villas," and "patios" where I and most "Anglos" live among neighbors who originate in Marrakesh and Casablanca, is of the second-thought '70s: low, open, and attractive. There has been a price, but a few lessons have been learned. Borders, clearly established, have been an Israeli obsession from the very start. Jerusalem used to enjoy them; Yeroham still does. No, they do not sit precisely where they did ten years ago. At that time our new house backed up against the very desert. It was not unusual to spot a Bedouin with 6–10 camels galumphing past our door. Now newer houses stretch to the east and south, a housing development which has transformed the once isolated town swimming pool from a bluish island to an inlet lapping at the peninsular shores of the new-built dwellings. And there, just beyond the last row of houses, queer with their chalet-style roofs, the last roads finger off and dwindle into the engulfing desert. No suburb, no agriculture—just beckoning space.

This sharp delineation provides a peculiar if intangible satisfaction. For Yeroham inhabits a space which is psychologically graspable. It is visibly girdled by an *eruv* which is checked for breaks every Friday prior to Shabbat. One consequence is that the town possesses a definition and integrity which elude Tel Aviv. It can be comprehended, touched, affected, and possibly changed just because it is still intact.

"Out there" the Negev looms like a limitless reservoir. I just don't mean the Machtesh Hagodol—the Great Crater, an aching depression in the earth just a 40-minute walk to the east past the soccer stadium and water tower, past the factories and glittering fields of broken glass, detritus from the bottle plant. Unlike Arizona's Grand Canyon, one can stroll out to the *Machtesh* of Yeroham almost any dawn, midday, or dusk with the assurity of finding undisturbed solitude. One lovely pipedream of the *garin* year of '78 was to invite Joan Baez during her scheduled Israeli concert tour to sing for peace at the rim of the *Machtesh* before an invited audience of thousands. La Baez, however, never did reply to our proposal. Disappointing at the time, it was surely for the good: the *Machtesh* remains beercan- and candy wrapper–free.

Nor do I refer to Lake Yeroham, the Negev's major body of

water (albeit artificial) of a scale to attract the migrating water-birds on the Africa–Europe fly route each spring and fall. No, I intend, rather, what is particularly needful for those of us for whom yawning, outstretched space remains the single, best, visible emblem of freedom itself. For many of us in Israel, more than the greenery of the Galilee or the white glints against the blue Mediterranean or the ridge-ribs of the Judean Highlands, or even the pulse along the Western Wall, it is the Negev that unfurls that compelling sign.

Of course I know that the vastness is illusory. There are seasons when the fire of automatic weapons from a training unit blurts just over the closest line of hills. But still the timid desert dogs howl stirringly in the night, and a 15-minute stroll will yield a featureless expanse given to reflection and to awe. On return, one can sense an almost magical Yeroham, like a prism as tactile as Wallace Stevens' silent jar in Tennessee, organize the spreading emptiness into order.

"Yes, my friend, but what do you *do* there? How do you fend off boredom and stagnation?"

I shall try yet again.

TAKE ONE: The week of Hanukkah at the home of Tsila & Max Stern. Thirty Yerohamites, half of us "Anglo," are gathered in the salon for an evening of music. As he does three or four times a year, Max has invited his musical friends—this time a pianist and a flautist from the Beersheba Sinfonietta and a young American soprano who recently made *aliya*—to play for us at his home in Yeroham. This evening, in addition to Bach and Mozart, we audition, a week *prior to* its world's premiere in Tel Aviv, Max's latest work—*Creation of the World.*

TAKE TWO: From next door we hear the beckoning sound of a guitar. Moshe Landsman is pecking away. When the little kids have been bedded down, Marcia, I, Moshe, and his wife, Leah (a member of the Yeroham City Council), conspire to run through our weathered, timeless repertoire of Weavers, Seegar, Kingston Trio, and early Johnny Cash till the children, fists rubbing their eyes, come wandering through in sleepy wonder.

TAKE THREE: It is the night of Purim. After attending to a reading of the *Megillat Esther* at the synagogue, I have returned home. From the bedroom, however, I am the only male auditeur to yet another reading of the triumph of Esther and Mordecai. For three months Marcia, daughter Jennifer (19), Leah, and Yaffa Shochet (another "Anglo" friend) have rehearsed the intricate cantillation for reading their sections of the *megilla*. Four other women, mothers of young children who could not easily manage to get away to hear the reading at Afikim Hanegev, are in attendance. This relatively unusual women's reading of *Megillat Esther*, to which I am an unintentional eavesdropper, is the fruit of scores of hours of practice and rehearsal. The next day of Purim eight more women come by to hear the subsequent reading. I don't know how many kosher women's readings were recited in all of Israel this past Purim; I suspect not more than several dozen. Two, however, were conducted in Yeroham. In our household, at least, it was a spiritual and cultural event of the first importance, the symbolic equivalent of bar mitzvah ceremony.

TAKE FOUR: A dozen of us are seated in the salon of Steve & Rona Roth. The former London rabbi has achieved enviable results teaching Bible to his students at the local (non-religious) high school: in the past five years, every one of them has succeeded in passing the nation-wide *bagrut* exam. He is also the possessor of a remarkable collection of opera and drama video-cassette disks. This evening we are watching Plácido Domingo in *Tales of Hoffman*. The Roths hold these soirées every few months throughout the year.

Such the sampling of "culture" that we Yeroham "Anglos" fashion, engage in, and support to keep our spirit rust-free. Of course, sometimes we travel to Beersheba, or even to Jerusalem, for a concert, a film, or a restaurant meal; but not really, to be honest, all that frequently. We are now accustomed to a more confined if perhaps a more participatory sort of cultural life. And it is, as may be ascertained, a cultural life much in a Jewish key. Only rarely do we feel a sense of privation at seeing fewer films and shows than formerly (touring theater groups do, in any event, play Yeroham's Cultural Center).

It is my fond, unsubstantiated suspicion that we outlanders not only listen to more recordings but compose more music, not only read more books but do more writing, not only observe as spectators but do more painting, potting, and sewing than any of us would were we living still where distraction feeds upon itself. That is what we do here. Since moving here a decade ago, Marcia and I have been at times elated, at times dejected, but stagnation and boredom have been among the most distant of afflictions.

Finally, we Yeroham "Anglos" lead our lives here much in the way folks lead theirs in Tel Aviv, Philadelphia, or Manchester. Only—may I be pardoned or humored for feeling that ours are, perhaps, just a shade more fulfilling than . . . well . . . just that? You see, that old clerk at the Diplomat Hotel had had it just right back in 1974. Struggling, untidy Yeroham, where we feel most wanted and needed, where we can most directly make a contribution to the development of Israel, is for us the most exciting place to live in the entire country.

Indeed, my fellow Zionists, if not here, where?

SCHOOLS AND
SCHOOLING:
NEW LESSONS

While during our first months in Israel in 1976 we were living as budding agriculturalists on Moshav Masuot Yitzhak, on several occasions veteran *moshavniks* regarded our quotidian, American-vintage family—one girl and one boy—with friendly consternation. "Here in Israel only two children, and especially just one son, is just not enough," Pnina, the mother of three boys and a girl who was assigned by the *moshav* to help us adjust, commented on more than one occasion. "Think about it!" Although fresh from America, we knew at once what she was referring to. Indeed, probably more than we were then aware—at the time we were mainly bemused by her readiness, like that of other veteran Israelis, to volunteer their expert advice about how we should lead our private lives—did it leave its mark. As it happens, it accorded well with some of our own recently rethought notions.

Marcia gave birth to Yishai in Beersheba in 1977 and to Miriam in 1979.

I think it can be justly ventured that for most married couples, more than anything else the measure of their real ground and temperament may be located in the education of their children; it is their reality principle par excellence. (I recall, for example, liberal senators in Washington of the '50s and '60s who voted consistently for school integration but were known to send their own children to private or suburban schools in Virginia.) For Marcia and me to have moved to quaintly Sephardic Yeroham as newlyweds or as retirees, though unquestionably less onerous, probably would have been less meaningful. On the other hand, for our children genuinely to suffer for our romantic idealism would have been painful, unjustifiable, and, finally, insupportable. We proceeded with our plans, but we were wary. Over the ensuing years several other "Anglo" families moved away from Yeroham (some to America, others to Jerusalem), most often "for the sake of their children's education." We have been inclined toward jaundiced skepticism. It was, we are sure, never really quite that simple.

After a decade's personal and secondhand acquaintance with Israeli schooling, I remain persuaded that differences in the school experience between Israel's Yerohams and Israel's privileged Elsewheres are much exaggerated. Generally much less than kind, they are also less of kind than of degree, and they may with a degree of parental effort be compensated for. Further, I am convinced that my kids have gained and are gaining much from the "special opportunity" of learning among kids who, albeit Jewish, are not just like themselves.

Still, that hump of incipient guilt from time to time still itches. No longer thrashing over the niggling indignities and long-range effects of Christmas caroling during school assemblies, I instead, when we felt compelled to withdraw him from an inept Israeli junior high school system, have had to spend hundreds of hours tutoring my older son. Of late we have spent hundreds of hours more teaching our two little sabras to read English. Scratching harder, I am most conscious of the irony that we feel constrained to ask our younger ones here in Israel how things in school "are going" far more often than we ever did our two older kids when they were learning in open classrooms in California.

On balance, however, things are going pretty well. Although some of the conditions and situations that we never anticipated before making *aliya* shadow our kids' footsteps in their days and lives at school, much else that occurs in and around Israeli classrooms is charged with success. The following three accounts are horizontal cross-slices at very different junctures, three direct incursions into the school lives of my two boys. Each pedagogical experience turned out to be a surprisingly poignant occasion for learning and reflection for me as well. As my daughters themselves would testify, I have of course been quite solicitous about their education as well, but because it seems to me that, like the Israeli social system at large, Israeli schools shield girls better than boys from some their more distressing barbs, I confess that I have felt a heavier anxiety about my sons. This apprehension has found a troubled echo in others. Though I have since 1980 published dozens of articles and reviews in the pages of the English-language daily *Jerusalem Post*, whenever I am introduced to new Israeli "Anglos," they almost invariably can place me not as that clever literary critic or that wry social commentator but as the chronicler of one particular personal piece that the *Post* editor labeled "Do-It-Yourself Education," a first, sketchy version of the "Junior Lows and Highs" which follows.

More than most Americans probably appreciate are their most intimate decisions influenced by answers to questions that never get asked in America. In restrospect, Pnina was right on target.

TRIPPING

WITH ALEPH

Three days before my first-grade son's annual class trip to Jerusalem in 1984, the radio news reported a bomb blast that killed two people in Ashdod. Closer to home, the incredulous sister of Leah Shakdiel, our nextdoor neighbor, was victimized *twice* within six months by successive Jerusalem bombings. Each time she sustained light injuries and broken glasses. Though I am quite certain that the streets of Beersheba are considerably less perilous than those of its sister city Seattle, together with the recurring threat of war, the random erraticism of *our* street violence engenders a higher measure of apprehension for our children's day-to-day safety here than I recall was common in America. Once or twice each year our turn, like that of all parents, comes to sit an entire day at the entrance of Kol Ya'akov Elementary School simply to watch for anything, anyone "suspicious." To date, I am pleased never to have sighted anything more suspect than some teachers dashing to the bank during the 20-minute class-break at 10:00 o'clock.

*I*n the front seat of the school bus, the M-16 bounced lightly against the knees of Yisrael, the young, bearded principal of Kol Ya'akov; as much as refreshments and a first aid kit, the rifle is standard apparatus for all such group excursions. Rolling north with my six-year-old son Yishai, his 18 classmates, the teacher, principal, and 14 other mothers and fathers, I could not imagine that the pupils in this first grade—*kitah aleph*—would ever drift, like me, in a buried vacancy of time. No, Israeli primary schooling is not necessarily a happier experience than is American. Our first peek into an Israeli office converted into a classroom years before had left us appalled: my older son's fourth-grade Beersheba classroom was now so tightly jammed with desks and chairs and students that there were no real aisles at all. Discordance and distraction reigned virtually unchallenged. The teacher's yelling only added to the confusion. Yet Rambam School had been touted to us as the best religious elementary school in the city. *And it was!*

Yishai's *kitah aleph* in Yeroham, however, was not only better than *that*; in significant ways it seemed to me a very model for the integration and transmission of community and spiritual values. This unevenness in Israeli schools is perplexing: far more than in America, less the school than the particular class proves "good" or "bad," and luck is important at every turn.

I admit it: my preparations for this excursion included a pair of army issue earplugs and a handful of aspirin. (Yishai swallowed a dramamine without demur; it would have been the better part of self-interest had I distributed tablets freely to the other chaperoning parents.) Neither my mother nor my father had ever accompanied me on *my* class's annual subway pilgrimage from the Bronx to the Museum of Natural History—

that mammoth repository of whale bulk and dinosaur bones, dioramas of Indians and Peter Minuit, stuffed deer and birds, all headed by Teddy Roosevelt on a wild charger challenging Central Park—that I came to know so well. I am sure I never blamed them a bit. (In fact, I cannot recall any fond fathers ever accompanying us.) The transparent function of the several parent–martyrs was to keep within bounds the gum-throwing in the night of the Hayden Planetarium and to keep us kids from being left behind on the subway platform when the doors of the Double C sealed shut. Though the ratio of Yeroham adults to Yeroham kids was almost one-to-one, could I possibly think that similar chaos would not ensue here? I accepted my aspirin and my appointed portion: two years thence, when our kindergartener Miriam would reach this pinnacle of *kitah aleph*, my wife's turn would come.

Save for the vaguest recollection of tears at the start and the gray visage of Mrs. Slattery, my teacher whose face looked just like that of George Washington standing up in a rowboat, my first-grade year at P.S. 86 is an almost perfect blank. Not so with Marcia's. It was Parents' Day in Fresno, California in 1948.

> I have a little turtle.
> I keep him in a box.
> He swims in the water,
> And climbs on the rocks.
>
> He snapped at a mosquito.
> He snapped at a flea.
> He snapped at a minnow,
> And he snapped at me.

She must have been a cheerful, well-adjusted charmer, my wife-to-be. Whereas my immemorable days argue a distasteful early dose of "life," Marcia can effortlessly unwind whole reels of time. Still, I too adjusted—and forgot; my fleeing year-the-sixth, uneventfully passed at Public School 86, The Bronx, was swallowed up alive—like a flea.

Kol Ya'akov is a state religious school; its class size is exceptionally small. Disregarding some rivulets, public education in Israel runs along three broad streams: state secular, state religious, and Arab. There is additionally an extensive religious school network run by various of the ultra-orthodox *haredi* communities both for their own children and, in places like Yeroham, as an outreach program. Many of the *haredim* believe and teach their children that secular Jews and even religious Jews who are Zionists are *goyim*—or the equivalent of *goyim*. These schools nonetheless receive regular governmental subsidies; in fact, thanks to the political power of the *haredi* block in the Knesset in the days of Menachem Begin, these schools used to draw even more in supplementary benefits, e.g., hot lunches and late afternoon classes, than the regular state schools! As a result, Yeroham's *haredi* Torat Moshe School successfully wooed large numbers of parents who normally would have sent their children to Kol Ya'akov. Hence, at least temporarily, for the lateral benefit of classes of Kol Ya'akov where many classes contain around half as many students as those in similar schools in Beersheba or Jerusalem.

Save for my son and a Yemenite boy—Yemenites are sui generis—all of the pupils in Kol Ya'akov's *kitah aleph* are Sephardim. Yishai's uniqueness was bothersome to him at first, but with time it had dwindled in significance. The main educational objective of *kitah aleph* for all Israeli children is to learn to read Hebrew. The night before this Jerusalem excursion, at the climax of a festive, public celebration in the Yeroham Cultural Center that featured that patented Israeli format of skits, songs, dances, recitations, and a speech by the town's mayor, each child proudly received his or her first real book—a *siddur*. All of the *siddurim* had been festively dressed in an embroidered bookcover, the work of the pupil's mother. At the climax of this bus ride, the children would pray from their very own *siddurim* at the Western Wall in Jerusalem.

Learning and communal objectives seem here to me wonderfully congruent and mutually supportive; even the still unhackneyed annual class trip is the felicitous outcome of individual and group achievement. Moreover, the interplay of parent–teacher–child that the earnest P.T.A. works so hard to foster in America here appears wholly organic. Imagine: 15

parents out of 19 choosing to come! There was no play-acting of "involvement"; indeed, there was no act at all. True, things begin to slide as early as *kitah bet*—I would needs be watchful—but for the moment, I was deeply impressed.

On the first stretch of the journey, Yishai and I noted, a bit self-consciously, whatever the passing scene could yield up. Determined not to act as silly as most of his classmates, in cahoots with his *abba* to make the outing convivial, Yishai devised an endless stream of questions about the army camps, the Bedouin girls and women tending herds of goats and sheep, and the enviable Bedouin boys prodding their camels. Camels are too common in Israel to rate zoo status, but I still gawk at their regal strangeness. For half his life Yishai's most consistent, unfulfilled request has been for an animal of his own to ride. The family cat and finches are of little account. Although we have scaled him down over time from a wild stallion to a donkey, prospects, we both knew, looked slim.

Still south of Beersheba, we passed the country's only prison to be constructed since statehood. The vast, square enclosure with (together we counted them twice) nine guard towers gripped Yishai's imagination. Who was kept there? Having learned of "robbers" through repeated, sad experience, he comprehended easily enough. As though the very embodiment of Bialik's sardonic prophecy about the tokens of "normalcy" in the State of the Jews, Jewish criminals are among the most potent Zionists. Just within recent months, *gonovim* had swiped his older brother's American Cub Scout belt that Yishai had borrowed, his little sister's doll carriage, and apricots from our front yard tree. Neither Yishai nor his *abba* can afford to be too naïve about the rotten fruit of Jewish normalcy.

"Arab terrorists"—*mehablim*—however, were something else again. Of course, he and his classmates had heard of them, but they inspire a kind of bewildered wonder for him—and for me as well. Unlike *gonovim*, these bespeak the permanent, mocking abnormalcy of us Jews, a belying of Bialikian and pioneer Zionist assumptions together. Yet if the Arabs in the Territories were of a mind, could they not have flooded this prison with so many as to make continued Israeli occupation of the Territories untenable? Of all peoples, we Jews would be the least capable of outfacing civil disobedients. Still, my point was not clear even to myself.

North of Beersheba sporadic singing broke out among the passengers (child and adult), some youngsters started wandering the aisles, oranges and thermoses were passed around, but no, I did not feel pressed to apply rubber stoppers to my ears. My mind stayed fixed on that fortress with the nine, armed turrets. I had myself not felt jeopardized by prison since that long night with thousands of others at the side of Washington's Pentagon in high-pitched 1967. During the past year, however, a former student of mine had served time. Micah, the top graduating student in Yeroham's high school, had refused to go to Lebanon. After several weeks in military jail, he relented only when he obtained a promise that he would be stationed north of Israel for a scant two weeks. On his tenth day he was seriously wounded; after several operations, he spent nearly half-a-year in Haifa's Rambam Hospital. Somewhat reluctantly, I had written for him a letter of recommendation to work as a counselor in an upstate New York Jewish summer camp. He was one of the finest youngsters I had come upon in Israel, but with an American girlfriend in Poughkeepsie, I was all too aware, he might well end up staying there. The ones who leave this country to make their fortunes do not really disturb me all that much, but could Israel long afford to drive away its Micahs?

Yishai was curious about our exact location. We had not headed due north out of Beersheba on the more direct (though twistier) route to Jerusalem, Derech Hevron. Understandably, no Israeli school buses travel unnecessarily through the Territories. On the back of an envelope, I drew a rough map of Israel and marked out for him our approximate route. He was fascinated, and it pleased me to recognize in my son my own lost self. For many years "cartography" had been one of my youthful passions: on my bedroom walls hung maps I had drawn, traced, collected from everywhere, many festooned with glossy maptacks that trailed blue, red, green, yellow explanatory threads to their wallboard borders.

I looked down again at my quick sketch and was shocked to realize that it registered more than mere geography, more than

I had intended. The eastern boundary of my Israel was an expedient vertical line, straight as a shot: my autonomous hand had overridden my ameliorative politics. (Had the turtle snapped again?) There was no bright, taut thread or explanatory tack. No key clarified just how far I had traveled from the American immigrant who seven years before had withdrawn from a settlement *garin* that had decided that the Gaza Strip would not be a bad place to strike roots.

To my surprise, after about an hour our bus turned onto a highway not normally used by Egged public transport, and I was treated to some unfamiliar scenery. Nevertheless, after some minutes I was half-adoze until I heard Yisrael, the principal, announce that the large building seated astride the hill to the right and dominating the verdant valley was "a *bet knesset* for the Christians." It was the Abbey at Latrun; palpably hushed, parents and children stared at the sprawling rococo building that seemed to beg for that wonderful statue of Rough Riding Roosevelt on 81st Street to set it off right. Some weeks before I had by chance read Amos Oz' disquieting story "The Trappist Monastery," which closes with two Israeli soldiers sighting this very structure, then in enemy territory, from their jeep. The Trappist vow of silence awes them; the story has much to do, in fact, with the inherent mendacity of speech. Though the Abbey reminded me incongruously of nothing more than one of the old-time Borscht Belt hotels in the Catskills remembered from my boyhood, it still retained an alien potency. We all, for a spell, were struck silent.

The final stretch of scenic twists and hills before arrival: three children threw up. Yishai, a trifle woozy, looked on with the pride of a pill-taker. Left of the roadside stood permanent, seagreen wreckage of tanks and trucks, monuments to the War of Independence campaign to break the Arab siege of Jerusalem. Yisrael, allowing little room for ambiguity, explained their significance to the children. Kol Ya'akov was no *haredi* outpost.

Jerusalem! Children and parents, the entire busload of us together broke into song, and we made our way on foot through the Zion Gate into the Old City. Wild cheers signaled our approach to the *Kotel*. Jewish Moroccan women's traditional yodel-whoops sound like nothing more or less than Indians of the Hollywood Tribe breaking out of ambush. The cheers were adventitious: our arrival had coincided with the celebration of a bar mitzvah party that, emerging from aperture on the far left of the Wall, stretched across its massive façade. At a distance from the *Kotel* behind the inner barrier of the yeshiva-lined open plaza that is Jerusalem's cozier version of St. Peter's, we arranged public benches into a rectangular island and named it "Yeroham."

There we were joined by Jerusalemite Ben Hollander, an American rabbi who with his family had lived in Yeroham for a year and taught at Kol Ya'akov School. He proffered words of greeting and Torah to heighten the significance of their pilgrimage and achievement for the children—but not without a brief skirmish. Twice when he launched our group into *Oseh Shalom Bimromav*, a song of peace and reconcilation, several Yeroham parents winged into a more militant ditty that urged spreading Torah throughout the four corners of the Whole Land of Israel. In the end, it was a good-natured standoff. In Israel, religiously-observant Americans bulk disproportionate among both the peaceniks and the not-one-pieceniks.

Yishai's peculiar dilemma was that whereas the *siddur* we had chosen for him followed the order of service of *nusach Sfard*, all the other children's *siddurim* were straight Sephardi. True, the *Sfard* hewed more closely to Sephardi than to outright Ashkenazi, but the pagination was slightly off, so until he got accustomed to it, Yishai would have to scramble nimbly to find the right place. I smiled: his problem would temporarily unite him (albeit unawares) with his *abba's* American pagehunting experience over the years many synagogues ago. At the same time, however, I could not help but wonder whether I would ever cease to feel twinges of guilt for the unease my own idiosyncratic choice always, it seemed, to live apart had conferred upon my son?

The bar mitzvah celebrants had dispersed. Our Yeroham Island was become the major tourist harbor at the *Kotel*. The camera-laden in black, paper *kippot* were taking dozens of snapshots of cute *kitah aleph* at song and prayer weeks later to exhibit to their friends back in Leeds and Akron.

Yishai and I had 20 minutes alone in which to explore the *Kotel*. I led him through the dark opening at the extreme left of the men's side, past several *minyanim* in amorphous, chanting clusters, to gaze down into the illuminated excavation that cuts through millennia at the very edge of the Wall. "How far down is it?," he inquired.

"Hundreds of feet and thousands of years."

At the bottom, dropped by visitors through the grate, twinkled distant piles of ocher and silvery coins. "Why?"

"People throw them in," I responded weakly.

"Yes, but why?"

"It's too far to touch or reach any other way. Maybe they don't know any better how to pray," I ventured. We both stared deep into the inverted sky, Jerusalem's unique planetarium, Yishai down into the past, I at my gazing son.

Outside, in the early afternoon brightness, Yishai used his new *siddur* to pray *mincha*. The little slips of paper in the crevices caught his eye. Some weeks earlier a friend of mine, a rabbi whose preoccupation is the covert activity of Christian missionaries among the Jews of Israel, had shown me a shoebox filled with little curled pieces of paper proclaiming Jesus as the true messiah. They had been discovered wedged between the stones of the *Kotel*. I fished around my wallet for an old business card on which I helped Yishai to write his secret prayer which he then inserted between the massive stones. While I sped through my own *mincha*, Yishai prayed for his very own donkey. As he himself must well have known, he had precious few prospects for getting one, but he shook back and forth nonetheless with real fervor. He had not lost faith in its coming. Perhaps the Trappists had, after all, a valid point about speech and silence. I added a prayer for peace. What could it hurt?

After we reassembled, our bus drove us to visit the Great Synagogue of Jerusalem. To my relief, that temple of marble and gilt was closed. Instead, for an hour the children ate and romped in Independence Park, just down the hill from Jerusalem's towering Plaza Hotel. While the kids scuffled and rolled down green mounds, I stretched out to nap on the grass.

Soon I was needed. Other parents had taken their youngsters to use the park facilities. Inspired, I grasped Yishai by the hand; shortly we were pushing together on the heavy revolving doors of the Plaza. (No, Marcia and I had never stayed overnight at *this* Plaza, but I often shamelessly exploit their facilities on my forays to the capital.) Downstairs, the fancy bathroom wall and sink mirrors dazzled him with the seemingly endless images of delighted Yishais smiling into infinity.

My own receding thousand faces hovering above my son's at some beady, diminishing point clasped in the frozen, floating past of that of another kid of six. A once-a-month, Saturday morning habitué of Angelo's Barber Shop under the el on Jerome Avenue, a long block down from P.S. 86, I am seated in the barber chair before the double row of green and yellow tonics, between the magic mirrors, to watch my hair get cut, snipped on my hundreds of heads, front, sides, and back. My father is sheeted in the adjacent chair, a hot towel across his face. Later the whole family would drive down to my grandmother's apartment close by the grandest place I knew— Yankee Stadium. Yishai had inherited a baseball bat from his big brother, Ted, but I did not believe that he had ever heard in his life of Mickey Mantle—or even of Babe Ruth. (Not so Joe DiMaggio. We had played Simon & Garfunkel's "Mrs. Robinson" too many times for that.)

The children were still lively. Ahead lay for them the day's grand finale: a visit to Jerusalem's Biblical Zoo, a "theme park" whose premise it is to house and display animals that prowl and graze through the Bible. Under the aegis of Isaiah's peaceable kingdom (spelled out in Hebrew, Arabic, and English), wolves paced disconsolately in the enclosure next to one that sheltered some complacent sheep. (The visionary time has not yet been fulfilled; the double fence was sturdy.) Deer roamed passionately beneath a rubric from the Song of Songs. And so it went from Genesis through Chronicles. However, there also perched and paced parakeets, bison, cassowaries, and other Darwinian evidence of a new or diverging Australian testament, all of which tended to dilute the zoo's original concept. It did not seem to matter to anyone else. Furthermore, compared to Israel's modern zoo and "safari park" in suburban Tel Aviv, this was really a raggle-taggle operation, but neither the kids nor the animals seemed bothered by the shoddiness.

We had a full hour; we two took off together, apart from the others. Save for a gaggle of dozens of Arab schoolgirls (all wearing gray skirts over long dark pants) whom Yishai seemed anxious to avoid, the zoo was largely empty of visitors. Like the museum, so it was with moving, breathing, crapping natural history: I can't recall my own father and mother, lifelong apartment dwellers, ever taking me and my sister to nearby Bronx Zoo. In the Sixties, however, when Jennifer and Ted were babies and Marcia and I had for three years lived in the Bronx, the crowded zoo, especially on Saturday, was our frequent destination. Unlike that vast animal reservation, Jerusalem's may be fully navigated in under an hour, and such seemed one of my son's implied intentions.

It was movement, indeed, that enthralled him; only reciprocal liveliness within the bars briefly halted our forward march across the biblical zoo-scape. A gibbon performed trapeze hieroglyphics with accompanying whoops that reminded me unkindly of our reception at the *Kotel* some hours earlier. A giraffe poked his (her?) head into a tree, then retreated from the sun into a silo-like structure. The path to the elephants, however, was blocked by a chain. Answering our entreaty, an attendant explained that because children had tossed so many objects at the elephants, one of them had started to retaliate by tossing things back. Why *did* Israeli kids throw so many stones? Yishai shrugged his shoulders.

We came upon three dozing tigers. Alone with my son and the sleeping cats, I was carried by a sudden impulse and flipped a small, smooth rock over the top of the high enclosure into the very middle of the tigers' water trough. The wet plop startled one of them to her feet. I looked around. No one. Yishai's gleeful giggle softened the stab of guilt.

With only ten minutes to go until time to reassemble, we crossed a narrow track into a desolate enclave that displayed a weatherbeaten sign—"Ship of Solomon." Four derailed cars of a kiddy train that had been sidelined for years stood unattended. Yishai explored the splintered deck of the beached vessel, for him inevitably a pirate craft—won't *someone* in the memory of a beloved departed someone contribute the wherewithal to refit the Ship of Solomon with a new coat of paint?— and then we withdrew to meet up with the rest of *kitah aleph*.

By the entrance, however, I halted to take closer note of the sophisticated signaling apparatus: WARNING, DO NOT PASS WHEN LIGHT IS RED was engraved above the deadened red, amber, and green circles. Below, in smaller letters, "Automatic Train Equipment Co., Rensselaer, Indiana."

Rensselaer, Indiana! A vertical shaft like a yawning fissure in the earth opened up at my feet. This Rensselaer place was the very hometown of Dick Sweeney, my bright, gangling grad school roommate of 24 years before. Twenty-four: a full day and night of hour-years since Sweeney had danced his Hoosier jig in A. D. Van Nostrand's Seminar in Literary Criticism, since Jerry Sternstein had smoked his reflective pipe among the lovely art students after lunch in the R.I.S.D. cafeteria (or since Paul had drowned himself in his Providence bathtub). It had been at least a dozen years since, at Detroit's Wayne State, I had seen Sweeney last. Both of us were there then, charting our courses across the career terrain of College English America. Peering intently, I could just make him out down there gazing up. His expression was puzzled, quizzical. (Who could blame him?) It was too far down to signal with words, with speech. Perhaps a dropped shekel, or just a stone?

Yishai and I were exquisitely conscious of having enjoyed each other's companionship, of having wordlessly chosen to spend the past hour apart from his classmates and their parents. Outside the front gate of the zoo, I turned to say something to one of the burbly cast of Yeroham mothers. Ahead lay the return trip of two-and-a-half hours of probable raucousness to Yeroham, but I was resolved at all costs not to regret that I had come.

Then, suddenly, I heard my son yelping in pain and turned to see him clutching his forehead. Another father reached him ahead of me. Yishai had been twirling on the guardrail near the entrance. Spinning, he had lost his grip while upside down, and his forehead had struck the pavement. There was a big bump but no blood.

Seated on the waiting bus, I cradled his head in my arms. I got a rapid overdose of conflicting medical advice from children, mothers, the principal, another father, and a ready candy bar from a mother. The last worked most promptly.

Eerily, it felt to me as though I had been clasping Yishai's hand for all of the hours of the day out of some veiled premonition of his vulnerability. No sooner had I let go . . . Despite the sporadic tumult of the busload of *kitah aleph* celebrants and their tired parents rolling southwest into the purple Israeli evening the long way around from Jerusalem to Yeroham, Yishai and I gratefully slumbered in each other's arms. We would both have to learn to manage to live with whatever Israel served up.

Later, when we recounted our exploits at home, Marcia supplied the final verse of her Fresno *kitah aleph* peroration. Yishai was delighted.

> He caught the mosquito.
> He caught the flea.
> He caught the minnow.
> But he didn't catch me.

My son learned it easily by heart. I can only hope that it works like a charm.

JUNIOR LOWS AND HIGHS

"You can't do it. Maybe it's okay in America, but here the bureaucracy will murder you. It's impossible."

This was the refrain Marcia and I heard not from one or two Israeli friends but from virtually everyone we consulted: a unanimous, well-intentioned chorus of cautionary incredulity. Such a drastic move, it was implied, would permanently impair our son's future. It was at best a retrograde step away from full absorption into Israeli society.

True, we had asked for it. Still feeling our way with fingertips extended after five years in the country, we lacked the confidence to proceed unhesitatingly with what in the States would have been merely a path less traveled, but one that had nevertheless already been pioneered by hundreds of other families. Indeed, it had spawned a movement, journals, a whole sub-community of devotees. Here in Israel, however, home learning seemed to mean nothing but failure at school. A child out of school was simply future welfare or prison-bait.

Finally overriding this prudential din, Marcia, I, and our 12-year-old son Ted (alias "Shlomo") decided together to remove him from his junior high school class in Dimona in order to take personal responsibility for his education.

When acquaintances discovered that we had actually done it, for our own good some had to vent themselves.

"It's against the law!" (True.)

"They'll send you to prison!" (False.)

"He'd be better off in the long run to tough it out!" (Nonsense.)

"They'll never let him back into the system." (False again.) After a few weeks, our craziness and stubbornness was an accepted *fait accompli*.

It is a small but telling consolation of being American Alices in *Altneu* Wonderland that many seasoned Israelis consider us more than mildly *meshuge* for dropping out of El Al 747s down into the Levant rabbit hole in the first place. It grants us, gratefully, a bit more room to maneuver, to proceed on our own set of assumptions over and against prevailing norms and expectations than is accorded sabras. "Crazy American" covers ground as diverse as recycling aluminum foil to concern for electoral reform, not to mention a host of other notions that ring slightly off-tune to Israelis of both Middle Eastern and Middle European origins. Not "deschooling," neither John Holt nor Ivan Illich has the slightest resonance here. For Israelis, suspect "home schooling" is cut from some defective bolt of cloth.

From our side of things, dropping Ted out was practical rather than ideological, a choice fueled quite as much by despair as hope. Fortunately, the astonishment of most Israelis was balanced by the supportiveness of the Yeroham "Anglo" community without whose active help and involvement we might have set out but could never have succeeded so well.

When we first moved to Yeroham from Beersheba in 1977,

it had been the "Anglo" friends we were leaving behind who thought we had gone over the brink. Disregard what gave promise of being meaningful work, discount the exceptional *hevra* of the five core families of *garin* Mashmia Shalom, overlook the clean air, the settling-the-Negev idealism: *the schools of Yeroham* (their trumps) *were notoriously deficient.* What would our kids *do?* Who would be their friends? How could we think so to jeopardize their education?

This attitude had left us somewhat bewildered. After all, in close to a year of living in Beersheba, our two older children had undergone enough "quality" local education to give them (and us) fits. How much worse, after all, could things in Yeroham be? The answer to that was much more complex than we had originally anticipated. For although the level of education in Yeroham (and Dimona and almost all the Negev development towns) *is* generally lower than in Beersheba, the difference, in reality, is no more than marginal. The coded message our Beersheba friends were really transmitting was that our kids would not find other "Anglo" or perhaps even Ashkenazi kids to befriend. We decided that *that*, at least, would not act as deterrent, that Yeroham would offer at least as much a cross-cultural opportunity as a drawback, and that our own attitude to the situation would probably prove decisive. On balance, on this we were not mistaken.

In retrospect, had we remained in Beersheba, Ted would probably indeed have "toughed it out," and our two-year experiment would never have taken place. We would have been the losers.

What actually happened? Well, I admit that we hedged. For our first two years in Yeroham, Jennifer and Ted, our school-aged kids, continued attending the school they were familiar with in Beersheba. Most days they bused roundtrip; one or two nights a week they stayed overnight with accommodating friends. After the sixth grade, Jennifer, still busing to Beersheba, transferred to a religious junior high for girls that seemed to fit her needs well. Thanks in part to what was occurring at this time in Yeroham's religious junior high, prospects for Ted were to prove less encouraging.

The following is a tale of subversion. Sadly, it is all too characteristic of the *Kulturkampf* and Jewish factionalism in Israel today. Many of the religious junior high school teachers were wives of fulltime "black coat" *yeshiva* residents in *Talat*, Yeroham's *haredi* community. The *Talat* community, planning to expand its own elementary school to include junior high grades, instructed all its women teachers at the school to refuse to teach mixed classes of boys and girls, which they had been doing for years. The grounds were, of course, *halachic* as interpreted by the rabbi of their community. The tactic worked. Because the state religious school was too small to support separate classes, it sealed the school's doom. The Department of Education would not continue to finance the operation. By the time Ted was ready to enter seventh grade, the "local option" had almost disintegrated.

We enrolled Ted at the largest state religious junior high school in nearby Dimona. This school was well-enough staffed, and it advertised an enriched curriculum for brighter students. In fact, that program, while functioning well enough for the girl students, flubbed sadly for the boys. Why? Because, in Dimona (as in Yeroham) too many of the brighter seventh-grade boys were bused daily to *yeshiva* high school in Beersheba, or even boarded away from home farther afield. With the passing autumn weeks, Ted's responses to our anxious "how are you doing?s" were becoming increasingly equivocal. Although he had been elected class secretary and was getting good test grades, he seemed to have very little homework, and scheduled classes seemed frequently not even to meet. In what purported to be his special class, he reported (at our prodding) such manic behavior that we could not conceive how normal classes could function at all.

The Israeli grade school year is divided into thirds: September 1st to Hanukkah, Hanukkah to Passover, and Passover to the end of June. At Hanukkah Ted produced a lovely report card garnished with tens, nines, and eights (ten is maximum), but our pleasure was sharply qualified when Ted admitted that what it chiefly signified was that he was not one of the troublemakers. After talking to his teacher, counselor, and principal, I adduced that no real improvement could be expected in the situation. After taking family counsel, realizing that we would be thought by some "elitist," and by others daft, we plunged ahead with the drastic step of removing Ted from all school systems and, with the promise of help from some of our friends, to take on ourselves the responsibility for teaching and learning. We would not have embarked on this eccentric road had we not concluded that to keep Ted within any of the ready options of the Israeli school system would have done him positive harm. What he had been learning in school was not to value but to waste his time; not to learn but to equate the numbers on tests and report cards with getting an education. These are, of course, familiar, indeed hackneyed American counter-educational notions. (We were not, by the way, committed to their tenets. On the contrary, what I really believe is that a good teacher will make any system look good.) Still we were reluctant; we had not, after all, come to Israel to be thought cranks. Nevertheless, in the absence of any serious hope of amelioration, determined not to send our 12-year-old out to board at some *yeshiva* a distance from home, we had backed up into our own cactus of *ein breira*; it prickled but it was sustaining.

A final preliminary: in all that follows it is important to bear in mind that while Ted is perhaps somewhat brighter than the average youngster, he is not an intellectual superstar. However narrow or broad, totally meaningless for Israelis or redundant for Americans the implications of our experiment may actually be, Ted, while of course quite special to Marcia and to me, is an ordinary young man.

How did we actually proceed? The point of departure was that it would not be wise or even worthwhile to attempt to replicate the school curriculum at home. Rather, we saw home learning as an opportunity for Ted to learn *how* to learn, how to take responsibility for his own education. At the start of each week, he made (in the first stage with my assistance) a schedule of hours of classes, study, and outside activities. The fulfillment of this schedule was his responsibility.

As one of his first and most important learning projects, Ted agreed to keep in English a daily journal. This became not only an instrument for self-reflection but also a self-check on his studies. It served another function as well. We had noted that many children of "Anglo" friends knew perfectly well how to speak English, but that their English reading ability was lower than it should have been. Moreover, as for their ability *to write English*, it was sorely neglected and often negligible. The journal would be Ted's prime means of mastering English composition and acquiring a style.

I surveyed our friends and acquaintances to discover which of them had the time and inclination regularly to teach a subject or skill about which he or she could be enthusiastic. We had an abundance of helpers; no one would accept any money. The resulting program would, I think, be the envy of most bright junior high school kids. Twice a week in the early morning Ted studied *Gemara* with our next-door neighbor Moshe (an American psychologist). With Moshe's wife, Leah, who has a degree in literature, Ted reviewed Hebrew grammar, read Israeli stories, and wrote short essays in Hebrew. Then there was the high school math teacher who met with Ted once a week; in return, he tutored her young son in English.

These, however, were only the more conventional areas of study. With Shmuel, a traditional scribe, Ted met weekly to learn the art of *sofrut*. Of course, before he could begin any writing, Ted first had to master the *halacha* incumbent upon all *sofrim*. Years later he still possesses the rudiments of this useful skill.

Our son developed his existing friendship with John Bernstein, an American student in Ramat Hanegev College's Overseas Student Program. John, an ecology major, was delighted to have someone to share his naturalist pursuits. At least once a week they would be off to Lake Yeroham before the dawn for a morning of bird-watching or for a hike to catch the sun's rising at Yeroham's crateral Machtesh Hagodol. Ted became proficient at recognizing and collecting desert plants, which later he and John studied under a microscope on slides they made themselves.

With me Ted studied literature. After some consideration, we decided to focus on Greek literature because it is sufficiently self-contained to be cohesive, it is significant and challenging, and it is usually neglected in the Israeli schools. For over 18 months Ted and I read through background material by the likes of Edith Hamilton, H. D. Kitto, and M. I. Finley. We were both excited. Our "texts" came right off my shelf, books I might not have looked at again for years—if ever: *The Iliad* and *The Odyssey*, the plays of Sophocles and Aristophanes (Ted didn't like Aeschylus), and the Platonic dialogues. After completing a work, Ted would write a paper, typically comparing some aspect of it to a biblical theme or character. As a result, Ted now enjoys some background and knowledge of Greek thought and literature and is able to compose a creditable essay in English.

Interspersed among the Hellenes, we read typically contemporary works like *Catcher in the Rye, A Separate Peace*, and a number of novels and stories by writers like Twain, Golding, Saroyan, and Thornton Wilder. In retrospect, I am amply satisfied that Ted has absorbed not only knowledge but, more importantly, a genuine love and respect for books and reading.

Was Ted cut off from his *hevra*? Not really! Or rather, not really more than he preferred to be. A member of the B'Nei Akiva youth movement, he took part in many of their Shabbat activities and longer excursions. He did experience a problem explaining to them—and occasionally to their parents—why he did not attend school and what he did at home. Usually he succeeded in steering clear of the subject. It was for them just too incomprehensible! His friends were particularly mystified when, during a prolonged teachers' strike, they were free to play all day and Ted was not. Our son's curriculum, of course, was wholly unaffected by the strike. His learning proceeded normally. It was an ideal object lesson, which he himself fully appreciated, in the differences between schooling and learning. Similarly, most of Ted's learning program was largely undeflected by summer vacation. This was not at our insistence; very simply, the *habit of learning* was being absorbed, and I expect that it will be retained for the rest of his life.

Early on in this period, after some reflection, I somewhat apprehensively approached the Ministry of Education office in Beersheba to inform the Director of Religious Schools in the South of Israel of our unorthodox doings. I fully expected to have a fight on my hands. To my astonishment, it was nothing of the sort. I explained our situation and with relative ease satisfied the Director that Ted was not being kept out of school in order to exploit him. Though the law could not strictly accept his extra-school status, as long as the Director received no written notice or complaint about Ted's situation, he would, he assured me, treat it with benign neglect. I was amply satisfied.

It would be misleading to suggest that everything went smoothly all the time, that Ted never felt isolated, never wasted an hour, that I myself felt no conflict between parental and pedagogic roles. It was clear from the very start, however, that my son and I had embarked together on an exciting experiment. Like *aliya* itself, it was a kind of joint adventure. Things went so well during Ted's seventh-grade year that when the following September arrived, we never seriously considered enrolling him in a regular school for the eighth grade.

Ted re-entered the system in the ninth grade. At 14, he was old enough and mature enough to board in a *yeshiva*. Both of us were persuaded that our experiment had been a success, but there were several factors encouraging re-entry, not the least of which was the need to prepare for the battery of matriculation examinations—*bagruts*—which all Israeli high school students must take in order to proceed (after army service) to university. It also seemed not unreasonable for an older Ted to test himself and what he had learned on the outside within the traditional learning environment. What we both knew, however, was that if he found learning in classrooms at *yeshiva* genuinely distasteful or seriously counter-productive, we would contrive means, in spite of the rigidity and uniformity of *bagrut* requirements, to continue outside of the school.

Ted's closest friends at Yeshivat Or Etzion turned out to be several of the staff. Though he enjoyed most of his studies, after nearly two years of learning on his own, he found the pace of learning within a class at times unbearably slow. With the beginning of the tenth grade, the *yeshiva* began to respond positively to Ted's unease. Three years after the Hanukkah report card which triggered our experiment in the first place, Ted came home for vacation with the news that he had been offered the option to skip the rest of the tenth grade and jump right after Hanukkah into the eleventh! He was apprehensive; nevertheless, he made the leap. It certainly proved a difficult spring. Suddenly Ted was thrust into an eleventh-grade classroom, among new and older fellow students, and facing four *bagrut* exams that very June!

His grades on his report card that Passover were lower, and there were many times that spring when he questioned whether he had chosen the right course. By the end of June, however, Ted had been accepted his new classmates, had succeeded in all his classes, and passed all his *bagruts*. He was ready for a vacation.

Six years later, I am certain that Ted and I are much closer than we would have been had I not been so intimately involved in his education. We recognize, of course, that what we underwent is not *the* solution to the spidery educational problems that face, particularly in the junior high years, many Israeli children and parents. Especially in seemingly brash but in reality unself-confident, conformist Israel it is easily subject to misinterpretation. Our Yeroham Dutch neighbors' oldest son, for example, has never adjusted well to school. Now 11, he neither regularly goes to school nor does any formal lessons, has evidenced ample anti-social behavior—in short, is plainly headed for more serious trouble. Yet his indulgent social worker father has twice commented to me that he did not think it potentially a dangerous situation. After all, had not my Ted also stayed out of school for months and months?

Still, despite this miscomprehension, I am encouraged that a pragmatic ("an American"?) approach to the problems of "the system," one informed by the traditional Jewish notion that it is, after all, the parents rather than the system that are ultimately responsible for the child's education, can prevail. Indeed, at each juncture in this account, the imposing system not only gave way: it actually accommodated us in our craziness.

I cannot predict what precise situation will confront Yishai and Miriam when they reach the shoals of Israeli junior high, but I am reasonably confident that means to avoid the necessity of moving away from Yeroham "for the sake of the children" can and will be found or devised.

BORDER CROSSINGS:
PUBLIC ARRANGEMENTS
AND PRIVATE

*I*t was an undeclared, informal, unheralded sort of milestone. Waiting our turn to be admitted by the guard through the security gate, Ted and I stood in line together behind three young Arabs in the courtyard of the stately American Consulate in East Jerusalem. Not yet 9:00 A.M.; it had not yet opened for business. Nowadays I usually get to see Ted at home in Yeroham only one Shabbat in every three, but since we both had matters to attend to in Jerusalem, we had made a date to meet at this unlikely place. Behind us an American Jewish woman, chatting with her friends, referred to the well-protected building on Nablus Road as "the Embassy." When I turned toward her quizzically, she smiled and corrected herself—"the would-be Embassy." Near the very front of the twisting line stood a young Orthodox couple holding month-old twins that a gray-haired couple from the American South, plainly not Jewish, cooed and dithered over. The day was warm for March. Lines generate moods of their own; this one seemed friendly.

More than half the waiting people were Arabs from Jerusalem or the nearby area seeking American visas. Clearly, the young Jewish parents had come to bestow upon their newly-borns American co-citizenship. In Israel, the American Embassy in Tel Aviv deals with American citizens *except for residents of Jerusalem.* Many Amerisraelis have a store of ready anecdotes to illustrate a pro-Arab tilt among Consulate personnel. Since Ted had recently entered a *yeshiva* not far from Jerusalem, however, we opted for convenience and to brave whatever crimson discourtesy or tape our choice entailed.

It was apparent that of all the people standing in line that morning, only my 17-year-old son had come to register for the

American selective service system. He was early—two months shy of his 18th birthday—because he had a prior engagement for that signal occasion: he and his *hesder* buddies from "the Gush" would be two weeks into their basic training with *Tsahal*—the Israel Defense Forces. Today's was merely an academic exercise in good (dual) citizenship.

"What if. . .?," Ted had ventured at one point, but before I could respond, he had himself severed the dangling question. "No, it's impossible." Still, even a hypothetical conflict of allegiance between the two military obligations, these two armies—especially in a family with such ambivalent military traditions as ours—struck us both queerly.

Suddenly a young Arab cut boldly in front of the new parents at the very front of the long line. "My business will only take a minute," he proclaimed with a rubbery smile. "I was here before."

The Americans in line were not mollified. Inasmuch as the Consulate had not yet opened its doors, just what sort of "before" was he talking about? Not on that day! The tall Southerner moved forward, tapped the dapper Arab on the shoulder, and loudly but courteously declared. "You're standing on United States territory, son. Why don't you just take your place at the end of the line before there's any trouble."

Ted, I, all the Americans beamed. A Lone Ranger rode! And, for a change, it wasn't an evasive Jewish pensioner feigning hardness of hearing or a cute *Tsahal* soldierette in a short, clinging skirt who had snapped the queue. A small but palpable satisfaction in that! Without another word, the young Arab retreated to the rear.

When we were finally admitted, the Consulate clerks handled Ted's business expeditiously. Prepared for the politics of hassle, we had been treated to a double dose of fair play and efficiency. What an unexpectedly star-spangled morning! "What if . . .?" Well, it *is* a tantalizer that twists like snakedance all around the heart of the matter of loyalty and personal identity. Still, it was much too hypothetical to cloud an altogether pleasant morning, was it not? In short order I was off to make my appointment, and my almost (?) grown-up son was

heading for the bus station to return about a dozen miles south
of Jerusalem to his studies and friends at Har Etzion, his *hesder
yeshiva*.

In the past decade, much of the élan of the Religious Zionist
Movement (N.R.P.) in Israel has been either frittered away
in political misdealings or hijacked by Gush Emunim—the
chauvinistic Land of Israel Movement. While the N.R.P., by
veering to the political right, had distanced itself hopelessly far
from my own political ground, still I had to admit that I and
my family had availed ourselves almost continuously of its
good offices: our first three months in the country were spent at
a *moshav* that was founded and still functions under its spon-
sorship, our own defunct *garin*—Mashmia Shalom—had
used its organizational umbrella for leverage, both Jen and Ted
had attended Religious Zionist (B'Nei Akiva) high schools, Jen
had volunteered for two years of Sherut Leumi (a program cre-
ated at the behest of the N.R.P.), and now Ted was a *hesdernik*.
Even my health plan—though this was a fluke, more a matter
of development town economics than ideology—was sponsored not by Labor-dominated Histradrut but by the Mizrachi-
N.R.P. I may have voted for Labor or Labor-affiliated candi-
dates ever since arriving in Israel, but how could I deny that I
was both in theoretical and in eminently practical ways involved as well with the interests of the N.R.P.?

To many of us, the *yeshivot hesder* are the last, wayward remaining hope for renewal within the institutional framework
of Modern Orthodoxy. If anyone, it is its graduates who will
form the nucleus of its regeneration. Though there are now a
good many of these Zionist *yeshivot* in Israel, as Ted would put
it, "there's only one Gush." His enthusiastic allusion is, of
course, not to Gush Emunim but to Gush Etzion, the group
of religious settlements that is the site of Yeshivat Har Etzion.

Har Etzion is reputedly the most intellectually demanding
of Israeli higher *yeshivot*. It is also the *yeshiva* from which, as
the toll of *hesdernik* casualties mounted sharply, issued forth in
1983 the first serious Orthodox criticism of Israeli adventurism
in Lebanon. Its rigorously rational, open-minded tone is set by
one of its two directors: Rabbi Aharon Lichtenstein. A product

of Yeshiva University *and* Harvard (Ph.D. in English), he is the son-in-law and major exponent of the philosophy of Boston's Rabbi Joseph Soloveitchik, America's pre-eminent Jewish theologian.

I had visited with Ted at "the Gush" for the first time just a few weeks before our Jerusalem date. Within one minute after making my exit from the Beersheba–Jerusalem *sherut* (intercity taxi) some ten minutes north of Hebron, I had an offer from a bushy-bearded rabbi in a new Opel to drive me the kilometer run up the hill to the *yeshiva*. (*Kippot*-wearers rarely have long to wait for rides along the roads in the Territories.) A small slip: emptying the back seat of bag, books, coats, and cookies for my son, I also hauled off the rabbi's raincoat. He had to hail me from a distance to retrieve it. It was a portent: I would be seeing him again.

Anyone approaching Yeshivat Har Etzion for the first time would be struck at once by its physical audacity. The central complex that comprises *bet hamidrash* (study center), classrooms, offices, dining hall, and library juts its chiseled, modernist faces toward the sky as if in a posture of stubborn perdurance. Though designed to impart less a sense of delicacy than of strength, its lines are clean and graceful. Both for Jewish and for Arab West Bankers, its impact against the gray hills of Judea is unambiguous.

In 1948, after fierce resistance which gave the Jews of Jerusalem time to prepare for its defense, all the religious settlements of Gush Etzion had been overrun by the invading Jordanian army. By chance, Moshav Masuot Yitzhak, the very communal agricultural settlement that served as our first waystation in Israel, had been founded by settlers who had been uprooted from this very site. Indeed, one of our closest acquaintances while living there, now a professor at Bar-Ilan University, had been captured here and spent more than a year as a Jordanian prisoner of war.

Shelving at least temporarily my lingering ambivalence about the awkwardness of its location, I found standing at the scene of Gush Etzion's resurrection unexpectedly moving. It was a chastening realization: though Gush Emunim had long seemed both simplistic and potentially dangerous, I discovered myself not immune to the force of sentiment that has fueled it. And now Ted was living here! Very little in Israel comes at one cut, dried, and permanently pressed.

Everything at Yeshivat Har Etzion, however, bespeaks forethought, calculation, a good plan in the process of realization: a rarity in the chronic Israeli state of slapdash or (putting a good face on it) improvisation. Facing the central core of structures rise well-designed dormitories that hug well-tended paths. Everywhere there were beds of red, pink, and yellow—flowers, flowers, flowers. I looked again: to be sure, I had walked right past several Arab gardeners at work—Israel's Invisible Men! Yet I, it struck me, could scarcely be cellophane for them. Indeed, is it not inevitable that I, that the hundreds of *yeshiva* students, that all of Gush Etzion would appear to them not so very different from the way the brash, young Arab would seem to me that morning at the American Consulate in East Jerusalem several weeks thereafter? And the Lone Ranger or a comic Tonto that is yet to be played out by the likes of Yassir Arafat? There could be nothing very funny for them in such musings.

Waiting for Ted to materialize, I was invited in for tea by two students from an adjacent room. Both Kim and Peter came from Copenhagen, and their stay at the *yeshiva* was to be the middle third of a year's study in Israel. Both were enthusiasts about the place; both planned eventual *aliya*. What about living—was there no neutral terminology?—on the West Bank? In Judea? In the Territories? *Here?!*

"When we're at the *yeshiva*," Kim said after a moment, "we don't much feel that it's the 'West Bank.' But even so, this area is special for us: six years ago, a Danish student was murdered here by terrorists. Coming to learn here is for us something like keeping faith with him." I said nothing.

Kim and Peter are among the relatively large number who come to learn at this *hesder yeshiva* for a short period—to study among young Israelis. They, however, are not properly speaking *hesderniks*. Moreover, any preliminary ideas of a resemblance between the *hesder* program and American R.O.T.C. are rather misleading.

According to Israeli legislation, full-time *yeshiva* students are entitled to a military deferment; probably most, with the encouragement (or collusion) of their rabbis, take full advantage of this. Many *yeshiva* students never serve in the army at all. For most Israeli secular Jews and religious Zionists, the abuses in this situation constitute a standing scandal. An alternative path for religious youngsters is *hesder*, which means "arrangement"; it is an accommodation between the army and the Religious Zionist Movement that permits draft-age youngsters to combine their obligation to study Torah with their obligation to defend the State of Israel.

The chief advantage in this arrangement for the *hesdernik* is that his actual time in uniform is reduced from 36 to 15 months, it is fulfilled in the company of fellow *hesderniks*, and the stigma of shirking his national obligation is assuaged. The gain to *Tsahal* is a cohesive corps of motivated young men who train to serve in frontline units as a matter of principle. In some ways, *hesderniks* are beginning to fill the army leadership vacuum that traditionally has been occupied by youngsters from the *kibbutzim*. In Israel's more recent wars, the prowess of *hesder* tank and infantry units has been notable . . . and their sacrifice disproportionate.

After Ted finally appeared, he introduced me to Rabbi Yehuda Amital, the co-head of the yeshiva. Embarrassingly, the veteran of the Battle of Latrun in the War of Independence turned out to be the very rabbi whose raincoat, now draped over a chair, I had almost commandeered. Smiling, he offered me a different seat. Yeshivat Har Etzion, he explained, had been initiated in 1967 after the Six-Day War. "The army approached me with the idea of creating a place where religious young men could both pursue their studies and fulfill their public service. We started here with just 21 students." He was soon ebullient: for the genial rabbi, *hesder* was plainly less an "arrangement" than an inspired synthesis and his major life-task.

"Studying Torah is the responsibility of all Jews; that's *halacha*, a religious injunction," he said. "At the same time, however, defending the nation is a task that cannot fairly be fobbed off on others. What sort of situation is it for the non-religious to do all the fighting for the religious? That position surely runs against what we find in the Bible. *Hesder* is our answer, our solution. Here Torah is studied for its own sake, but in time of need, our boys are ready and the first to go. There was at first serious resistance to these ideas. It hasn't entirely been dispelled, but we feel that our success has been remarkable. Not," he added swiftly, "that we are satisfied. But then again, what teacher is ever satisfied?"

We arrived at the recently dedicated library, funded (seemingly like half the structures in Israel) by donations from overseas. Of the approximately 500 students at Har Etzion, costs and Har Etzion philosophy conspire to attract a substantial number—115 currently—from the United States. (Ted's closest pals, in fact, seemed to be American.) "It costs us now around $120,000 to operate every month. The Israeli students can pay only about $300 a year; the Americans pay ten times that. But there's much more than that to our large American component," he hastily added. "We number over 80 *olim* among our former students. We *want* Americans to study with us here . . . and to fall in love with Israel."

I paused at an alcove and read three names on a plaque: Asher Yaron, Sriel Birnbaum, Avner Yonah. And at the next library alcove was affixed a similar plaque with the names Rafael Neuman, Binyamin Gal, Ramy Buchris—in all, twelve young *hesderniks* from Har Etzion who have fallen in time of war. A number of them were tankists who, in a well-known, harrowing occurrence from the early days of the Lebanese invasion, were killed in the same incident.

We passed on to *bet hamidrash*, the hub (& -bub) of the *yeshiva*. Over 130 Har Etzion graduates are now working in Jewish education; while the *yeshiva* professes to encourage its students to pursue their own paths, it was evident to me that Jewish Education gets special emphasis. "Jewish life in the Diaspora is ebbing," I was reminded. (From the perspective of Israel, this is simply a self-evident truth.) "Our job is to do what we can to keep the flame kindled for as many young people as we can reach. So we don't merely receive students from America. Each year we export young men to the Diaspora on special educational missions. We receive requests from all over the world for our graduates, and we've had particular success with projects in California—especially San Francisco and Palo Alto."

I was directed to some likely future emissaries for such projects. Danny Epstein, a bearded, 24-year-old former Brooklynite, was actively planning to work to reverse assimilationist currents among American Jews. "Har Etzion," he said, "is integrated into the real world. The emphasis is on the student's developing his skills of analysis and conceptualization. That makes it very different from most other *yeshivot*, both *hesder* and otherwise. Moreover, there are *yeshivot* that espouse a philosophy that some people on their own staff don't really believe or live. Here everyone is fully committed, and a real concern for moral and contemporary issues is the norm. And I don't mean only Jewish issues, per se: we've had public discussions recently on world hunger, on Cambodia, on other matters. That sort of thing is almost unique in the Torah world. Further, the most talented young Jewish minds in the country can be found right here. You know, it's not for nothing that they call Har Etzion the Harvard of the *yeshivot*."

A shade less gushy about "the Gush" was stocky, 27-year-old Hershel Summer. He too found Har Etzion uniquely satisfying, but stressed the intrinsic tension between alternating cycles of studying *Gemara* and packing an M-16 on Israel's borders. "It exacts its price. A friend of mine is leaving the *yeshiva* next month. Too many cross-pressures." He touched on a sensitive point: learning Torah and manning roadblocks are neither naturally complementary nor neatly reconcilable activities. *Hesderniks* tread a finely drawn line that continually threatens to eclipse religious sensibility or to dull moral awareness. The passage from yeshiva student to soldier and back . . . and back . . . is not negotiated without heavy personal cost.

Summer noticed that I was distracted by the constant din of over 100 buzzing students at their paired-off studies. He smiled: "Oh, you get used to it. It's not a bother at all." Ted at home had once made the same claim of his life here, and, of course, it must be so. Within earshot all those boyhood years of the song of the Bronx I.R.T.'s Jerome Avenue el, I recalled how conversation would automatically accommodate itself to the periodic roar. Still, the cultural gulf between the intense chatter in the *bet hamidrash* and the characteristic hush of the university library seemed broad and deep. Did it not perhaps bode something unbridgeable? Not exactly disinterested, I suddenly entertained the nettlesome notion of my son's moving in a direction that could swing him irremediably beyond my sphere. What if . . . ? It was not, after all, so very entertaining a prospect.

Just 15 minutes before his weekly lecture on the teachings of Rabbi Soloveitchik, I entered the office of his son-in-law. High forehead prominent, Rabbi Lichtenstein cuts an austere, formidable figure. What, I wondered, had brought him to this chilly bluff in the Judean hills?

"More than other alternatives, Har Etzion suited my ideological needs. Only a few of the boys arrive here with a clear sense of purpose. The challenge is to inculcate them with a passion for Torah."

What about flak from the Torah world for his public criticism of Israel's Lebanese involvement?

"Rabbi Amital drew more criticism than I. People already knew my position, but they assumed that he differed, that he was at bottom 'one of them.' They were somewhat surprised. But you know, there really is no 'party line' here at Har Etzion. Many on our staff view the world quite otherwise than I, and they are provided the fullest opportunity to present their views. In fact, I suspect that most of the students probably don't agree with me politically. There's nothing wrong with this; save for the fundamental commitment to Torah, our aim here is for openmindedness.

"[As for American Jewry,] what is happening is that while the base of Jewish life is contracting, the center is solidifying." There was no need to add that among his own and Har Etzion's highest priorities is to produce a cadre of young men committed to attracting the very best from that periphery as adherents of a broadening mass at the center.

In the cafeteria, I rejoined Ted who was eating with David Nelson, a *yeshiva* student acquaintance of ours from his volunteer days two years before in Yeroham. The talk turned to the contrast between the intimidating Lichtenstein and warmly buoyant Amital. What was clear was that beneath the striking opposition of personalities lay a commonality of character and ideals. The former was less aloof than reserved; the latter quite capable of intellectual brilliance. They had struck a remarkably successful working arrangement. I optimistically suggested that their harmonious relationship was an emblem, perhaps, to more than the atmosphere of intellectual caring that Har Etzion radiated. Might it not possibly be seen to embody a fruitful reconciliation between contraries not only for *hesdernik* part-time students / part-time soldiers but even perhaps for Israel's fractured body politic as a whole? No one else, however, seemed on that almost messianic wavelength.

"Have you noticed what this place resembles?," David provocatively queried. A pyramid? A unicorn? I was stumped. "It's more like an American college campus than like the other *yeshivot*. And I think that that's intentional," he pursued. "What Har Etzion is saying is that it is ready to compete with the finest American or Israeli universities for the best Jewish minds out there—that Har Etzion is *the* address for Jewish higher education."

When later that day I turned to wave goodbye to my newly vegetarian, *hesdernik* son, I had to grant that, however probable the future widening of the gap between us, it was already implicit in the "arrangement" I had made with my life when I packed us all off to Israel in 1976. A consolation: had we remained in California, would not the breach likely have been far more sharp and grievous?

It had started to sprinkle. The weather in the Territories is different from the weather in my Negev. Why indeed had I not brought along my own raincoat?

B etween the time of my visit to Yeshivat Har Etzion and my morning with my son at the American Consulate, a car bomb exploded at Metulla in the North. Twelve Israeli soldiers were killed. Ted called us a few days later. He had been the day before to two funerals: one in the morning in Jerusalem, a second in the afternoon in Haifa. (It is such a small, small country we inhabit.) Two *hesderniks* from Har Etzion, while out on patrol the day *after* the car bomb explosion, had been killed in a light arms clash. Both were third-year students. From time to time, Ted had played chess with the one from Haifa. Something of immense value had been cashiered as casually as a rumpled raincoat from the backseat of a car. There was no clear way to make retrieval or reparations.

In the future, the names of Daniel Moshitz and David Cohen will be added to the somber, growing roster of supreme "donors" on a plaque in the Marcos Katz Library of Yeshivat Har Etzion. As for Peter and Kim, so too in all likelihood for Ted as well. With the passage of time . . . and blood . . . it will be increasingly difficult not to view his area as so "special" as further to delimit—or eliminate entirely—the possibilities of effecting any reasonably satisfactory "arrangement" with the majority of its inhabitants.

Almost a year after these two funerals, Ted, having completed his first arduous phase of military service—nine months of training and active duty in *Tsahal's* elite *Givati* unit—was just barely a month back at his studies at Har Etzion. Our soldier son was once again a model *yeshiva* student. He arrived home for Shabbat in the middle of February looking well but disturbed. Israeli forces were just returning from more than a week in Lebanon in search of terrorists who had recently abducted two Israeli soldiers. In their primary mission, they had been unsuccessful.

"Dad," Ted said softly after dinner Friday night, "those two soldiers who were kidnapped were *hesderniks.*" He paused for a long moment, then continued. "They were our replacement platoon. Their platoon is led by our old officers."

When poet Yehuda Amichai is questioned about his "politics," he simply points to his life: "I live with my family here in Jerusalem." Yeshivat Har Etzion in "the Gush"—a Jewish patch on an Arab garment—fits the ideological needs of another Jerusalemite, daily commuter Rabbi Aharon Lichtenstein, better than the other options. The teacher of my son, a man who commands the Torah world's and my own great respect, he is mistaken about everyone knowing his politics well. I have found myself puzzling over them ever since our too-brief meeting.

Jews and Arabs, all of us here in Israel are nationals both of the Land of the Head and of the Land of the Heart—two faces of a coin that purchases both hope and desperation. I would, I think, be a fool were I surprised to discover that one day, perhaps totally unawares, as with so many other dual citizens of this torn land, I had passed through an undeclared, uncelebrated, informal sort of milestone at a border crossing of my own.

ON RESERVE:
THOSE WHO STAND
AND WAIT

At the western edge of Beersheba's "Old City," the grid of right-angled streets once holding 2,000 Arabs which was left deserted after the War of '48, is laid a cemetery. I enter its grounds three or four times a year. It lies close by what is now the "Negev Museum," a mosque dormant for almost 40 years whose telltale minaret spirals into the sky just across from Beersheba's main immigrant absorption center— most recently a first Israeli home for hundreds of immigrant Ethiopians. The plaque on the outside wall reads BEERSHEBA WAR CEMETERY; English, Arabic, and Hebrew proclaim that this parcel is "a free grant from the people of Palestine . . . for the perpetual resting place of those of the Allied Armies who fell in the War 1914–1918." The precise, round-shouldered, white stones stand at splendid attention.

Whatever ragged image the blurry phrase "people of Palestine" summons to mind, *this* formal place could never be mistaken for a Jewish cemetery. In fact, a recent Jewish cemetery may be found within a kilometer of this site. As in all traditional Jewish cemeteries from Vilna to Queens, one senses within it what almost seems an intentional deficiency in plan and design, a mazy slide toward jumble; it is, in fact, redolent of post-'48 Jewish Beersheba itself, a celebrated blunder of city ill-planning, whose streets arc and spiral about obscurely like gross question marks. Not unlike wary, self-protective Judaism itself is Beersheba: if you don't already know the territory, if you do not get assistance from a long-time resident, you will spend a long, long time finding your way.

I always navigate through the silent ranks toward a certain gravesite—very front row, second from the right. I once roughly calculated that at least 1,400 men lie at permanent inspection here. Nearly all of the stone markers in the Beersheba War Cemetery bear a cross. Front and 2nd right, however, is the final resting place of Captain S. I. H. Van den Bergh of the Middlesex Yeomanry, who, as any casual observer may discern from the engraving, was the son of Henry and Henriette. He fell in battle in September 1917 at the age of 27. To his right is the grave of a Private of the Somerset Light Infantry with the unlikely name of I. Suarez; to his left: "A Soldier of the Great War Known to God." Both are buried beneath the cruciform. Among all the 1,400 soldiers who lie in this cemetery, Captain Van den Bergh is the only known-to-man Jew.

Beneath the six-pointed Star of David a chiseled inscription patiently awaits me: "So far from home / yet so near to those who love him." This sentiment always evokes a queer frisson: it expresses with precision the self-same feelings of my own parents who live in North Miami Beach. I have a strong intuition that Henry and Henriette Van den Bergh once, surely at least once, journeyed from Middlesex to Beersheba. They passed through the heavy metal gates and past the phalanx of crosses in the BEERSHEBA WAR CEMETERY to stand here before the remains of their son, just where I myself periodically station myself. One time I impulsively troubled the obliging Moroccan caretaker for information. Noting that very few make inquiries about soldiers who fell in the Great War, to my astonishment he was able to produce a Kensington address for the Van den Bergh family. My letter never earned a reply. Even to myself, my motivations for writing were murky.

This cemetery, beautifully maintained by the British Commonwealth War Cemeteries Commission, is a green island along my dusty way to the pickup point where I catch a ride to the military airbase where I must report for short- or long-term *miluim. Miluim*—reserve duty—is one of those Hebrew words so endemic to life in Israel that even the newcomer, though he himself is exempt from its force for at least his first three years in the country, uses it exclusively from the very start of his tenure as an Israeli. One serves, health permitting, in a regular unit until the age of 50, and then till 55 in *haga*, a "home guard" unit.

Miluim has punctuated my life, and with equal strength the lives of Marcia and the children, since 1980. Each stint is heralded about six weeks before by the arrival of a small, brown envelope, which may call for four days of training, a three-day exercise, or up to a month's active duty: normally, 40 days a year. Particularly at the time of the war in Lebanon, the flow of these brown-skinned missives was one of citizenship's most insistent and ambiguous bonds. It sometimes feels as though most of the time I am doing *miluim*, not long returned from it, or on notice to report. A free grant from the people of Palestine.

This particular occasion, a prototypical 23 wintry days and nights, passed as 1983 faded into still Lebanon-tainted 1984. Together with the pilgrimage *hagim*—Pesach, Shavuot, and Sukkot—for most Israeli families, *miluim* taps out the rhythm of the year. I have never escorted any tourist or Stateside visitor to the Beersheba War Cemetery. What would it signify? At bottom there prevails, I think, a gnawing incommensurability between the tourist's, even the sensitive tourist's, encounter with the tokens of our reality and its grainy texture for those of us who live it.

Preliminary calculations: if I am stationed in the Northern Negev, I should be able to wangle a pass home at least once a week. No need, then, for many books. But two years earlier I was sent to an airbase not far from Eilat, and in the fall of 1982, I found myself incredulously attached to a security unit whose mission it was to guard from interlopers the airport at Beirut. One could never be certain. I settle for Yehuda Amichai's only translated novel. Also a pocket *siddur*. No neophyte, I include an extra battery for the transistor radio, Uncle Harry's navy long johns from World War II, my older son's woolen muffler, sucking candies, toilet paper. My overnight bag is packed before the small children return from school and kindergarten; the final afternoon and evening are reserved for a last round of Junior Scrabble and *The Little Engine That Could*.

On the 5:30 A.M. bus ride from Yeroham to Beersheba, I

divert myself with number games—a private *gematria*: I am 45, my father 79. When he was 45, ever a shade beyond being nibbled up by the encroaching of the draft—he was an air raid warden—I must have been 11. My own sons are 6 and 16, my daughters 4 and 18—a pair of parentheses, perfect symmetry. Arriving in Beersheba with an aerogram in hand to send flying to North Miami Beach, I detour slightly to locate an unjammed letterbox (yesterday was the postmen's turn to be on strike). At the site of my modest pilgrimage, I startle a recumbent crew of Arab gardeners resting not far from the eternal bed of Captain Van den Bergh. I flash them a sign that I have not come to bother them. Beersheba chores accounted for, I hitch a lift and passively deliver myself into the hands of *Tsahal*—the Israel Defense Forces.

A small room crowded with middle-aged men being processed by three girl soldiers in their late teens. Mind buttoned-down for the usual muddle, I encounter (as usual) a revamped system, which (for a change) seems really to function smoother. More to the point: while others are being directed to a waiting bus headed for the North, I am assigned to the group that is to remain here. I feel intense relief: I must have been more anxious than I knew. Straining memory for names, I grin and nod at faces familiar from past tours of duty.

The next two hours pass as if just backstage in a prop & makeup room. I am bestowed with an M-16 and five clips of bullets, blankets ("How many?" I raise three fingers), sets of fatigues (two fingers, please), coat (minus a hood, I half-heartedly complain), stocking cap, and an assortment of clattery gear (ammo pouches, canteen, etc.). Together with my bag from home, it is a clumsy burden I lug the kilometer or more to the tent where that night I'll be sacked out. A good sign: for a change I contrive to adjust the straps and hooks on weapons and belts without nicking my fingers. Outfitted in the same brand of fatigues I wore for three years as an American recruit, I stretch out on a cot and for 20 minutes doze as if I hadn't a care in the world.

Imperceptibly, the regimen of *miluim* creeps over me. If at home my rest is broken, it takes an hour's reading before I can return to sleep. Here I snooze at will and at all hours. Refreshed, I exchange greetings with some other reclining *miluimniks*. During *miluim* my native taciturnity is accentuated. In part it is because the Moroccans and the Russians gravitate toward themselves; as is often the case, I am the only "Anglo" about. It is, however, also a conscious maneuver that suits me, my tested, Maoist military strategy: withdraw, observe, retreat. Indeed, I can feel myself palpably settling into a privateness, rehearsing amidst the sprawling men a singular reserve of my own.

The massive dining hall is a brisk, 20-minute walk from the barracks, a factor to be weighed against fatigue, rain, and threat of rain. Some veteran *miluimniks* who make a practice, almost a ritual, out of cooking their meals at eccentric hours over a burner in a tiny kitchen off the dayroom rarely appear in the dining hall. Not I. True, unlike the U.S. Army messhalls I recall from the early '60s, there is scarce choice and certainly nothing exotic. Still, the noon meal is generally ample and sometimes quite palatable.

A scattering of us new-arrivees sit among the young Air Force trainees. They seem like large boys, which, indeed, *is* the easily forgotten case. Platters of chicken—one piece parceled out per diner—and spaghetti with pitchers of apple juice are served up mainly by young women soldiers, none of whom seems overtly conscious of sex-role stereotyping. There is some playful flirting. On balance, the presence of the teenage girls in uniform seems to me salutary, something tending toward the normalization and universalization of *Tsahal*. Many of the girls, of course, perform more vital functions than this. Still, I am not displeased that my own daughter has chosen to perform her two years of alternative national service through Sherut Leumi. One burning generational chasm: most of the youngsters pass over the thick soup. Not we chill-boned reservists.

The first, dozy afternoon: reorientation. About sixty of us men assemble, and respond to our names; pronouncing the several ". . . schvilis" from Soviet Georgia gives the sergeant the most grief. I note dourly that about half present have lighted up. The mission of our unit is to secure this vast base from subversion and infiltration. The likelihood of such activity seems remote, but it develops (our ears perk for this, the highlight of a soporific business) that two Arab suspects had been caught at the perimeter fence three months earlier and, more recently, a German tourist was nabbed snapping photos at another Negev airbase. Nearly all windows are shut; noxious smoke has filled the room. I recall many of the men, but most faces are new. I sit by a window, but nothing truly avails. I could use that gas mask *now*. The week's password—"fresh sardines." A lecture–demonstration on first aid follows the fire prevention expert, and finally we are dismissed until 6:15 the following morning.

There's a long wait at the phone, but I ultimately succeed in reaching home. "No, not Lebanon . . . a slight head cold but no real problems . . . I'll try to call tomorrow whenever I can." That evening I prove an easy mark for the long-limbed charms of Julie Andrews in *Victor, Victoria*. Back in the tent, however, it is chilly. Awakening at 3:30 A.M., I am beneath three woolen blankets shivering from the *cold*. Next morning, replacing the previous cycle of *miluimniks*, we trudge into the barracks, but too late for me—my nose is drippy. A bad start. The week prior to callup I'd spent two days in bed on a hot-water bottle—my temperamental back. Sunshine and Ben-Gay, Ben-Gay and sunshine: my private private's litany for getting through these next weeks.

The following morning disposes of the last preliminaries: I am wedged into the rear of an army truck, the M-16 askew between my knees. My eyes close. The vehicle jounces over newly worn ruts—it had rained a week before—and time and my bones arc the two decades back to basic training at Fort Dix. Thanks to Dix, I do things that are quaintly inappropriate for *Tsahal*. I may be Israel's only *miluimnik* who neurotically doublechecks his pockets and fly to make sure they are all buttoned. I am ever choking over an impulse to salute each passing officer in this haven of classlessness. The Moroccans and Russians possess wondrous wit and discretion at needling authority. Real aptitude. Among them, I parade about like an understudy, squarishly Angloid, a Van den Bergh among the *goyim*. Lunch, and then, in queer Hebrew letters, the duty roster stares my own name back at me. The afternoon shift of five hours of guarding in the South Lookout Tower. And again tonight from 2:00 to 5:00 A.M. on jeep patrol. A reasonable facsimile or the self-same I, "Chertok, Haim" is officially here.

A time for revelation, the guarded truth about this guard duty that has fallen to me as the given portion of my late-in-life Zionism: it may be otherwise for others, but, if surely not an unalloyed pleasure, *miluim* still functions as a not unwelcome break from everyday routine. What would not have happened to me at Fort Dix had I been discovered guarding with a novel in hand or portable radio at ear? Here, they are mere accessories, props. I am surrounded in my tower by 12 thick plastic panels. I pry one out for better ventilation, check in on the two-way radio, and scan the brown rolling Negev hills with the powerful German binoculars. The perimeter fence of intricate barbed wire twists off for several miles in both directions. At night this fence is studded with squinting owls. Soon I am familiar with every knoll, every tree (there are only about a dozen all together), every turn and bush. In the foreground is the hulk of an old Arab-style dwelling, a picturesque ruin. Nothing stirs on the roads that parallel both sides of the fence. On the BBC, Flanders and Swann offer a commentary on the laws of thermodynamics. And I crank up Yehuda Amichai's *Not of This Time, Not of This Place.* I can think of many less pleasant ways of passing a sunny, winter afternoon.

Solitude. It was only after four weary weeks of basic at Dix that I discovered an underground delight in guard duty. General Orders committed to memory—12? 13? Can I really have forgotten how many there were?—I strode my post the better to keep warm and hummed the night away. For the first stretch in an eternity of drilling, eating, sleeping in company, I WAS WONDERFULLY ALONE.

In truth, a blissful simplification transpires during *miluim.* Nowhere else do I, can I so dutifully observe the principal precept of General Thoreau—*Simplify!; Simplify!; Simplify!* Daily life in Israel is often a tangle of half-done tasks, strikes, bureaucratic miasma, delay. There is no *time,* but here I have nothing but time. Indeed, life narrows to one particular thing at a time, and I have both inclination and uninterrupted opportunity to observe, to take note, and to think. At home Marcia must manage alone with the bank misstatements, notes from teachers, children's squabbles while here I sit for five-hour stretches protecting Israel with my very gaze. These Negev Highlands bear an uncanny resemblance to the foothills of Central California. The landing jets swoop in low, disturbing the graceful formations of dark birds in their ascent from their barbed wire perches. Thoreau sat guard for nearly two years. Amichai and Flanders & Swann are competitors for my attention. As the sun descends, a tiny jeep, like a windup toy, begins to edge toward me in my tower from the left.

My relief!

Asleep by nine, I am roused at 2:00 A.M. My partner is Slonim, a burly engineer from Leningrad. It is cold—very cold. Over our coats, we don hermonits—flight suits. Our mission is to follow the perimeter of the fence that surrounds this huge base; another pair had set out in the opposite direction about an hour before and another will leave around an hour from now. We each make as well a return trip. My tasks: looking for signs of breaks or incursions, to gaze myself dizzy on kilometer after kilometer of barbed wire, periodically to radio in our location, to direct the spotlight at obscured sections along the fence, and to open and lock behind us the heavy double gates along our route. After just a few minutes, fingers (though gloved) and face (albeit scarfed) chafe from the freezing wind that lashes us in the open jeep. A quick tabulation: three pairs of shifts a night make it nearly 400 kilometers of nightly surveillance. Few have to be persuaded that averting intrusions that might in some emergency delay the takeoff of our jets is necessary. Slonim drives; I ride behind the mounted machine gun.

After only 20 minutes, the two-way radio calls up back. A first-night snafu: neither of the other pair possesses a driver's license. Since it increases my chances of finding myself motorized on Shabbat, I am in *miluim* a reluctant driver. Nevertheless, I switch seats and jeeps, and am accompanied along an unfamiliar road by Eli Malka, a Moroccan of uncertain years who has staked out the privileged barracks role of elder cook and statesman. Stretches of the dirt road dip, swerve, trail off unexpectedly into mud. We make several wrong turns and have to snake back in reverse. Fingers and nose numb from the cold wind, I also find myself feeling exhilarated. *It is fun!* I'm reminded of the Stay-on-the-Hiway game I used as a kid to love to play at Coney Island. Would not the folks who line up at Orlando and Anaheim wait for hours for a shot at the "Negev Nights Jeep Patrol"?

With dawn I *daven* just outside the barracks (the base *bet knesset* is located kilometers away). After breakfast and a short nap, I forgo the first morning's bull session—would America or Russia win World War III? I heed instead the classic counsel of the Fort Dix recruit: Get the hell out of the company area! A bit of reconnoitering discloses two sanctuaries. Close by the permanent party billets sits a usually deserted playground, a gift of WIZO, West Germany. A few quiet hours before lunch with my book restores my well-being. Other days I stake out a patch among the pines in a small grove that has been planted behind the *bet knesset*. Despite the night games, I have so far held at bay my incipient head cold.

In the coming days I talk at some length with almost all of the 20 reservists who at assorted hours are awake when I rouse in the barracks or who accompany me on eating or perimeter jeep jaunts. The cot to my left belongs to Daniel, a prematurely white-haired kibbutznik from Brazil. His grandfather, thanks to Baron de Hirsch's generosity and anti-Zion Zionism, had been moved there from Russia at about the same time that *my* non-Zionist Russian grandfather had bid farewell to his Palestine-bound brother and had set sail for Boston. Like me, Daniel has the sense of being a participant in historical rectification and closure: he has connected Russo-Israeli family threads that had been severed two generations earlier. He is quiet, competent, and, despite the serious economic problems on his kibbutz, smiles easily.

Another Dani, a *moshavnik* from Iran, lies in the bunk to my right. Just across from me wisecracking Leonid from Lvov tells a sad tale: Five years ago his father refused to sign a permit for Leonid's departure from the Soviet Union. Father and son had to disavow each other; he hears from his mother only. Armand Biton, a Moroccan factory foreman from Arad, wants to talk to me about Judaism. He grew up observant. No longer. He doesn't really believe all that the prayers say. Do I? Yes and no. Not good enough, he pursues. Yes is yes; no is no. I try again to explain why, how his questions miss my point. It is friendly but fruitless. Who among us is as incomprehensible as Haim, the immigrant *from* America? Some of the Russians prefer vodka, but Eli Malka each night nips at his bottle of arak. Earlier in the evening he dispenses syrupy Turkish coffee and his Casablanca-distilled wisdom to all comers. About a week into our *miluim* cycle, when I arrive at the South Lookout to relieve him, I am confronted and startled by the sight of seven stony mounds, each precariously balanced to the height of three-to-four feet, each crafted lovingly. Malka had spent his five-hour shift raising pillars which must have resembled those Jacob and Laban erected at Gilead. He smiles shyly at my bewilderment and jeeps down the rutty road.

By general consensus, the most helpful, the most professional reservist among us is Almanzor, a Soviet Georgian with dandy, graying mustachios. Even in the mud, his boots sparkle. His voice is never raised; he even occasionally spells other reservists and works extra hours. Almanzor is the perfect antithesis of the stereotypical *Gruzini*. These fellow Jews are Israeli types I do not normally encounter in the run of daily life. Several times a year, however, the lottery of *miluim* tosses me haphazardly among them. A paradox: though too frequently disappointed, depleted by the uncivil encounters of Israeli civilian life, I have never yet failed to emerge from a stint of reserve duty impressed with the diversity, strength, and good humor of my fellow *miluimnikim*. And I, oddball voluntary immigrant, Quiet American, son of Florida Flo & Sam, am of them among the most exotic.

Midmorning in a tower; I am reading my Amichai. His protagonist, a Holocaust survivor, returns to Germany to seek vengeance. Off to my right, Israeli pilots, touted as the world's best, twist through the sky on maneuvers. Cynthia Ozick's new book, which I just reviewed for *The Jerusalem Post*, also features a survivor. (Are novels still written that don't?) Unexpectedly I discover tears welling up in the corners of my eyes. The planes slant down like skyskaters, one in every five or six nosing up instead of landing on the strip that hides just beyond my field of vision. Last month a touring, prize-winning Israeli play, *Pilots*, which aims at the immorality of dropping bombs on civilian targets, played our Yeroham Community Center. I check my non-digital wristwatch: an hour yet of Amichai in the dimming light before my relief chariot will swing in from the left, coming for to carry me home.

First Friday: weekly inspection. The queerness of hearing Russian has mellowed. I studied it for a year over two decades before at the U.S. Army Language School in Monterey, California; I can still follow conversational snatches. There's something lovely about these Israeli airbases being guarded around the clock, around the calendar, by dozens of ex-Russians in G.I. fatigues. I have cleaned my rifle more than strictly necessary. Gun-oil's whiff packs Proustian potency. At Monterey the precious weekend pass could be put in jeopardy by a misaligned toothbrush or razor in the footlocker display, an unbuttoned breast pocket, or an inopportune smile or (Heaven Help Us!) giggle. Keeping a face inspection-straight while braced at attention opposite Pvt. Frentz and Pvt. Butterfield was not always a simple matter.

Different to be sure, but things here can be equally comic. When the young C.O. objects to a roll of toilet paper that sits posed for a still-life atop a locker, he becomes the target of *chutzpah* and laughter crossfire. The real point of *this* inspection, however, is to talk over first-week-on-the-job snafus. A sure token of well-being: after lunch I catch myself warbling "Bye-Bye Blackbird" in the shower.

Friday night, a *miluim* Shabbat: an officer and I are the only *datiim*—observant Jews—in the unit. I don't expect to be removed from the duty roster but, without checking with me, the officer has arranged it. I am grateful but suffer, to be sure fleetingly, from classic guilt: someone else is jeeping that night in my place. In the base synagogue are assembled about 75 Jews, mostly young airmen. There is one girl soldier, probably from a religious kibbutz. It strikes me that I am the oldest person in the room. How do I appear in their eyes? Yeats's public man "Among School Children" clashes mildly with *Adon Olam*.

I eat that evening and Saturday morning after *kiddush* with Gerald Blidstein, an ethics professor acquaintance from Ben-

Gurion University whose *miluim* duties for *Tsahal* are to function as itinerant rabbi. Shabbat afternoon I enter *my* pine grove behind the synagogue to doze beneath the branches and startle a rabbit. Blidstein's talk prior to *ma'ariv* service deals with the need for the Jewish people to treat with compassion and justice the strangers within our midst. This is not the sort of theme most of these young men, graduates of yeshiva high schools that generally stress the *Jewish* rights to the Land of Israel, are accustomed to hearing.

Returned at nightfall to the dayroom, I come upon a knot of eight fellow *miluimniks* who are closing out their Shabbat engrossed in the charms of TV's "Wonder Woman." We exchange greetings of Shavuah Tov, and I zip into my hermonit for another chilly four hours around the base.

I have a strange altercation with Slonim. He has made a brief visit to America and has heard that any American Jewish soldier making the request is supplied with kosher food. It is all too easy to summon the acrid taste of bacon grease in the eggs, potatoes, beans. Somehow every mess sergeant I ever encountered hailed from Tennessee or Carolina; lard infected everything. Slonim insists. It had never even occurred to me to request a kosher cuisine. I demur. Like many Israelis, Slonim is the greater expert. Tiring, we let the issue lie fallow.

New Year's Day in the North Lookout Tower. Israelis, many of them, celebrate an indeterminate solstice with "Sylvester" festivities. Many of us do not. It is a divisive time. The BBC overdoes the dawning of 1984 and Orwellmania. A revolution has hit Nigeria. Also, Eric Williams, author of *The Wooden Horse*, a best-selling novel about an escape from a Nazi prisoner-of-war-camp, has died. I cock to attention. What novel! *The Wooden Horse* was true! The exciting exploit by Williams was the very first book I selected when as a ninth grader I was finally admitted to the downstairs, adult section of the Fordham branch of the New York Public Library. I had by then almost read through the young adult offerings upstairs. There were here so many more shelves, so many books. The librarian escorted me to the section of Non-Fiction Adventures. *The Wooden Horse* had really happened: that had been a matter of tremendous importance to me.

Had I been tricked, cheated? Could it, in fact, have been a novel? Yet could anyone familiar with Amichai's poetry not hear the same voice through that of the protagonist of *Not of This Time, Not of This Place*? Together, memory and craft blur the line between fiction and fact, true and *truth*. How many civilians does it take to render a target "civilian"?: 50?, 45?, 40?, 30?, 20?, a barebones 10? Attached to the Israeli Air Force, I, my father's true son and seed of Avraham Avinu, am an inveterate groundsman, one of the Yeroham Yeomanry.

Days, nights, days of jeeping, sleeping, reading in my Joycean lighthouse tower. Every so often I recall the two suspects who were collared some months before and scan the horizon. Always stillness except for the dark, nervous birds that circle at dusk in the softly setting sun. Dani has taken the trouble to inform me that he feels bad about the porcupine that our jeep had pointlessly smashed, that this had not been the real or true Dani. He had stopped and backed up after the collision so that we could look at the writhing creature. The bristling apparition in the night's cold drizzle fixed crazily in our headlights; the plump 3:00 A.M. crash had opened a sudden chasm between us. *Lama*—why?—was all that I could utter. Recoiling, I had little stomach for small talk for the remainder of our circuit.

Second Shabbat of *miluim* is my 48-hour "vacation"; after inspection, I am skipping off for Yeroham. Home for Shabbat. My gift for the kids is modest: a can of *Tsahal* halvah. They are delighted. I have developed, in fact, a taste for halvah sandwiches before my 2:00 A.M. excursions. Marcia presents the week's accumulation of mail among which I find an Israeli weekly that has printed a short, reflective article I had written to order about the anniversary of the assassination of John Kennedy. The editor has cut some of the meat, but I am pleased nonetheless. That dividing, so far and close year of '63 was when Amichai's *Not of This Time, Not of This Place* was first published. It was also a time when I wore the uniform of another country. I adjust to the family's Shabbat rhythm, and they readjust to mine.

Two days later, the morning sun appears a bit after 6:00, but only around 8:30 do I feel its first warmth radiate to me in my cold tower. "Ineluctable modality of the visible" strikes first. Warmth and the smack of jets follow in light's wake like ideas that congeal around scattered impressions only later, in the act of writing. Of what good or use is "feeling bad" about bombs and porcupines? I sorely miss my typewriter; indeed, I find I can scarcely think at all in its absence.

Around the barracks these days of routine the men play at *sheshbesh* and cards. A Rumanian lawyer produces a tattered copy of *Playboy*. "At your age, Shmuel?," someone jibes. "At my age especially," is his laughing retort. The *dati* officer, a Swiss, confirms that at least in Europe, *Chabad* (Lubavitch) supplies American G.I.'s so requesting with kosher meals. Slonim, admirer of Rabbi Meir Kahane, was possibly right after all! Here indeed was a gambit overlooked by Pvt. Max Klinger of M*A*S*H in his campaign to get back to Toledo. He should have slipped off his stockings, slipped on his *kittel*, and insisted on his gefilte fish and horse radish with pumpernickel. (But wasn't he supposed to be a Lebanese? Innocuity itself is an endangered species.)

Just three nights to go. With so little time left, I am determined to ignore a twitchy pain that grips my chest whenever I breathe in hard. Around 12:30 A.M. in our jeep, Almanzor and I are radioed that a suspicious vehicle has been spotted near the fence. We shoot off down a bumpy access road. I clutch the M-16 at my right side and hold a clip at the ready in my left hand. If whoever we encounter does not respond correctly to the new password—Red Sun—if he does not stop on command, I know that I am fully prepared to shoot: "First shot in the air, next shot anywhere below the waist. Don't miss!" After eight or ten kilometers of pursuing the air, we return to our checkpoint. Nothing. We are not at all disappointed.

My final morning in a lookout tower. The long johns I am wearing have inhabited other towers. Marcia's Uncle Harry worked in the 1930s as a firewatcher in Montana for the C.C.C. So that teachers would not become eligible for tenure, in those years they were fired every year. For almost a decade, every summer Uncle Harry and Aunt Irene had to move on to a different town, every fall to a different school. The tops have ripped; odd that they should end up here in the Negev, a place for which I freely surrendered my tenured position at a California college.

Our barracks hosts its traditional end-of-*miluim* party. No dining halls this night: all day Eli Malka, Biton, and some others supervise the food preparations. By evening the dayroom, with streamers aloft and cloths covering tables that are anchored by dozens of bottles, looks positively festive. All of the officers make an appearance. The C.O. of the airbase, a general in his mid-30s, is here. While we all dig into the salads, dips, pita, wine, and beer, everyone in turn says a few words about himself and his feelings about his waning tour of *miluim*. The general, even taking a few notes, seems to attend closely to what is said.

Leonid is cut off by the entrance of Eli Malka who announces that the grilled meat is ready, but the general insists that Malka too say a few words. Malka throws the general a wizened look and, after a dramatic pause, on the balls of his feet slowly approaches to within a foot of the seated general. The room hushes. "You know, this year I will be 56 years old. Over the limit. I don't have to be here at all." There was total silence.

"But," he proceeded, "I come because I love it here . . . and I plan to come to *miluim* till I die." With that Malka reaches out, pinches the startled general's cheeks with both of his hands, and backs away in triumph.

Later, after the officers have withdrawn, we *miluimnik*s all sing sentimental Israeli songs (most of which seem to have Russian melodies). Then most of us offer at least one ethnic tune, most in ensemble. Being the only "Anglo," my ace in the hole was a solo rendition of Guthrie's "This Land Is Your Land"—given the occasion, a somewhat ambiguous entry. While a skeleton crew rotates as the night's least tipsy guardians of Israel, beer, wine, and arak gradually disappear. In the tents behind the barracks sleep chilled men who tomorrow will replace us in the jeeps and towers for the month to come. Yet later the most determined roisterers blanket-toss those of us found presumptuously in the sack. No need to doze before the final 2:00–5:30 A.M. turns around base perimeter. I can make up my losses the coming night on civilian time.

The next day the skein unravels: rifle and clips, fatigues and stocking cap get returned, forms are initialed. Now in jeans, sweaters, denims, and pullovers, Daniel, Leonid, Eli Malka, I, and all are, until the next time, demobilized. "Make my bed and light the light / I'll arrive late tonight / Blackbird, bye-bye."

In all my visits, I have never encountered even one other visitor between the rows of the Beersheba War Cemetery. The caretaker said that once a year the British Embassy sends some people down to Beersheba for a ceremony. Captain Van den Bergh, fallen at 27, would be an old man in his 90s today. When I was 27, our first daughter was born, and Marcia and I registered as potential *olim* at the San Francisco office of the Israel Consulate. Eleven years were yet to pass before our dare, our threat would take wings. Apparently, Captain Van den Bergh never married, was childless, and certainly never registered anywhere as a potential *oleh* to Israel. Yet here he resides, the only Jewish *oleh* among the 1,400 other fallen.

Beersheba is merely a normal, poorly-planned city of around 115,000 Jews. Except for its Thursday morning Bedouin market, it boasts scarcely any attractions to divert curious tourists. The Beersheba War Cemetery is for permanent party, not for passers-through. Inside its walls I say my brief prayer several times each year at the gravesite of Captain Van den Bergh. Better for me than the more public, formal ceremonies that Israel has instituted, through this I renew a link to the anomaly of his fate, to that of his parents (and to my own), to the Jews of another time and place—that ashen reservoir of unready, un-done *olim*—who lacked a nation and an army to forfend their annihilation, and to the anomaly of my own.

PART THREE.
PERSISTENT
RESERVATIONS:
NOT HERE ALONE

When a stranger resides with you in your land, you shall not
wrong him. The stranger who resides with you shall be to you
as one of your citizens; you shall love him as yourself, for you
were strangers in the land of Egypt: I the Lord am your God.

Leviticus 19:33–35

If you look at prewar Zionist literature, you will find hardly a
word about the Arabs.

Chaim Weizmann

I went over to Abdul-Karim's body and turned it over. He
looked as though he had seen me swimming in the pool a few mo-
ments ago. His was not the expression of a man who had lost.
   There in the courtyard, it was I, all of us, who were the
losers.

Benjamin Tammuz
(from "The Swimming Race")

The erosive grit of the day-to-month Israeli round—the harder grind to earn a slimmer living, the raising of children amidst unexpectedly problematic circumstances, the continual public and private discourtesies—are the aspects that undo most of those American Jews who come here for a short while (generally less than two years) and, often with distaste and ill temper, toss it all over as a bad show. No *oleh* can honestly claim full immunity to its cumulative effects, but as long as one's fundamental ideological premises are not jarred too sharply by larger disturbances, the daily dissonance tends to be counterbalanced and neutralized. In itself, it would not, I think, make potential *yordim* (of either the body or the spirit) of those committed to the survival and flowering of the Jewish people in our own national homeland, i.e., Zionists who actually live in Zion.

However, Israel, like America, is earthquake country. Over the course of this decade, many early complacencies have sustained repeated shocks that honesty requires recording. Nontransient aliens in our midst include both outsiders and insiders; both sorts offer or imply genuine challenges to my own underlying sense of what this place Israel is all about. It takes its toll. There have been encounters and re-encounters with the Arabs, with the Bedouin of the Negev, and with American blacks whose Zionism makes a parody of my own. There has been the multiform specter of intramural Jewish fascism abroad within the land and disclosing larger designs on other lands. Finally, there is the livid memory of those who have abandoned the struggle and turned or returned to the Diaspora, those who are openly or secretly planning to follow suit, and those who would like to but will live out their acerb lives in Israel. Some of these less than others but all to some degree are felt co-presences with me in Israel; their unassimilable premises I may dispute or discount, but only at serious risk can they be overlooked.

As I say, it takes its toll.

BEIRUT BLUES
AGAIN

Waves slapped softly against the beach about 100 meters off to the right. The mild, 1:00 A.M. sky was starry over the Carpenters whose low croon "Bless the beasts . . . and the child-ren" treacled from the mouth of the battered transistor—a deceptive link with home. "Home"? Eyelids lightly closing, I could easily have been out camping beneath the eucalyptus trees with Marcia and the kids at the state park south of Morro Bay along the Central California coast. (Indeed, one summer evening we had driven over the hills from Coalinga all the way to Paso Robles just to see the inane movie that had introduced that song.) Suddenly Abu, a cheerful Moroccan from Dimona, gently nudged me awake. This was our 16th day and 16th night of guarding the access roads leading to the airport outside of Beirut. The "kids" were now 17 and 15, California was a distant dream, and sleep was a dangerous shadow. I hummed old tunes and, sometimes, needed to bite toothpicks or my own cheek to banish sleep.

We hunched low in our jeep—Abu behind the wheel, I legs astraddle a Browning machine gun—eyes straining at the southern approach to what I had heard is the longest runway in the Middle East. I did not doubt it; it must have surely been, in fact, the longest dormant runway in the world. The five-kilometer strip pointed like the "up yours" of an extended middle finger at the leggy sprawl of darkened West Beirut. Not yet curled into an attitude of accusation, it was just a steady pointer to the west. Between the two of us and the beach ran the quiet, or seemingly quiet, coastal road. A few hours earlier it had fidgeted with restless traffic in both directions: fruit &

vegetable delivery trucks, tanks, mottled vehicles in dire need of paint that flew the arboreal flag of Lebanon like a college football banner, vans crammed with assorted furniture, army trucks carting P.L.O. booty south of the border. Despite my mumbly doodle-dee-dooing, it was not "Mex-i-co Way."

Our orders were clear: stop absolutely anything that dumb-blundered onto our newly-cut dirt road. At night, nothing should pass. Our makeshift roadblock was a dozen strands of barbed wire strung like innocent thread between telephone wire wooden spools and anchored by a metal bedstead. Short of a tank, it would, we thought, stop anything.

Two nights before in Jerusalem, the last night of my two-day break for Rosh Hashanah, my friend Jeff had noted that the American army considered the Browning "an obsolete weapon," a World War I antique, but at my touch it felt potent, heavy, and quick. Not for nothing had I spent scores of Bronx Saturday matinees at the RKO Fordham or under the make-believe clouds that float forever over the twinkly stars of the Loew's Paradise night. Except for the goopy interludes with tight-sweatered Denise Darcel or clinging-slipped Corinne Calvet, the best movies were always the war extravangazas: *Battleground*, *The Audie Murphy Story*, or even *The Sands of Iwo Jima*. Rat-tat-tat: no P.L.O.-RPGers would make it past *this* roadblock. Since midnight I had counted 14 sets of headlights, their eyes fixed and steady, prowl up or down the beach road. Nothing, no one—no erring poor bastard of a Lebanese civilian, no P.L.O., no Denise Darcel—had strayed toward the comforts of our flagellant's vision of a bedstead.

Just three nights earlier, the Sunday after Rosh Hashanah, I had outwrestled fatigue to watch with my family in Yeroham a television showing of Simon & Garfunkel's grand reunion concert in Central Park. Still at their harmonies after all these crazy years, S. & G. were attended by a court of over 400,000 on the Manhattan grass. 400,000! Quite a few seemed to be "older folks"—like me. The last time I had been a celebrant in Central Park was in 1968. No, we could not have been nearly that many, but the music—Joan Baez and Richie Havens—yes, the music had surely been just as fine. I would wager that we made at least as much noise. Our occasion, however, carried no tinge of nostalgia.

> What do you want?
> PEACE!
> When do you want it?
> NOW!
> What do you want?
> PEACE!
> When do you want it?
> NOW!
> What do you want?
> PEACE!
> When do you want it?
> NOWOWOWOWOWOW!

What the hell were my middle-aged bones doing at the Beirut end—the My Lai end—the massacre end of Operation Peace for Galilee?

In 45 more minutes Hananya and Prosper, two other Moroccans who were now sleeping in a tent in the culvert behind the jeep, would take over the nightwatch. *Michigan seems like a dream to me now* . . . Meanwhile, too weary to be distracted by riffles of mockery, I would grasp at friendly fragments of so-familiar songs as for old, old companions in the night. A pair of headlights floated past. *Counting the cars on the New Jersey Turnpike* . . . Soon Prosper would man my turnstile and tally the night while I succumbed to lovely sleep.

Six years previously, my compulsive search for aimless Amer-rica had run into plush cul-de-sac California. Aside from family and friends left behind, we had departed with few misgivings. All those queer vehicles sporting pennants of green trees, were they not on the trail of a "Lebanon" whose very quiddity had imploded, blown, and flown like grains of dust? But was that not, sorry bastards, *their* business? What could I defend as mine except frustrated rage and confusion, the rancid fruit of Ariel Sharon's blustery deceit, Menachem Begin's vacant histrionics, and the blood of the dead Palestinian grand-

fathers, women, and children at Sabra and Shatilla: "terrorists," mothers and lovers of "terrorists," or "terrorists" of the
future?

Of course, I could finger pretty closely what had got me up
here. Had I not known when I came on *aliya* that it would
entail periods of military service? Of course I did, but I was fit,
I was willing, and I had few serious doubts that, in a world of
causes none of which can afford to remain pristine, the Zionist
cause was sufficiently just to call my own. Besides, conscrip-
tion would occur only after we had been living for over three
years in the country, too distant a consideration to matter
much. I would be all of 41 before being called up for basic
training! How likely was it, after all, that one of the best armies
in the world would feel constrained to toss overage me onto
the sands of Iwo Jima! Besides, the hard ambiguities and en-
during reservations had finally to wear the brackets of paren-
thesis: the bottom line—to defend the State of Israel against
the genuine, continual threat to its very existence—well, I
could imagine no serious compunction about doing whatever
Tsahal would ask of an old hand like me.

To be honest, however, there was more to it than that. What
I had actually *felt* almost three weeks before was raw, adolescent excitement and—yes—*pride* at having been chosen for
inclusion among the special force of 22 out of the 60-odd men
who had reported in for *miluim* that day at our home base near
Beersheba. Everyone of us had been given the option of back-
ing out at the very start; Captain Paz made it amply clear that
he wanted no one in his unit who had serious reservations
about this assignment to Beirut. Yes, I was apprehensive, but
no, I could not truly claim that either politics or morality had
played any part in my deliberations or that I was the least bit
reluctant to be included in the action. Would Crane, would
Hemingway, would Mailer, Plath, or even Capote have backed
away from an encounter with "raw experience"? No sirree! It
was, to be sure, late in the day, but Shemesh was even older
and creakier than I. It was not too late for the real action, for
Battleground, for—who could predict?—even Denise Darcel.

I called Marcia from a phone at a bus stop en route to the
North. "You'll never guess where I'm going."

"Lebanon?," she weakly responded.

"Well, you guessed! Yes . . . Lebanon. An airport detail in Beirut. I'm feeling okay, and I'll be careful. Kiss the children. I'll call as soon as I can. I have to run. I love you. Goodbye." I was acquainted with only two among the 22 reservists from previous *miluim*. Captain Haim Paz, a rangy Argentine, had recalled, however, that one rare day during training I had shot particularly well. It was true: I have those afternoons when eyes and fingers click just right. Still, I was the anomaly among them: one of the two avid readers, one of the two beneath a *kippa*, the only "Anglo," a mysterious notebook scribbler, and a troubling disposition to withdraw into my recesses. Moreover, I had faulty wiring for the Israeli army. Three years as an enlisted man in the U.S. Army in the early Sixties had left in me a fixed reflex against fraternizing with rank. Here, however, the line between *us* and the officers was blurry, and the *hevramen*—like streetcorner guys in the Bronx—established the tone. They were affable, they were fair, but they really didn't at all fathom me.

But I, I did dig them, this mélange of 30- and 40-year-olds, mostly sabras and Moroccans garnished with three Russians and myself. They were gregarious and capable, generous and funny; in short, a world removed from the usual behavior of equivalent citizenry in typical Israeli offices, factories, and schools. Each morning in our quarters, whoever of us awakened first routinely swept and sloshed the floor of our makeshift sleeping area without need for any special word. Unfailingly, we relieved each other from duty on time. We bought each other cans of Lebanese Pepsi and took care to permit each other the maximum of sleep possible. Amazingly, among the lot of us could be found not a single slacker.

Our quarters were, in reality, the airport's fire station; it sat across from the ghostly, damaged main buildings of the Beirut Airport Terminal. An improvised synagogue and adjacent bathroom were situated down the hall to the right. Our security detail's row of jeeps sat parked just past the shoulder-high wall that enclosed our rows of cots. From behind the machine gun emplaced on our rooftop vantage, we could just make out the signature on the Terminal Building: WELCOME TO LEBA-

NON!—BIENVENU AU LIBAN! Finally, beckoning on the far horizon, a Manhattan to our Queens, West Beirut.

Come on, baby, let's go down-town . . .

When we had first arrived here, things appeared positively cushy. Israeli tanks guarded the airport entrances and all the access roads. That left only the fire station itself, some internal roads, and a nearby helicopter strip for 22 of us to patrol. Hardly a taxing burden! After the first three days, five of the men, the start of a roster, were already being sent south to Israel on a four-day break. As for me, I lacked neither sleep nor books. I was doing all right.

On our first Monday in Lebanon, I and four others were included among a larger group of Israeli military personnel for a nine-hour excursion that would cover almost the entire breadth of the country. Starting in hilly Christian East Beirut, where the lights at night hovered over the bay like those of a magically transposed Oakland–Berkeley Eastern Shore over the Bay of San Francisco, our truck climbed into Catskill-range rolling country. Even nearly four months since the arrival of *Tsahal*, the beautiful little Lebanese kids tirelessly smiled and waved their fingers at us.

In the midst of a Christian village, we stopped at a large, natural cleft in the rocks where icy water from a mountain spring poured down from the heights above. We bathed our arms and legs and relaxed at a nearby café. An old woman appeared from nowhere urging pears and apples on me. Not Denise, but who needed Greece? It was so pleasant to envision driving up here some day on a camping trip with Marcia and the children. Was it not a real possibility?

The truck rose higher, passing Israeli tank emplacements, and we exchanged greetings with Lebanese patrols. Lebanese? Phalangist? Haddad's men? No one seemed quite sure, but it did not much seem to matter. All were, after all, our allies. At one checkpoint where we briefly paused, I heard a voice call out my name. Smiling and gesturing in my direction was a vaguely familiar, tall Israeli tankist. Suddenly I recognized him: it was a former Yeroham high school student of mine, also a Haim, from two or three years before. We had just time to clasp thumbs before I had to return to my vehicle. Haim's hair had been cropped. Only later did it register that he was no longer wearing a *kippa*. We kept climbing higher, and the highway narrowed till it seemed that our truck hugged the very side of the mountain. There were no guard rails on the other side. Finally we reached a pastoral region of mountains and cedars much resembling the Lower Sierras. Then, as we dipped to a sudden flatness, below lay the Bekaa—a flat sliver that ran between the heights like a reduced facsimile of California's San Joaquin Valley. We got out; in the hills across we examined Syrian positions through binoculars. It was still too soon, perhaps, to be booking reservations for the family. We had reached our day's limit; it was time to return. There was a more immediate danger: our driver seemed so passionately bent upon skirting the very rim of the roadway, I preferred to clench shut my eyes than to admire the scenery coming the other way.

We stopped only once on the long descent to Beirut: when our vehicles encountered a funeral procession in a Christian village. The men bore the casket down the middle of the road; the women trailed behind. But I had passed an enchanted day and—a tourist, was I not?—I felt only moderate curiosity in the local burial customs. The possibility of ending up myself a traffic casualty was the only thing that dimmed my high spirits.

The idyll blew to a thousand pieces in the middle of the very next day. I was on duty on the roof of the fire station, looking in the direction of West Beirut, when a shattering explosion crashed from *the wrong direction!* With the killing of Bashir Gemayel, Menachem Begin's designs were blasted as thoroughly, and our soporific operation was jolted to the alert. Within three hours, dozens of Israeli-manufactured Merkava tanks were deployed on the expansive pavement of the airport: the Middle East's longest strip was now transformed into a vast staging area for the forward advance into West Beirut. The rest had been so much foreplay. What we did not at first apprehend was that moving up as well were all those comforting tanks which had been deployed at the access roads and entrances to the airport and had been performing so much of our detail's job for us.

Had *Tsahal* known from the start that these tanks would be moved up for the advance on West Beirut which merely awaited the drop of a pin or a bomb and that we 22 would then be needed indeed? I do not know. Suddenly, though, our reduced detail had *four additional posts to guard.* There would be no more daytrips to the far Bekaa. I calculate that, grabbing food and sleep on the run as best I could, I was actually on duty over 20 of the next 38 hours. Fatigue had descended upon our unit like a fog. Finally, on mid-Thursday, several of our men returned from their breaks at home, and, with immense relief, I and three others took off for Lod on a Dakota transport. Wedged in between two generals, I was off for Rosh Hashanah with the family in Yeroham.

The brief respite at home was a round of sleeping, eating, sleeping, praying, and sleeping. Dwelling on what was circumstantial or fortuitous, I steered conversation away from the subject of danger. I talked about the NBC newsman Tony Hillman whom I encountered most evenings when he arrived at the Beirut Airport with his day's quota of film to be shipped on the regular night flight to Ben-Gurion Airport. A pleasant sort, he kept me well supplied with Paris *Herald-Tribunes.*

Then there was the pleasure of working on a peace operation under a captain named Paz. Paz, in fact, was a good officer, the hardest working among us. He would lie down but never really sleep at all. During one 3-hour stretch of night-guarding that, because of our reduced circumstances, I was doing alone, tired Paz joined me for an hour's conversation just to help me relieve the boredom. He was intelligent and resourceful. Unfortunately, also comically, his voice gave way in the night damp, so that the midnight command took on the grotesque flavor of a Latin-American squeal. (It reminded me of nothing more incongruous than one of Señor Wences' hand puppets whining orders.)

I described the nightly airport cosmetic ritual necessitated by the marauding mosquitos of Beirut: white repellant lotion smeared over our face and hands. (After a time, most of our meals seemed seasoned from the same dispensary.) Truth to tell, our quarters at night resembled a morgue; recumbent bodies were sheeted from scalp to toes. Nothing really availed:

still the mosquitos scored. One morning I counted 14 tender bumps on my forehead.

My *pièce de résistance*, however, was the Chabadniks, a sort of serio-comic subplot to the main business at hand in Beirut. Before my three-and-a-half weeks were to elapse, no fewer than *five formations* of these pests, each containing 3 to 5 Chabadniks, would have descended upon our helpless, hapless unit. I could only assume that *Tsahal*'s compliance with this black-coated fraternization had something to do with the government's wheeling-dealing with the *haredi* parties. We reservists were the helpless pawns. At the first arrival, I must confess that I had not been displeased by the diversion. If, by the time of Rosh Hashanah, my initial positive predisposition had already suffered a sea change, by the very end of our Beirut mission, I would be settled into a permanent seething fury at the very whiff of a Chabadnik.

In that first week, however, I was not reluctant to share a glass of Chabad vodka (plied with liberality), to contribute a nominal sum toward Chabad's Torah scroll writing campaign, and to chat of matters eschatological with some black-suited young men from Massachusetts. They seemed harmless enough. I even briefly cavorted about with them and some of the kitchen crew (you can reliably uncover some *datiim* among the kitchen crew in most *Tsahal* units) to Lubavitch horn and clarinet. By the final week, they had grown as bad as the mosquitos. Ten A.M., 4:00 P.M., 2:00 A.M.—it made little difference! There they were, woodpeckers in crow's dress rapping away with ideological fervor to anyone of our drowsy company they could collar. Their dearth of human sensitivity was beyond measure. One wave of them, after praying *selichot* service, felt moved one midnight to sing and chant loudly without a thought to the men of our unit, groggy from hours of standing guard, who were trying to catch some sleep.

On the night of Yom Kippur, though more than two-thirds of those present were Sephardim, another phalanx of five of the black-coated visitants seated themselves in the very front row and rammed through the Chabad *nusach*. The startled Sephardim were manipulated and cowed into sullen silence. Photos of Menachem Schneerson, their St. Nicholas–looking

Rebbe, looked out upon our operation seemingly from everywhere: the synagogue, the sleeping quarters, the bathroom, the dining room. Indeed, it was much as though neither Begin nor Sharon but rather the Rebbe himself was the presiding spirit of our Beirut operation. Indeed, a fitting emblem he turned out to be, because the ubiquitous Chabad literature and *siddurim* that were distributed were so poorly bound that they fell apart at the very turn of a page.

And the point, the climacteric of all the vodka and spiritual bullying: *He was coming soon. Very soon! We want mashiach NOW! We want mashiach NOW!* I can still with nightmare clarity visualize patient Paz slumped over some charts at a table at 2:00 A.M. while an 18-year-old, black-suited *pisher* held forth about the pointlessness of peace treaties. After all, who needed a treaty with Egyptian *goyim*—or even peace itself!—when *mashiach* was coming so very soon. Among the 22 in our unit was a barrel-chested, soft-spoken Moroccan from Dimona whose name just happened to be Mashiach; he, like all the Moroccans, kept his distance from the Lubavitch crowd.

That *something* had happened on Rosh Hashanah I could read on several ashen faces, but at first I could not figure it out. It was like that Shabbat four months earlier when, while I was on my sabbatical leave from the weekly world of telecommunications and transportation, I could nevertheless sense that something unusual was astir. It was Yair Cohen, not a Shabbat observer, who told me when I happened to see him late on Saturday afternoon that over 200 Yeroham reservists, himself included, had been contacted door-to-door and would be busing out that night "for the North." Indeed, did it not also bizarrely resemble the inside of my boyhood Beth Shraga synagogue in the Bronx during the High Holidays, which God decreed should always coincide with the World Series? Whispers would start in the back near the door, and pass from mouth to mouth to attentive ears. Finally, I too would get the news: "A clutch hit by Henrich." Or "DiMaggio's homered in the 10th."

But no, this time it was nothing so innocent as that former time. Faces blanched, and I had need to add an unpleasant new word to my Hebrew vocabulary—*tevach*. There had been a massacre of P.L.O. women and children in Beirut; somehow *Tsahal* had been implicated. Suddenly, little else seemed to count. Before returning me to my unit the following morning, Marcia fashioned for me a slim, black band to wear for the remainder of my time in Beirut. Pinned around my wrist, for all the world a watch-guard, it was for me as a vital reminder and a sign. What insane larger design had I let myself so unthinkingly become enmeshed in?

I recalled the first days of the Peace in Galilee Operation when Chaim Herzog, not yet then President of Israel, formerly a general, had each midday analyzed the military maneuvers and larger situation on Israel's English-language radio. After the fourth day, his expertise was strangely exhausted. The stated military objectives of the operation had been attained, and yet the tank columns kept pointing toward the North. He confessed to mystification. The stench of déjà vu for me had been acrid. One Vietnam was surely enough for a lifetime, was it not?

I left home the next morning in a private fog. Bumped that evening from my Monday return flight from Lod to Beirut, I was graced with an extra night of leave time; too distant from Yeroham, I spent it with American friends in Jerusalem. From Jeff and Judith I learned that shock and disillusion were widespread. Judith told of demonstrations of *datiim* before the leadership of the Mafdal. Could anything really be expected from that compliant quarter? I was dubious. Indeed, for all I knew I was the only *kippa*-wearer in all of Israel who had voted to the left of Labor in the previous election. Anomaly in America, anomaly in Israel; why not, after all, in Beirut as well?

I had not landed and returned to my unit for 20 minutes before Paz tapped me for a jeep to escort a tour by some generals of newly Israeli-occupied West Beirut. It was a city-scape pockmarked with destruction, a realm of gaping holes. Not a single building along the once-handsome beachfront was wholly intact. Though I was fully aware that most of the destruction I was viewing had not recently been inflicted, that Lebanon had suffered through more than seven years of civil war before Israeli forces entered the picture, I still felt like a defendant. Was I not guilty as charged? No kind old lady materialized to offer us any pomegranates or bananas. No smiling children waved. Treating us as if we were invisible, the occupied city appeared too preoccupied with itself. Studiously ignored were the innumerable clusters of tanks, the checkpoints, the careening jeeps. Occasionally, pathetic little white flags could be seen dotting a field or a heap. I really could not determine for myself whether they were the residue of children's games or of that of adults. What, I wondered, could these people have committed to warrant such havoc?

The generals we were escorting were inspecting former P.L.O. arms depots. Four or five times, at double-time, I followed Paz and the generals' party into the night-dark subbasements of apartment buildings, like the holds of vast ships, where we discovered sweating *Tsahal* crews who were sorting and piling immense quantities of confiscated arms for reshipment south. Aware that our groundtime in Beirut was not unlimited, the crews were working around the clock. Returned to the jeep, we passed fixed Phalangist units at intersections in silence. Our erstwhile allies? Our murderous cohorts? Everything was happening too rapidly to be put in focus. Were they here, what would I say to Harrison Lee, to Frentz, to Rita, to Beaulieu, or to Ira—old army friends, former Movement comrades in America? Had not the very meaning and shape of my newly-chosen life in Israel become wildly distorted?

A new day. Abu, Hananya, Prosper, and I attended closely to the voice of opposition leader Shimon Peres being interviewed over the transistor. One government minister had defected; still, neither Peres nor the pundits expected this government to collapse. Like unshored pillars, the ministers depended upon each other for balance. "Too much is at stake," declared a different, authoritative voice. My mind tuned out.

> Shout about it, shout about it, anyone you choose,
> Anyway you look at it you lose.
> Where have you gone, Joe DiMaggio?
> A nation turns its lonesome eyes to you
> Oo oo oo . . . oo oo oo . . .

Later I asked some of the men who had been here what they had seen and heard. No one said very much. The airport had served as the staging ground for the Phalangists. Then they moved out. Mashiach thought that he had recognized Colonel Haddad at the airport after the Phalange had moved out. That was all anyone could say.

Injuries were starting to turn up in the unit: Abu's bad leg, Shemesh's back, Gaby's hand, several sore throats. I was depressed, but my body, springing lively to its own perverse, lively beat, kept on with its hearty eatings, its instantaneous dozings, and sudden awakenings. It was healthy. Who, where was the distant drummer?

Hananya claimed to understand the Phalangists and the *tevach*: "If the P.L.O.'d been fucking you over for eight years, you'd get them too, the first chance you had," he opined. Five of us in a circle heard him in silence. Then no one concurred: not like this, not old women and children.

My previous worst moment in the Israeli army had occurred during the final ten days of my basic training two years before, and it had had nothing to do with being an achy 42-year-old recruit. I was manning my first roadblock; it was north of Jerusalem at Beth-el, a place near where Jacob had had his odd dream about angels flowing up and down a ladder. This time, thanks to *Tsahal*, Beth-el traffic was flowing much more sporadically. Before we succeeded in getting them checked out for arms or explosives, vehicles containing frustrated, distraught Arabs were lined up for nearly an hour's delay. Naturally, others displaying "Jewish license plates" were waved right through.

Uri, my 21-year-old sergeant, twice bawled me out for not keeping the barrel of my M-16 at the horizontal forehead-level of the parked Arabs. "They have to be afraid." (I did my best with the men, but I refused to oblige him with the old women and little kids. Fuck you too, Uri.) So this was life under military occupation. It stank, stank, stank!

After five sweaty hours of hoarsely shouting threats and waving my M-16 threateningly in order to prevent furious Arab drivers either from turning around entirely or slicing off onto a side road that, 100 meters in front of our roadblock, inconveniently branched off from the main highway, I was praying for relief to arrive. That evening I officially informed my C.O. that I would refuse to do that again. In my remaining time there, he was good enough to oblige me.

Beirut days and nights had become almost indistinguishable: a succession of hours passed staring at the road, the darkness, the ticking at my black-draped wrist. We never missed the hourly news report. At all daylight hours, random explosions punctured the air in the West. After a while, most of the men no longer even turned heads in their direction, but I usually watched the dreamy smoke—usually white, sometimes brown—rise, congeal, and softly dissipate into the faultless sky like an ethereal ballet. It reminded me of my old fascination with the smokepuffs from Camels cigarettes that floated out from the huge male lips of the giant billboard over 44th Street and Broadway. At night, automatic weapons clacked from any of a dozen quarters of East Beirut.

At the main entrance of the air terminal, a dog had settled at my feet. She was formerly a denizen of nearby, ghostly Bourg-al-Bourajneh. Now she barked at stopped vehicles whenever I rose from my seat at the checkpoint. Suddenly my English had assumed a distinct value. While in their Moroccait dialect our unit's Moroccans at the gate usually dealt with the entering and departing Lebanese terminal workers, I was handling most of the Phalangist officers, newsmen, and—toward the very end—the Americans. Once I chatted briefly with a sergeant, an explosives expert from Georgia. He showed no surprise that an American in *Tsahal* uniform was manning the gate. American personnel were planning to move in here soon to help make the airport functional again. I wished him luck. Usually, however, the range of intercourse at the gate was much more narrow. At night, no traffic at all was permitted to come this way.

Night again. I was explaining the mystery of my *aliya* to Yisrael, the other *dati* member of the unit. It had first emerged as a serious option, replete with a visit to the *Aliya* Office in San Francisco, when in 1965 Secretary of Defense McNamara had publically threatened to activate the reserves for a war that I already knew too much about. I paused. Yisrael softly, wryly laughed. I joined him. Our conversation had faltered, but I appreciated his being so laconic.

Another day. I was returned to observing the traffic along the coastal road. All day long Israeli tanks in groups of five or six were aimed toward the south. Each open tank was studded with its crew who looked like tall, absent-minded children: multi-headed mammoths breathing power. That night around 2:00 o'clock the Army radio station—Israel's most popular— played Janis Joplin wailing *Busted flat in Baton Rouge* . . . She sounded so fine that it surprised tears to my eyes. I was grateful for the dark so that no one noticed. Why, I could not determine, was I so strongly moved? On the following night, Saturday, more Israeli military traffic was headed south, south, south. Only south. Finally, on Sunday morning our weary quartet was relieved in time to shower before the advent of Yom Kippur. A battery of telephones awaited us at the fire station. I managed a 30-second talk with Marcia for the first time in a long week. . . . *and Bobby McGee-ee!*

Yom Kippur eve was a Chabad-inspired shambles. I was actually pleased when seven of us from the security unit who were attending services were recalled for an urgent meeting. We were on full alert. And then what I had been witnessing for the better part of the week finally fully registered: all those tanks, trucks, and troops that were withdrawing from West Beirut headed south had left our security unit of 22 at the very forward edge of the Israeli presence in Lebanon! There was nothing between us and whatever was still out there of the P.L.O. At the airport there still remained staff people, support personnel for the planes, and the kitchen crew, but our unit was now the frontline defense. A new password was issued. The worrisome danger was that the P.L.O. would try to make an R.P.G. extravaganza of the Israeli withdrawal from the airport.

I was listed on the roster for guard duty between midnight and 3:00 A.M. For the sake of safety, we moved all the cots from the outside into the interior hallway of the building. For the first time since my arrival at Beirut, I could not doze off even briefly before the beginning of my shift. Reclining in my boots on my cot, I sensed a curious inversion: in place of actual safety couched behind putative danger, beneath the bland façade of another routine night of guard duty there now lurked the serpent scent of real peril. That night eerie flares went off at regular intervals. I strained at the suddenly illuminated darkness, and my fingers played ragtime on the safety switch of my weapon.

Yom Kippur Day in Beirut, 5742/1982. The noise of *shachrit* filtering down the narrow hallway roused me, and soon I joined the odd congregation. "For the sins we have committed knowingly, and for the sins we have committed without knowledge, save us, redeem us, forgive us, our Rock and our Redeemer."

A rumor spread rapidly that we were to be flown out in two days, on Tuesday. It proved false. On Tuesday I sat for five hours in a jeep with Be'eri, an Agrexco exporter. We guarded 19 dark-skinned workers who, wielding large brooms, swept clean a wide stretch of runway. Yes, the Americans would soon be arriving; Middle East Airlines would again be aloft. Be'eri was impressed when the workers continued with their sweeping even when their white-shirted supervisor had departed from the scene. "Israelis don't work like that anymore," he tersely commented.

At 4:00 P.M. the natty boss reappeared. He looked displeased. "These Pakistanis are lousy workers," he remarked. "In the old days, the Syrians really did a job." At Be'eri's behest, I told the Lebanese in English that Israel really did not covet any Lebanese territory, that Israel only wanted peace with Lebanon, that the Lebanese should perhaps be a trifle grateful to us for cleaning the P.L.O. from out of their midst.

"Oh yes," rejoined the boss smoothly, "you are like the cleaners. Very good. Things are much better now. But you know, when the bombs were falling, we were afraid. There were so many of us in each building. Now it's okay. All Lebanese have money. We will build everything nice again. You will come as tourists to our beautiful Lebanon, yes?"

We shook hands fleetingly, but among the three of us, no two pair of eyes flicked together. It was all mendacious. I myself harbored no fond illusions about returning here as a tourist. Whatever history would decide had been my mission to Lebanon, I could not any longer believe for a moment that it had more than momentarily turned the screws in this gimcrack place. It was not even very clear whether we had loosened or tightened them.

Under the pillow at my cot rested four copies of *The Jerusalem Post* for September 26th, the entire airport allotment falling to the lot of its only remaining Israeli "Anglo." They were a nourishment and a feast. Headlines proclaimed "400,000 RALLY AGAINST GOVERNMENT"! *Four Hundred Thousand!!* In Israel! Was it truly conceivable that 1 of every 10 persons in the country had attended this rally? However great our sins, both knowing and unknowing, this sang to me, however faintly, of hope. I read the entire item through twice and almost cheerfully joined some of the others for a cup of Turkish coffee.

Late the next morning we and all of Israel had indeed almost reached the end of the Beirut road. Most of us, perspiring freely from the hot wind that blasted us out of the exhaust of the Dakota's engines as we boarded, crowded into the belly of the aircraft for what would be the final Israeli flight from Beirut for a long, long time. Newsmen and camera crews dogged our steps. Abu and Hananya stopped to strike an accommodating pose for a photographer who claimed that they would appear on the cover of *The New York Times Magazine* the following week. (My promise to them to have my sister mail a copy was not to be.) The year before, making it home from *miluim* had been a family concern; this year it appeared to be an international preoccupation! We were a smiling, much-relieved group of men who, after three-and-a-half tense weeks, were en route home to our wives and children.

A final glance behind at the familiar fire station, the terminal building, and at the panorama of West Beirut. Bye-bye, Beirut. The final word I voiced over Beirut was a simple, prayerful *shalom*. It has thus far had little effect. Just over one year later, a blast at the airport I had come to know so well killed 241 American military and civilian personnel.

Returning the two jeeps that belonged to our Negev home base, Captain Paz and four other men drove back to Israel along the coastal road I once so avidly had scanned. It took them six hours longer than the rest of us to reach Israel. Paz was surely as eager to get out of Lebanon as anyone; he did not have to go that route.

I later recalled a particularly infuriating time fully 20 years before when, prior to being flown to my post in the Far East, I waited at Travis Air Force Base near Sacramento more than 20 hours for a military hop to the East Coast. It would be a last, brief visit with my parents until my return nearly two years later. Finally, the loud speaker announced a flight for Wilmington, Delaware. I dashed to the desk. Yes, there was plenty of room. Unfortunately, the young woman ruefully explained, only officers would be permitted to board. It took off without me, half-empty. The food in *Tsahal*, albeit kosher, may be neither as varied nor as plentiful as what was available at Fort Dix or the Presidio at Monterey, but *Tsahal* does enjoy some powerfully redeeming features.

At the base I bore witness to a stunning, never routine metamorphosis. My unit turned in its gear, and we rapidly changed into our civilian clothing. Uniformly competent comrades somehow dwindled before my eyes into ordinary, variegated civilians: there was loquacious Lach, now a balding engineer; Amihud, suddenly simply a genial chemist; Asher, again a near-sighted, graying technician; generous Mashiach; Shadni, the crane-operator who advocates Dale Carnegie. These were the middle-aged, mostly paunchy Jews who had just returned from defending the very front line of Israel's northern presence! *This* was one of the world's best armies! The enormity of it! Could the Syrians, the Iraqis, the Jordanians possibly realize any of this?

But suddenly, unexpectedly, I found myself looking *through these figures* at a room filled with the large-sized uncles of my childhood—Uncle Ben, Uncle Mac, Uncle Leo, Uncle Abe, Uncle Izzy, Uncle Leon—card-playing, joking, gregarious men who sold apparel, insurance, and charm. One by one, almost all those old men, my potbellied, laughing uncles, had flowed away from the edges of my life; however, here these others—and I among them—had made our strange descent. Indeed, we were all, properly speaking, rung-by-rung descendants together. I could not fix my vision any more clearly in focus than that, but I sensed its effect for many days afterward.

I felt, there at the very end of our adventure—for it was, at the least, that—a fresh advent of affection for this almost random group of Israelis and Jews. I was strongly aware that when

I would encounter one or another of them on the street in Beersheba or the plaza in Dimona, we would smile, shake hands, and would not have all that much to say to each other. It would, however, have to serve. It would *have to be enough* to enable me to hold firm a vision of Israel which had been under heavier duress, in more serious jeopardy than I could have dreamed possible even a month earlier. I had, however, to admit to myself that I did not know how strongly or how often I could call upon the residue of such feeling to sustain me in the future. Something fine had transpired and been confirmed in Beirut, but something else had taken a beating and been shaken loose.

Where have you gone, Joe DiMag-gio . . .?
Well, somber Beirut had yielded forth some tangible clues. The least I could be sure of in my bones was that His working address was neither the Knesset in Jerusalem nor Eastern Parkway in Brooklyn.

Dressed again in my own clothing, hiding out in my Russian grandfather's mustache and my Polish great-grandfather's beard, a lanky 44-year-old was finally—O YE-AH—finally, homeward bound.

BEACHCOMBING
IN THE DESERT:
CONSCIOUSNESS
RAISING ...
AND DEPRESSING

No more than in America are there in Israel to be found any real retreats. Unlike the children in Kiryat Shimoneh and the other northern settlements our kids in heart-of-the-country Yeroham are not periodically obliged to take cover in their *miklatim*, Israel's ubiquitous underground shelters, from the thud of whistling katyusha shells. All the action, however, is scarcely reserved for some distant elsewhere: Yeroham's somewhat older children are the active, flesh and bleeding instruments of Israel's immediate retaliations over its borders. Still, even in the face of pain, illusions do persist, and sometimes even retain a special force. Though most Yerohamites perceive their isolation and feel its burden more as a deprivation than a refuge, there is hardly a tide when the sudden tensions, ambiguities, and underlying conflicts that afflict all of Israel do not wash up on Yeroham's inland reaches.

PILOTS

The absorptive capacity of Establishments to co-opt, corrupt, and neutralize dissent is no less incessant in Israel than in America. Naturally, they do not always at first or at the last succeed, but the reflex seems almost inevitable, and time and cash are on their side.

Less than a week after I had watched admiringly how a road company of Tel Aviv–based Neve Tsedek, a left-leaning political theater commune, had mounted their prize-winning production *Pilots* in our Yeroham sticks, I noticed in *The Jerusalem Post* that Oded Kotler, its founder and, until he subsequently took over directorship of the Israel Festival, its guiding spirit, was one of the honored recipients of Israel's 1984 "Quality of Life Award." Kotler shared his prize with a less controversial company, among them, Father Marcel Dubois (a Catholic scholar who chairs the Philosophy Department at Hebrew University), a furniture store owner who had initiated a successful traffic safety campaign, and the founder of an organization which aids and encourages *yordim* to return to Israel. More than an honorific, its value of $10,000 is in Israel a very substantial sum indeed.

It all gives one pause. Could the presenters not have been aware that the Neve Tsedek Company plays its road audiences consciously, indeed exhaustingly, so as to achieve one overriding goal: the subversion of their established preconceptions dealing with authority, Jews and Arabs, Israeli democracy, and (particularly at that time) the war in Lebanon—preconceptions which hold especially strong sway in Second Israel's hinterland?

The awards committee itself, chaired by former Speaker of the Knesset Menachem Savidor and including a former Israeli Supreme Court justice, could scarcely have been more mainstream Establishment. I wish I had been privy to what Kotler was thinking when he heard suave politician Savidor remark that "a prize award for those who cherish the quality of life is like an outcry against the ugliness, the disparagement of values, and the erupting violence within our society." A figure like Liberal Party veteran Savidor surely could not have been discovered too many evenings, second row center at the Tel Aviv showcase of Neve Tsedek. Almost surely he would have found too ample cause for offense; indeed, *Pilots* is cut from the same bolt as the "disparagement of values" that he decried in his presentation speech.

I suspect that the irony could not have been wasted on the sharp-witted Mr. Kotler.

For the Neve Tsedek road company, playing the Yerohams of Israel makes for a long, long day of theater. This sort of road program, and I am referring in Israel to over 2,500 annual theater road productions and another 800 of music and 600 of dance (1985 figures), hits the road under the auspices of a program characteristically labeled *Omanut La'am*, "Art for the People," and falls under the Ministry of Education and Culture. A cultural lifeline for those of us removed from the country's cities, of late it is only about 30% government subsidized. The evening performance of *Pilots* had been scheduled for 9:00 o'clock, but the real show—the participatory theatrics—started in mid-morning, soon after the actors had arrived in town. Indeed, while it turned out that the elongated one-acter by Dr. Yosi Hadar is an effective but rather one-dimensional piece of political theater, the unsubsidized, agit-prop warmups by the actors were considerably more fascinating to observe.

At 11:00 A.M., the kids from Yeroham's Shoshana Sapir High School were trooped over by their teachers to Yeroham's Samuel Rubin Cultural Center to meet with the cast of the all-male production. The teachers, of course, aside from breaking both themselves and their students out of Sapir's four-walled classrooms, simply intended for the youngsters to get a taste of the cosmopolitan. Faultless pedagogy.

For Neve Tsedek, however, this was their best shot to broadcast that their show had hit town, to drum up local interest in the evening performance of *Pilots*. Of at least equal importance for the cast, however, was to soften up the kids for the evening by exposing them to their "radical" ideas—to reach them. For Neve Tsedek's *raison d'être* is political theater, and *Pilots* is nothing if not "socially relevant." Its message is the immorality of bomb strikes over civilian or, at the least, problematically military targets. Its concern is with men at war who question and even refuse to obey orders. Ultimately, subversive-as-hell *Pilots* poses the conundrum of the morality of making war even for a society whose neighbors are permanent belligerents. And Neve Tsedek fully intended to press its theme both on stage and off.

The actors were knowledgeable, committed, experienced, and professionally facile, so they held almost all of the trumps for putting forward their controversy-laden themes before the unprepared, unsophisticated high schoolers who treated them at first with a mixture of deference and suspicion. Few seemed inclined to bite very hard on the actors' leading questions. A few teachers seemed detached; most, however, soon looked disturbed.

"But you can't have pilots who refuse to fly their missions. The country would never survive!," an annoyed teacher finally blurted out.

"Then the generals had better make sure that the missions are really military and genuinely justified," an actor retorted. Time was too short for many to get caught up in the web of the incipient dispute. Still, the students now had some notion what *Pilots* and its cast were up to. Most seemed a little puzzled but not ill-disposed. They had cause to be grateful. After all, these young guys had come down to Yeroham all the way from Tel Aviv to perform and to tell them something, and it was one sight better to sit in the Cultural Center than in a high school classroom: for distraction, Sam Rubin has it all over Shosh Sapir.

Thirty minutes later, two other actors faced much longer odds. A group of middle-aged Moroccan housewives that normally comes to the Cultural Center four mornings a week for Hebrew lessons was led in to sit before them. Morality of bomb strikes? Refusing orders? The poor women just did not or would not get the point. Finally one hair-covered housewife hesitantly asked how pilots managed to get their heavy planes off the ground into the air, anyway. It was a frustrating session all around.

Not so at the 2½-hour, late-afternoon marathon encounter: about 30 people—mainly young religious women who are Sherut Leumi volunteers—together with a contingent of high school students (including some returnees from the morning) and two teachers sat rapping with actors Ezra Kofrey and Noam Cohen. *Rapping!* Yes, indeed, and as the hours ground on and additional people wandered in to replace those who drifted away, heated voices were increasingly raised in disagreement, anger, or occasional concurrence. The scent of déjà vu grew positively pungent. It was like being transported again to the unjaded, urgent Sixties at campuses in Ohio and Oregon. Since my coming to Israel, never before, not even during the dislocating bewilderment of the weeks in Beirut, had the parallel roles of Vietnam and Lebanon in the national psyches and situations of my dual-cit. countries seemed so poignant.

Noam Cohen, open-faced, in his mid-20s, recounted the plot of the drama; he pointed out that the group of pilot buddies were intended to represent a microcosm of Israeli society. Some are troubled by the war but gamely carry on with their bombing missions, others merely follow orders unthinkingly. One cracks up; another ultimately commits suicide. What was unique about Lebanon was that it was the first of Israel's wars whose necessity was dubious and the first to drag on seemingly without end. There was patent restlessness in the circle of listeners. Did, he wanted to know, they think it was somehow perhaps improper to raise these matters in public or on a stage?

Response at first was hesitant. After a first thrust, and then another, to Cohen and Kofrey's evident satisfaction it turned into a torrent. One pretty volunteer, Hadassah, thought it was reprehensible, especially while our boys were still dying, to raise these issues at a public forum. (She wore a ring. I recalled that my daughter had mentioned that this Hadassah was engaged to be married and planned to live in a new settlement on the West Bank.) "But where should they be raised?," came Cohen's riposte. She was not sure—but not there. "Not while our soldiers were fighting," another girl chimed in. "But the war's been going on for nearly 20 months! When would it be 'proper' to discuss them? In history class 20 years from now?" Again, no direct reply.

Moshe, an able teacher whose right hand is withered, did not raise it before he barked that people like Eli Geva were undemocratic, even traitorous. Why? "Once the government is elected and the Defense Minister gives the orders to march, discussion should cease."

"No matter that the Minister is a fascist!," Cohen retorted. Four people were now yelling simultaneously; comprehension was canceled utterly. Though things were getting warm, however, the actors still held the chair and control of the proceedings without challenge.

To my surprise, Zahara, a heavy-set woman in her 40s who works at the Cultural Center, spoke out in support of the actors' position. Too many sons and husbands had been killed— and for what? Another woman, this one in her 20s, rose to agree. Could there really be greater antiwar sentiment in Yeroham than I had anticipated?

For a favorable spell, Cohen and Kofrey sat back cautiously, more than content to act the role of moderators. At a later juncture Cohen countered a critic with the disingenuous contention that, after all, he was only raising questions; he himself had no final answers. It was the only plainly false note that he struck all day. A newly-arriving high school student argued that soldiers cannot be bothered with such questions. Kofrey, alluding to Guernica, responded that he was first a man, only then a soldier. Not for the last time, a shouting match briefly ensued.

In the course of the next hour, virtually everyone in the room delivered some variety of opinion. After a time, the new arrivals were treading over familiar ground, but the two actors, though an evening performance loomed ahead, seemed to relish the repeated confrontations. There was one striking, perhaps foreboding divergence, however, from the American precedent: it was the younger participants who were far more likely to argue against protest. Those even a few years their senior were the war-doubters and the supporters of the right to question even in times of war the morality of policies and actions.

I chatted afterward with Noam Cohen. Was Yeroham typical? Indeed! Everywhere Neve Tsedek toured, people were eager to give vent to their feelings but lacked an appropriate forum. Relevant theater could provide the vehicle for debate and for change. He too noted the generational split and thought its implications for the future ominous. The youngsters seemed increasingly attracted to "King of Israel" strongmen like Begin, Rafael (Raful) Eitan, and, most pernicious of all, Ariel Sharon. Perhaps they would outgrow it in a few years, but it frightened him. He himself, "in order to register a protest," had voted for Likud and Menachem Begin in an earlier general election. Then his older brother had been killed in the Yom Kippur War. Change *was* possible. He himself had changed!

That night at 9:00 the Samuel Rubin Cultural Center theater was filled. The audience was young: students, unmarrieds, and young married couples. I did not spot any of the morning's middle-aged Moroccan housewives. Let it be noted that under adept direction, the pacing of the production of *Pilots* on the nearly bare, Yeroham boards was perhaps a bit rushed—after all, there was that return, two-hour bus trip to Tel Aviv to close a long, long day's work—but it was professional, smooth, and well-received.

The play by Dr. Hadar is, however, a limited vehicle. The pilots are flattened figures; each occupies a discrete niche on a response-to-authority spectrum. The main protagonist, brooding over the death of his closest buddy, hunkers moodily about the stage. He is inarticulate, plainly something of a case. Still, though all the "normal" pilots in the squadron are broadly painted stereotypes, I was conscious that the audience was extremely attentive. They laughed appreciatively at the barracks banter and could not help but descry the thematic point of the play. Only the final metamorphosis of the indecisive hero into a proto-fascist monster seemed to leave them (for good reason) more confused than moved or involved.

For many more months both before and after its Yeroham performance, *Pilots* played to good houses in Tel Aviv. Hardly likely to survive as a permanent addition to Israel's dramatic repertoire, its long run appears to sustain Noam Cohen's contention that Israelis had need of theater as an auxiliary forum to air their doubts about their longest-run war. As with America's Vietnamese "Incursion," the longer "Operation Peace in Galilee" ran, the less were "the hearts and minds" of those involved—the Maronites, the Druzes, the Sunis, the Shiites, and finally us Israelis ourselves!—won over to see things from an official perspective.

A facetious fancy: Could we have done worse with "hearts

and minds" if, after a point, instead of sending north more platoons and planes, we had tried our luck with a road company? Just possibly the Ministry of Education and Culture would have been willing to take on the job. I suspect it would have cost much less both in shekels and in blood.

Only two weeks prior to that Neve Tsedek performance of *Pilots* in Yeroham, Defense Minister Yitzhak Rabin had come down to address an older, better-dressed crowd of Yeroham worthies who had gathered at the festively rigged-up Shoshana Sapir High School gymnasium. It was a celebration of the Labor Party's victory in the recent municipal election runoffs. Bucking the trend among the development towns, Yeroham's slick, young, newly-elected Moroccan Mayor Baruch Elmakias was not a Likudnik!

Twice, in his opening remarks, Rabin, perhaps from the journey down looking quite tired, reflectively referred to himself as an old man who had witnessed much in his lifetime. Then, unfortunately, the former Prime Minister demonstrated that it might indeed be the case; he gaffed classically by announcing to the assemblage how much it pleased him again to come to Dimona. *Dimona!* Doing his best to recover, Rabin spoke of other cabbages and kings, but not at all of any of the issues that were to be raised by the Neve Tsedek players. Indeed, he looked and performed like an old man!

Then two weeks after *Pilots* had scored its success at the Cultural Center, Rafael (Raful) Eitan made *his* speaking appearance in our town. Many of the same young people who had attended the play sat in his audience as well. Moreover, the talk by the Army Chief of Staff for Operation Peace in Galilee could not help but impinge from the other direction on the very questions raised by the Neve Tsedek performers and Yosi Hadar's play. As Noam Cohen had remarked, there is now underway in Israel a long-term struggle for the very heart, mind, and soul of this Israel, which the more tried and tired mainline politicians seem hardly able to address. They had to be learned soon.

Pilots may not rise much above a piece of popularized propaganda. Still, for the Neve Tsedek journeymen to have brought their cultural artillery to Yeroham just actually may have made a small but real contribution toward sustaining "the quality of life" of the moral polity in this, our deeply disturbed country. Those were, I think, 10,000 well-directed dollars.

A PETTINESS

The June 1985 dedication of Yeroham's million-dollar Fay and Joe Ain Library was to serve as the climax of the fruitful, five-year relationship between our small Negev *shtetl* and the Jewish community of Montreal, our giant "twin" under Project Renewal. Inevitably, only a small minority of the Jews of Montreal have in reality involved themselves in this program, but in the course of their activity, these well-intentioned, well-off few have done much to alter for the good the external face of our little town.

Until this time, Yeroham's municipal "library" had been a single large room and adjoining alcove in the town's Cultural Center. It contained a curious assortment of books, not merely in Hebrew but also French, English, and Maharati (for Yeroham's Indian citizenry). More than the usual case in a similar American town, the one-room library afforded local junior and senior high school youngsters from large families and overcrowded apartments a spot of afternoon quiet to do their study and homework. Overtaxed and much-used, the library space in the Cultural Center was plainly inadequate; a new facility was one of the highest priorities of the Project Renewal planners.

Now, at this time, wholly innocent of Project Renewal's plans and good works, Pauline and Maurice Gaba, a retired couple of Scottish *olim* living in Jerusalem, had read an article about Yeroham and its needs and decided that they wanted to do something for the town's children. After visiting the town and Yeroham's two librarians, they fixed upon a very handsome donation that would enable the library to purchase books, an encyclopaedia, and games for the children. (It had been more than five years since the children's librarian had

had the funds to replace even a single game.) That these materials would soon be housed in an elegant, new edifice was to the Gabas a pleasant surprise. All they asked was that their donation be designated in honor of their departed parents. Preparations for the June 19th dedication were typically, comically confused. Visiting dignitaries would include the President of the United Israel Appeal of Canada, the World Chairman of Keren Hayesod, and a delegation of Montreal Jewish leaders, including, of course, Fay and Joe Ain—the major benefactors. Although dozens of Yeroham mothers are fully capable and willing to serve up tasty, sumptuous spreads for over 100 people, the municipality and Project Renewal officialdom decided to have the occasion catered by Beersheba's swankiest establishment, the Hotel Neot Midbar. Pavement that had already been installed around the building was dug up in order to replace it with yet fancier paving—and then not quite finished in time. Welcoming banners were spread; a blue ribbon that begged the cutting was strung. And invitations were funneled to important local and regional officials. Quite naturally, the two Yeroham librarians did not neglect to include on their invitation list those generous Jerusalem friends of the library, Pauline and Maurice Gaba.

For some hours that morning, the company of visitors was escorted about the town and shown other evidences of Project Renewal and Montreal's niche on the townscape. Then, at the appointed late-morning hour, the outside host was directed to the town's new "Cultural Plaza"—a not quite completed, ornately lighted, planter- and sundial-bedecked patch between the Music Conservatory, the Cultural Center, and the new Ain Library—for the grand ceremonial ribbon-cutting. Before the distinguished guests and visitors were admitted inside for the buffet and a round of gracious speeches, however, there occurred an incident so small that probably few or none at all of that delegation from Montreal are aware that it ever occurred. Yet for those of us who knew of it, that brief incident was not trivial; indeed, the thought of it flares like a crimson canker. Like the *Midrash* of the tortuous hospitality with which the ancient Sodomites were accustomed to accommodate their overnight guests—to fit in a standard bed, short visitors were stretched and tall ones were relieved of surplus leg with an ax—it seems too typical of a corrosive, bureaucratic spiritless-ness that at times threatens in this land of Israeli officialdom to sink us all.

In those final minutes before the snipping of the *cordon bleu*, a Keren Hayesod functionary, who together with Edit, the head librarian, was checking the readiness of the library interior for the imminent, august onslaught, happened to no-tice a small brass plaque which the librarians had ordered and hung near the children's section in order to honor the parents of Pauline & Maurice Gaba. It had been placed quite apart from the larger, dark plaque that Keren Hayesod itself had pro-vided, which honored the building's major donors, the Ains of Montreal.

"What's that?," the bureaucrat peremptorily demanded.

Edit briefly explained who the Gabas were and what they had done, but the man was neither impressed nor mollified.

"It's impossible! Take it down! That plaque looks nicer than the plaque for the Ains."

"Who's fault is that?," Edit retorted angrily.

The functionary was adamant. "Take it down!" he yelled. "Who invited them here, anyway?" Without further debate, he reached up and removed the offensive plaque from the wall with his own two hands. In his haste, he scratched the plaque's brass surface on a protruding nail. Both Edit and the man were then urged by an emissary from the frontlines to come outside at once; the ribbon was about to be cut.

Distraught, Edit grabbed the plaque from the functionary's hands. "*I* invited them. They are friends and guests of the City of Yeroham." But there was nothing for it but to stow the brass plaque behind her front desk and to join the public festivities.

Now, let it be recorded that much went very well that day. The ceremony began and almost ended on time. The food, if not as hot or tasty as it would have been had local talent been permitted to shine, certainly was sufficient and *looked* properly exquisite. Speeches were short. (Yeroham's Moroccan Mayor startled everyone by speaking for five solid minutes in, for the first time in anyone's recollection, carefully rehearsed English.) The town's children's choir under their Russian maestro charmed us all.

Pauline and Maurice Gaba were seated next to me. They plainly were genuinely delighted with the occasion. After the speeches were concluded, Edit and I tentatively showed them their plaque, explained what had happened and indicated where it would be hanging after that day. Whereas we were still incensed, the understanding couple from Scotland seemed fully appeased, was not in the least offended. Nor, for that matter, have I any reason to believe that Fay and Joe Ain, the Canadian benefactors, would have suffered offense had Keren Hayesod protocol not been so forcefully served. To our relief, all ended more or less well!

These days the Fay & Joe Ain Library, free of all ceremony, is busily hosting its intended clientele. The two plaques, good neighbors at a room's-breadth distance, both hang on display. A slight scratch on the one is barely noticeable. But it is to me, when I pass it, a livid, permanent scar. I do not know why it is so, but there seems to abide among us Jews here in Israel a chronic, endemic pettiness that clings like an officious, Sodomite crab to the very coattails of our spirit. What is the source of this aridity at the main course of feast, this unwonted meanness that besmears so many of our more generous works and days? The question leaves me baffled and depressed.

PATROLLING

THE GREEN

The short item in *The Jerusalem Post* (8/20/84) was headlined GREEN PATROL CONFISCATES BEDUIN SHEEP, GOATS, CAMELS. It had been positioned just above FATHER, SON CHARGED WITH LOD MURDERS, and for nearly all the skimming and skipping morning *Post* readers, it surely made the same negligible impact. Divided into eight major tribes, the 50,000 Bedouin of the Negev frequently serve in the army, often as scouts for the Border Patrol. Although an increasing number are being settled in two quasi-urban conglomerations, one between Beersheba and Arad, the other between Beersheba and Kiryat Gat, many others prefer their traditional herder and tent style of desert life. For American Negev-dwellers, the parallels between the Bedouin and the Navajo or Sioux are, though occasionally misleading, both inevitable and of service. The overwhelming majority of Israelis, however, Jews and Arabs alike, don't give a passing hoot for the present trials of the Bedouin.

Here is the lead of that *Post* story: "Beer Sheba—The army and the Green Patrol yesterday confiscated more than 200 sheep and goats and 30 camels from the Beduin Al Azazma tribe near Yeroham and brought them to the district veterinary compound here where they will be held until the court decides their fate."

That Sunday morning at around 11:00 o'clock, our Yeroham neighbor Leah Shakdiel had burst into our house. Could I hurry at once to accompany two Bedouin herders back to their pasture? Their pickup was parked on the street; highly distraught, they were currently sitting next-door in her salon. The Green Patrol was at that very moment rounding up their livestock. Leah, a Labor Party member of the Yeroham City Council, is the Bedouin's most sympathetic local ear in high places; indeed, this was the first time in recent memory that the Bedouin knew that they had a person in Yeroham with some measure of authority upon whom they could call in times of emergency. Since the Camp David accords, this has been of increasing importance, for, with their conflicting claims and needs for overlapping stretches of the Negev, the Army and the Bedouin have been colliding with increasing frequency. It is an unequal struggle.

I indicated that I was ready to go immediately. "I'll join you as soon as I can," she yelled over her shoulder. "I have to call Shavit [the Bedouin's lawyer], *Ma'ariv* and *Ha'aretz*, the Association for Civil Rights, and a babysitter. Take your camera and all the pictures you can. And be careful!"

The Green Patrol—paramilitary, ecological gangbusters

of the Negev—had undertaken a similar operation several months before. According to Shavit via Leah, however, I had understood that until pending legislation between the Israel Lands Authority and the Al Azazma tribe was concluded— and it could take years—the courts had explicitly forbidden the Green Patrol from further harassment of the Bedouin. From the Bedouin point of view, it was essential that some sympathetic Jews be present at the actual scene of any encounter. Even just *one* would be a 100% improvement over the current situation at the scene of the roundup. Bedouin, sometimes for good cause, have a difficult time getting themselves believed in an Israeli court of law.

I sat wedged between Hassan Awad Almared and Haid Asayek, Al Azazma tribesmen, in the front seat of their pickup as it careened out of Yeroham onto the road toward Dimona. Several additional Bedouin, heads covered by red-fringed kaffiyehs, hunkered in the rear. Asayek, so overwrought he could scarcely speak, managed to convey over the noise of the vehicle that the Green Patrol had begun its roundup in secret, very early in the morning, at the edges of the grazing area. He swore that the stock had not been set out to graze on military land; in fact, it had been the Green Patrol jeeps that had driven the sheep, goats, and camels onto a firing zone in order to justify the operation. According to his account, in order to prevent the Bedouin from being alerted earlier, the Patrol had taken a young shepherd, really just a boy, into custody. While Asayek drove with one hand on the wheel, I covertly watched his other hand playing with the sheath of his ornate dagger, the sort worn by nearly all Bedouin men at their corded belts.

His story was not implausible. Neither, however, was it possible to verify. For some years even before Camp David, the Green Patrol had been carrying on with their own style of vigilante campaign against the Negev's indigenous Bedouin, presumably in the name of land conservation. Although the matter is unproved, the popular belief remained strong that the Bedouin's overgrazing of the largely barren land with their black goats was a principal cause for the northerly advance of the Negev sands. When the Green Patrol came under the jurisdiction of Ariel Sharon in his capacity as Minister of Agriculture in the Begin government, the Patrol became virtually unrestrained. Currently it acted with greater caution, but its animus against the Bedouin always has been undisguised, and its operations occasionally downright ruthless.

The pickup passed several *Tsahal* military installations, those *other*, more familiar tent-dwellers of the Negev, along the ten kilometers of Arizonan landscape between Yeroham and Dimona. It certainly was not unlikely that some Bedouin livestock could have strayed onto military turf: so *much* of the Negev now was military, so many of its roads were dotted with signs proclaiming DANGER: FIRING ZONE ON BOTH SIDES OF THE ROAD. At any time of its choosing, a pretext for a Green Patrol foray was readily at hand. This particular operation was being carried out at the suspiciously expedient moment when the court in Dimona was out of session for two weeks of summer vacation. For Leah to locate a judge in Beersheba who would issue a restraining order for her would not be an easy task.

The pickup stopped abruptly for a young Bedouin wearing an Israeli army uniform. He hopped onto the rear of the truck and yelled out directions to Asayek. We cut east of the highway. In the distance I could just make out a little Bedouin boy running after, or perhaps toward, something. Just two minutes from the highway, the desert, to my grossly untrained eye, seemed both featureless and infinite. Suddenly once again the familiar tents, flags, and a few jeeps loomed and shimmered beneath the noontime sky. It was startling how ominous they could seem when sighted from the front seat of a Bedouin pickup.

We stopped and on foot approached a small cluster of soldiers, army trucks, and jeeps, two of which were marked with the Green Patrols' distinctive green coloration. Wordlessly, the Bedouin deferred to me. I gathered myself and announced to a surprised lieutenant that I was a Yeroham resident for seven years and a journalist. My pen scratched nervously over my notepad. What was happening here? Did he have a written order? How could it be that in spite of a written court order to the contrary, Bedouin livestock were being confiscated? Where *was* his written order, anyway?

I sensed that I had caught the lieutenant, who may have had little heart for his morning's work anyway, offguard. He was abashed and confused. What sort of unexpected development was this: interference from a bearded Jew wearing a *kippa* and (by chance) a red shirt! "What's your name, lieutenant?," I demanded.

"I don't know about a court order," he muttered. "Lieutenant Ofer Bardan, and this is now a firing zone. They [he vaguely indicated my Bedouin associates who hung a few steps behind] have to clear out of here. Those are my orders. You as well. That's all there is to it."

"But," I persisted, beginning to warm to my role and scrawling imaginary notes in dangerous English on my pad in front of his eyes, "where *is* your written order? According to the courts [I prayed that I had this straight from Leah, from Shavit], you are absolutely forbidden to act in this way as long as the Bedouin Lands case is undecided by the courts. Aren't you aware of that?"

I was, I felt, carrying the offensive reasonably well when out of the dozen or so onlookers a husky fellow in a T-shirt stepped forward. "This is a firing zone," he barked in a clipped manner. "What's your name?"

"Haim. I live in Yeroham. Who are you?"

"It doesn't matter who I am, Haim. If you don't get the hell out of here, you'll be arrested. Do you understand?"

"But do you have a written order to move this livestock?"

"Haim, you have no right to be here," he responded in a voice quiet with Dan Duryea menace. "I'm telling you nicely for the second time, move on or you'll be arrested."

I and the two Bedouin deliberated only for a moment, then slowly backed up some 50 meters toward the parked pickup. Unlike Ofer, the T-shirted Greenie was not about to be cowed by the likes of me. We loitered uncertainly in the shadow of our truck, a bit like street-corner types. Behind the shield of the Bedouin and the pickup, unnoticed I thought, I snapped off a quick, unfocused photo in the direction of the Green Patrolmen, their jeeps, and the distant soldiers of *Tsahal*. Perhaps I would be lucky. Just the very day before I had received my own notice for reserve duty—26 days in October. Soon I would again be wearing the same uniform as Lieutenant Bardan, my first adversary of the day.

I had a hunch that I could guess what had probably happened. Lieutenant Bardan had said that the area was *now* a firing zone. In all likelihood, a desert stretch to which the Army and the Bedouin both laid claim but which had not been used by *Tsahal* had been declared "a firing zone" a day or two before. The Bedouin, knowing nothing of it, had not moved their goats and sheep. The day's fracas, probably Green Patrol–inspired, perhaps not, was the result.

Heading back toward Yeroham, our truck encountered Leah being driven in our direction by another Yeroham neighbor (and former comrade in *garin* Mashmia Shalom), social worker Hans Levy from Holland. They were accompanied by two of Hans's young sons and some additional Bedouin. Although our *garin* had been officially defunct for several years, we ex-*garinikim* were aware that in situations of this nature, we could depend upon each other and no local persons except each other. We all smiled when the vehicles stopped. I was beginning to feel like an impostor: the day might well spell a serious setback for the harried Bedouin, but it gave increasing promise of a desert outing, a heady adventure, a participatory reunion, and an extended anecdote for a future evening's telling for us former members of the *garin*.

Leah had been elected to the Yeroham City Council a year earlier. On a former occasion when the area Bedouin had been similarly vexed, she and her psychologist husband, Moshe, had acted as their spokespersons before a magistrate in Dimona. The Green Patrol had, apparently with dubious legality, "arrested" some Bedouin for disobeying Green Patrol–issued directives. Moshe and Leah actually succeeded in obtaining the release of several of the illegally arrested Bedouin from the Dimona jail. In the process, they acquired the status of heroes among the Al Azazma tribesmen.

On a later occasion, when local Bedouin had been discovered breaking some water pipes outside of Yeroham so that their stock could drink, it was Leah who had prevailed upon Yeroham's City Council to investigate the cause before they took punitive measures. What developed was that whereas

years before a compassionate Israel Water Authority functionary had had a tap placed in the line for the Bedouin's use, a
recent successor without prior warning had it turned off. This
had left the Bedouin without any water at all for their animals.
They had resorted, predictably enough, to breaking the lines.
With Leah's intercession, a tap with a meter was installed.
Everyone was immensely pleased with this simple and peace-
ful solution.

In general, relations between the Al Azazma Bedouin and
the Jews of Yeroham have over the years been unstrained.
There are, in fact, local people who have expressed a willingness to support in court the Bedouin contention that they were
acquainted with these particular Bedouin families and that
they have lived in the area at least since Yeroham's founding in
1951. If and when the issue ever gets to court, such testimony
would undermine the Green Patrol's contention that, respond-
ing to the availability of water in the area, the Yeroham Bedouin had arrived in the vicinity only since Israeli independence and therefore had no prior claim to the land. If such were
the case, it would render the Bedouin right to graze there
highly problematic.

I switched vehicles, and shortly we all arrived at the scene of
my earlier engagement with Lieutenant Ofer Bardan and the
taciturn creep from the Green Patrol. There were now in view
not one jeep but three. Our Bedouin informant told us that
seven additional jeeps were now out in the desert rounding up
the Bedouin livestock for delivery to the quarantine station in
Beersheba. A group of soldiers sat suspiciously guarding several dozen camels, as well as a large number of sheep and
goats, in a makeshift corral. A Bedouin woman in black, full-
length robe—the sort, save for the intricate embroidery, that
nuns used to wear—was screaming some choice Arabic im-
precations at them. Several rows of practice target dummies
were lined up off to the left. I could not recall seeing them
when I had been there just minutes before.

Leah, hair anomalously covered in the shawl that identified
her as "religiously observant," a *datiya* in this land where head
coverings are like wingtip coloration for ornithologists, argued
more loudly, more effectively than had I with the T-shirted,

soft-spoken menacing patrolman. Several times a pot-bellied soldier stepped forward to intervene in the argument.

"Things were fine around here until you strangers came along to try to run our lives," Leah was yelling.

"Strangers!," countered the unrestrainable fat soldier. "Who's a stranger," he asked, pointing toward a quiet Bedouin, "me or him?"

"You, of course," Leah retorted. "I *know* him. He lives here." Annoyed by the intrusion, the Green Patrolman elbowed the soldier to the rear. He had had enough of talk.

"If you don't all leave at once, and I mean right now, you'll all be subject to immediate arrest." He turned toward me standing, I thought, innocuously at the fringe of the action. "This marks the third and final time I'll be telling *you* that, Haim."

We protestors made our reluctant departure, but, feeling eyes trained in the back of my head, I made no further attempt to snap another one off with my camera. On the trip back to Yeroham, Salaam Muhammed solemnly informed me what would happen: the Green Patrol would haul his camels, goats, and sheep to a quarantine station outside of Beersheba. He then would have to pay a large fine in order to retrieve them. "They told us that it will cost us more than the animals are worth," he stoically related.

In Yeroham a quarter of an hour later, Leah was again on the telephone trying to reach the press, lawyers, and a stay-at-home judge. In a country where "connections" are usually of vital importance, even temporarily delaying this Green Patrol operation seemed like a hopelessly complex task. There is in all of Israel just one Bedouin doctor and not a single Bedouin lawyer. Shavit, their Jewish attorney, lives in Jerusalem. Successful at last in reaching him, Leah copied down his dictated text of a restraining order. Now she had somewhere to find a judge willing to sign it. Meanwhile, Shavit would speed down to the Negev as soon as he could. A distant relative of mine happened, in fact, to be a Beersheba magistrate, but I also knew too well that Ya'akov's politics are aligned to Gush Emunim, so I did not offer to push my own few "connections." I contacted *The Jerusalem Post* and watched as Leah drove off toward Beersheba.

Five minutes later, her husband, Moshe, already apprised of the crisis by some Bedouin, drove up. It took him three minutes to formulate a new strategy. He filled his Subaru bubblecar with his own five children. "They won't arrest the kids," he explained. Our own 7-year-old Yishai and his pal Baruch jumped in, and off they drove.

Half-an-hour later Moshe returned with an empty Subaru. He had left standing as close as they were permitted access to the cattle roundup all the kids in the charge of his 12-year-old daughter. "They're all right," he smiled. "Just lined up along the edge of the highway." Then Marcia, another former *garin* neighbor woman, and six additional kids, most belonging to our former Mashmia Shalom enclave, all crowded in with Moshe into the Subaru and headed down the road toward Dimona. They too could serve, if not on a witness stand in court, still as potential "Jewish witnesses" to the day's mayhem, perhaps (who could tell?) even frustrating it. Just before the car pulled away, I handed our camera to Marcia.

The final paragraph of that *Jerusalem Post* story reads as follows: "Marcia Shertok [sic] of Yeroham reported that she and a neighbor went to take photos of the incident, but the local police snatched their cameras and confiscated their film, saying it was illegal to take pictures in an army zone."

Moshe and a local police vehicle returned to Yeroham with the jubilant children about 2:30 in the afternoon. Moshe looked very distressed. They had not been permitted to get very close to the scene of the animal roundup. The police had, in fact, been angered by the presence of all our children, some of whom had unfortunately behaved like *chutzpanim*: "I can't see that we accomplished anything," he complained. "All that I did was damage my relationship with some police from Dimona whom I've known for over ten years." Leah was still out on a judge-hunt somewhere in Beersheba. Marcia and her friend were still in police custody in Dimona. We learned over the phone that Shavit had driven all the way to Beersheba, could not locate Leah anywhere, and was currently returning to Jerusalem. "The awful thing," Moshe bemoaned, "is that when the Green Patrol decides to strike, there's not much a person can do to head them off. Everyone is so helpless."

An hour later, Marcia arrived at home clutching the camera, minus the film, in hand. "It was a stupid thing," she sadly confessed. "I was really just trying to get a shot of all the Mashmia Shalom kids together. I wasn't at all thinking about it being a military zone. I don't think I took any shots in their direction, anyway. If I'm right, they'll return the film after they have it developed. The police were very nice about the whole thing. Look at the bright side of it: it will save us the cost of developing the roll."

"Yes," I offered ruefully, "but I *did* get a shot of the Green Patrol guy in the T-shirt."

"Oh," she said grinning sheepishly, "I did forget about that."

The last returnee of the day was Leah. It was 5:30. She had finally found a judge who would sign the restraining order, but not until all the camels and sheep and goats had been unloaded at the Beersheba quarantine station. "What a day of frustration," sighed the mother of two, foster mother of four, Yeroham's only city councilwoman in recent memory. We all rather grimly concurred.

The following day some Bedouin came around to visit with us. A big fine had already been paid; all the livestock had been restored. Smiling, Marcia pointed out that 6-year-old, corntassle blond-haired Baruch Levy was holding hands with one of the dark-skinned visitors. It struck us both that just possibly the previous day's children's crusade had not been entirely futile. There were now at least a few Yeroham Jewish kids who did not automatically perceive *all* Arabs, or at least all Bedouin, with instinctive hostility.

Moreover, it seemed of some note that our Al Azazma neighbors knew that they had a second address to come to when next time unexpected trouble struck. As seemingly comic and unavailing as our efforts had been, all Jews were not quite the same as the husky glob in the T-shirt who the day before had been calling most of the shots in the desert that is the Bedouin's only home.

This could yet be a matter of some importance. In the general election of 1984, the Labor Party, while still the major vote-getter among the Bedouin, lost considerable support. Although Ezer Weizmann's new Yahad Party list did surprisingly well, support for the Rakah Communist Party and for the new

Palestinian nationalist P.L.P. list was substantially higher than ever before. Who, really, could blame the hapless Bedouin for shopping around? Six weeks later the Dimona police telephoned: our roll of developed film was ready to be picked up. It turned out that my photo of the early stages of the encounter *had* come out, but the distance was so great that the toy-like jeeps and camels looked like incidental props in an art-shot of the rolling desert wastes. The Dimona police, if they ever figured out what the photo was all about, had rightfully concluded that it was of little value to anyone. Still, I presented it to Leah for whatever future purpose it might have. At the least, I was not very worried that her taste of public office was likely to co-opt, corrupt, or neutralize *her* commitment.

There was no word of further follow-up to the incident in the press. This was no surprise. There is in Israel hardly any general consciousness of the special problems facing the Bedouin. Worse, if they were whales or pandas or exotic birds there would be a greater awareness that their very presence in our midst is actually a significant enhancement in the quality of our lives. For the vast majority of Israelis, except for their ability to attract large numbers of tourists to the Thursday morning *souk* in Beersheba, the Bedouin of the Negev provide more of a bother than even a mild distraction.

"MY HOME IS
OVER JORDAN"

*T*hat Jewish nationalism—Zionism—is more a species of "racism" than any other nationalism, than American patriotism, pan-Arabism, or Swissism, is an anti-Semitic carnard too specious to warrant rebuttal, but this United Nations–fostered cuckooness has had a useful, personal side-effect: it has encouraged a modicum of personal introspection about black people. In my 36 years of living in the United States, the years of my life before I emigrated to Israel under the aegis of the "racist" Law of Return, just how many American blacks had I befriended, anyway? There were some pleasant fellow black caseworkers when, between graduate school and the army, I had worked briefly at New York City's Department of Welfare; blacks sticking to blacks in the Army; black colleagues at the five campuses where I taught for different spells; blacks—always too few—in the Movement; 15 years of black students sitting (mostly indifferently) in front of me, a rare black neighbor, but in all that time, *only one black friend*, Lionel Williams. It does seem a paltry tally. Is that crux personal, universal, American, merely accidental; or is it perhaps also, somehow or other, Jewish after all?

MESSIANIC BLACKS AND
SUCKER JEWS

*E*xcept for a handful of non-Jewish students who briefly studied art at Ramat Hanegev College when it still boasted an

Overseas Student Program, until February 1984 Yeroham, with its 5,000 Moroccans and Indians, its 1,500 miscellaneous Persians, Rumanians, sabras, Yemenites, and "Anglos," had always since its founding been a wholly Jewish town. In that month, however, Yeroham's first *goy* began, for an indeterminate period, to live in a house in Sh'hunat Ben-Gurion, one of Yeroham's newer neighborhoods. His name was Melvyn Coleman, and he was a 31-year-old black man from the South Side of Chicago.

Coleman, whose fluency in Hebrew surpassed my own, had lived in Israel since 1971 as a member of a sect popularly known as the Black Hebrews (among themselves, the Nation of God) under the moniker "Shamur"—the Preserved One. About 1,200 of these Black Hebrews live just to the north of Yeroham in larger Dimona. Perhaps another 300 may be found in Mitzpe Ramon and Arad, towns to the south and east. Until that February, however, none had ever actually resided in Yeroham itself.

Not that Coleman was, rare Gulliver, the very first black person ever to enter the town! Yeroham is the traditional Bedouin site for where Hagar discovered a well in the desert wilderness from which her son Ishmael could drink. Each year the Bedouin celebrate that event near the *tel* just outside of town. A surprisingly large number of these Negev Bedouin are black, a residue of the still-thriving (albeit no longer within Israel) Arab slave trade. Moreover, Black Hebrews have, from time to time, been employed by the town of Yeroham to sweep its streets. Dressed in gaudy-colored dashikis and fancy, distinctive knit caps, like disinherited princes behind their long-handled street brooms, the tall black men—most were at least six feet—seem disinclined to talk with any residents. Nowhere have more regal garbagemen ever plied their implements than here in Yeroham.

In 1978, during my first full year of living in this town, I initiated a conversation with a Black Hebrew seatmate on a bus ride home from Beersheba. (At that time, the No. 057 bus from Beersheba arrived in Yeroham only after first making its depressing circuit of Dimona.) I was frankly curious about the man's black community. His response was a canned, half-hour monologue about America-the-despoiler of the world's resources; the poisoner of earth, water, and air; the subjugator of the black man's mind and the black woman's body. By moving to the land that God and the Bible had promised to *them* and by their close adherence to God's law, the Nation of God was fulfilling holy prophecy. By the time the No. 057 had arrived in Dimona, though we had yet not touched upon the Hebrews' claim to be descended from the Jews of the Bible—to be the authentic Jews—I was amply satisfied that the Ministry of Interior had not erred in refusing them admittance to Israel as Jews under the Law of Return.

Still, I had to acknowledge to myself a certain resonance in the man's pitch. After all, if he were totally deluded, what might I be? Little that he propounded was so vastly different from remarks that I had heard myself deliver, perhaps with greater éclat, on various occasions in American years past: variations on the themes of disillusion and *aliya*. What dark caricature had I engaged, what odd mockery had I invited and entertained on a bus ride home to Yeroham!

For several years thereafter I traveled at intervals to Dimona in order to purchase the whole wheat flour, wheat germ, and granola dispensed at the health food store run by the black sect which at that time was still unobtainable in Yeroham. Relations were cordial but confined themselves to wholly granular matters. I was aware that the Hebrews organized themselves something like a kibbutz. They pooled their income. Their kids marched through the Dimona streets to their own school: boys in cutdown versions of their fathers' colorful garb; girls, like their mothers, in long, flowing gowns. Aside from the store which I frequented, they had a soul band (for weddings and bar mitzvahs!), they made and sold earrings and pendants at bus terminals and *souks*, and they fielded a basketball team. Such was my knowledge; such was their public, stereotypical face. Still, the Black Hebrews, a people apart amidst a people apart, seemed under the special discipline and dictates of their spiritual and maximum leader, Ben-Ami Carter, to be making it in Israel.

In fact, I could not help being a trifle envious of some of the things they seemed to have attained. After all, Marcia and I had come to Yeroham as members of a *garin* that espoused communal principles. After more than three years of frustrating efforts combating too many centrifugal forces, we had determined that living within a town was too powerful an impediment to our continued communalism. We decided formally to disband our communal experiment. Now, the Hebrews gave lively evidence of *bizarrerie*, to be sure, but after more than a decade together, there they were, against the odds—still together! Even sweeping our streets, they held their heads proud. Amidst the not unusual shove and shout of the Israeli bus queue, never once had I seen a Hebrew jostle or raise his voice in anger. They stood aloof—and united. Perhaps their secret ally had been adversity itself.

From time to time I heard about friction between the former American blacks and their Moroccan Jewish neighbors, but Ben-Ami Carter's good working relationship with Dimona's Mayor Jacques Amir kept relations from getting explosive. Then, suddenly, the Hebrews' health food store was closed, and for some years I grew less conscious of this largest concentration of American settlers (*olim!*) in the Negev. That they were here illegally, that through threat and artifice they evaded deportation proceedings, that they were a permanent problem and minor international embarrassment for Israel, really seemed of relatively little consequence. After all, the addition of a little social diversity made Dimona seem almost interesting. What harm were they doing, anyway?

In 1980, a special committee of the Knesset under M.K. David Glass of the National Religious Party studied the Black Hebrew situation, listened sympathetically to their requests, and issued a report that was surprisingly favorable to their aspirations. Its conclusion was that the sect should be resettled somewhere in the Arava tableland of the Southern Negev as an independent community. The Glass Report also urged that sect members should, conditioned to the premise and the promise that their illegal immigration would cease, be granted some sort of regular status under Israeli law. The Glass Report's recommendations were acceptable in full to the Nation of God. Interior Minister Yosef Burg (also of the N.R.P.!), however, peremptorily rejected the proposals and refused to implement them. Shortly thereafter, the sect was moved to an abandoned absorption center at the edge of Dimona, and their legal limbo has prevailed until the present. Like its donated ambulances and F-16s, America has exported not only a contingent of urban blacks to Israel but a strategy of "benign neglect" for handling them as well.

In the spring of 1967, Marcia and I subwayed from the Bronx (where I was then an English instructor and involved in planning an experimental college at Fordham) to the Upper West Side apartment of old friends Bob and Patricia Johnson. It was to be a friendly, social evening with them and a third couple, Richard and Judy Goldberg. A typical night out for us in the Sixties: for three earnest, sodden hours we found ourselves deliberating how we six could establish a network of whites that, at short notice, when Harlem's turn to burn it up, baby would come, could position itself prophylactically between the cops and the blacks. We even began to make lists of possible participants. Duty and conscience demanded a nonviolent buffer between the pent-up People and the oink nightstickery.

Unaccountably, Harlem declined to follow the lead of Newark, Detroit, Hough, and Watts; our third-force pacifism died still-born. We were, it is plain, merely ridiculous but *not*, I think, flat-out dopey. That *was* how things felt and were. At just about the same time in hog-town Chicago, Ben-Ami Carter had a vision which informed him that the time was at hand for American blacks to return in mass numbers to the Promised Land. So commenced his career of preaching and organizing the Nation of God. After establishing an organization and a network of disciples to carry on in America, the first contingent of black pilgrims set out. There was a layover in Liberia, from where they were expelled—Liberians being well-known for their "racism"—and then the Black Hebrews began making their high-profile appearance in Israel.

Rabbi Shmuel Golding, a former Yerohamite who has achieved considerable notoriety in Israel for his controversial anti-missionary work against proselytizing cults and sects, informed me of his willingness to house one Melvyn Coleman, a Black Hebrew defector, in his temporarily vacant house in

Yeroham. Apparently, Coleman had not merely broken with the sect but had spilled the goods to the authorities about the Hebrews' secret connections with the patently anti-Semitic American Black Muslims, about the appalling health conditions under which they lived in Dimona, about their past and present criminality, and about the security dangers that they posed for the State of Israel.

Golding was somewhat apprehensive about the reception Yeroham might afford this American black. It seems that Coleman along with 79 other sect members, in order to make any deportation proceedings as tortuous as possible, had publicly renounced their U.S. citizenship back in 1973. He had been stateless ever since. Would I help Coleman to get established locally until he could wangle permission from the Embassy officials to return to the United States?

My four children were openly fascinated by our Friday evening guest. Melvyn Coleman was polite and neatly-attired. Although most of the Black Hebrews tower over most of us Jews of the Negev, Coleman was short, almost diminutive. None of us was clear whether he still considered himself in some way Jewish. He ate no meat, sported no head covering, did not (I think) join in our table blessings.

He spoke softly with little trace of black intonation. Earlier in the week after he had moved into the Golding house, I had twice spoken with him. Now I was hearing again his set-piece of disillusionment with the Nation of God: "Ben-Ami Carter teaches everyone that money and material possessions are evils. So all the money goes to him. No one else can own a car, but *he* drives the Lawdmobile." We all laughed appreciatively. Coleman seemed clever, perhaps intelligent; he had certainly worked up a lively routine and could put on a fine performance. "He's got lots of folks sleeping on the floor, but on the inside of *his* house it's like a mansion."

Coleman, short of money to provide clothing and food for his three wives and many children (just *how* many he never made precise), had been advised by Carter that if he used his "God-given brains, the Lawd would provide." Taking Carter at his word, Coleman, who was then the manager of the Soul

Messengers (the Hebrews' band), used his brains to appropriate
the proceeds of a concert for his own urgent needs. "The Lawd
provided, but Ben-Ami Carter sure didn't like it much." Again
we all laughed right on the cueball, but I could not help but
wonder what Coleman's defection was really all about. Had he
finally after twelve years of a dream of gullibility come broad
awake, or had he simply embezzled Nation of God funds? It
was more than I could clearly resolve. No matter: although I
could not accept Coleman's extravagant evaluation of the danger the sect posed to the very security of the State of Israel,
neither could I resist liking the man and feeling sympathy with
his hunger to retrieve his lost identity and to return to his first
home in Chicago.

Just that very next week, after a lengthy hiatus, 15 or 20 Hebrews suddenly reappeared on the streets of Yeroham pushing
their brooms. I wondered whether Coleman, whose major activity seemed to be exposing his former comrades in the press
and over the airwaves, might be getting a mite nervous. A
cover story featuring Coleman had appeared in an English-
language Israeli newsweekly. It revealed the names of members of the Nation of God wanted by the F.B.I. and made
charges that disclosed details of the sect's alleged involvement
in the rackets in America. Apparently an earlier defector named
Cornell Kirkpatrick had been murdered at Carter's order in
1972. Coleman shrugged off the danger. "They won't touch
me," he smiled.

Late one evening in March, a neatly-attired Coleman appeared at my door accompanied by an employee of Amidar,
the government housing authority. Yes, I could vouch for the
fact that Coleman lived in Golding's flat with Golding's knowledge and consent. But did I not know that to sublease Amidar
rentals was strictly forbidden? Well, yes (why was I the defendant, anyway?), but I was certain that Coleman was a guest
rather than a subtenant; he had paid Golding nothing. Moreover, sublessees abounded in Yeroham. All too plainly, Amidar's uncharacteristic hewing to the letter of the law in this
instance had its unpleasant roots elsewhere. I was disturbed.
Whereas evictions in tenants-rights Israel are normally almost
impossible to undertake, it might prove very different with

Coleman who had no official status in the country—or any other. Coleman, however, looked calm as could be.

Two days later, while I was accompanying my daughter Miriam to her kindergarten, a black streetcleaner went out of his way to strike up a conversation with me. In fact, Amadiah Ben-Yehuda was downright chatty. Had there been a shift in the tactics of the Nation of God?

When in 1969 we crossed the George Washington Bridge and left New York City 3,000 miles behind, the impulse that had twisted the key in the ignition of our Volkswagen was neither pure nor simple. Goodbye to all that was romantic, self-serving, protective, and reactionary. *That* included drugs, pollution, noise, triple-locked doors, blacks—and Jews. At the time, we were not particularly aware of all this. We were very tired of certain political complexities and urban knots. We longed for "a nice green place" to withdraw to in order to raise our family in peace. The contradictions that we carted along with us to our life in rural California would ultimately eject us all the way to the Negev. Who could have dreamed that the preponderance of former Americans we would encounter in our Negev would be blacks so disgusted with their lives in Detroit and Chicago that they (like myself!) would change their very names upon arrival? And what could have been quite as just?

Melvyn Coleman was becoming one hot yam. Twice Washington without explanation had rejected the recommendation of its Embassy in Tel Aviv that he, on humanitarian grounds, be permitted re-entry into America. In close touch with his parents and sister in Chicago, Coleman was apparently working to rouse some black and Illinois Congressional pressure on his behalf. Though he knew the angles, one week's assurances dissolved into its successor's disappointment. Meanwhile, however, he was proving adept at making some other friends in Yeroham. One day he borrowed a small sum of money from me; a few days later, he returned it in full. I was curious how he was subsisting, but thought it the better part of wisdom not to pursue the matter. Aside from that one incident with the Amidar employee (which came to nothing), Coleman's Yeroham reception was friendly. One day at an accidental meeting at the bus stop, he assured me that he "was doing jes' fine. The vibes in Yeroham are good, very good."

Amadiah Ben-Yehuda dropped by for a glass of water. (As strictly as the Latter-day Saints, their former fellows in polygamy, do adherents of the Nation of God refrain from brews of caffeine. He would drink nothing but water at my house.) A bit too casually, Amadiah asked whether I happened to know where Melvyn Coleman was living these days. Sensing that he already knew, I did not hesitate to tell him Shamur's current whereabouts. "He's not Shamur any more," I was corrected. "He goes by Coleman, his slave name again." Save for this peevish touch, Amadiah was amiable.

That evening, feeling a bit uneasy, I dropped by the Golding place for a visit with Coleman. He was just concluding what seemed like a long-distance phone call. On the dining table he directed my attention to a detailed street grid of Dimona. Word from the Embassy that week had been highly encouraging. "They want to know who in my family would be coming with me. My three older boys want to come, I know. But not their mothers. So it's up to me to get them out. The Embassy won't lift a finger."

I followed *his* finger while it traced an escape route. "A car's got to go real slow past this store. Friday's the best time, in the afternoon. My boys'll be waiting right here." He indicated a spot at an intersection of two streets. "The brothers'll be playing baseball back this way. A car's got to drive slow along this street . . . and then speed away around that way." I could not help but wonder whether Coleman had seen some of the same gangster films as I or whether just perhaps he had participated in some heists himself. Still, they were his kids, and he was in a difficult spot. I promised Coleman that I would ask around for someone who might lend him a car for the kidnap operation. I confess that I was less than frank: I ended up asking only one person and did not urge him very strongly at all.

More expansive than usual, Coleman talked about his years growing up in Chicago. His grandmother had cleaned house for Jewish people on the North Side. "Nice people. Whenever it snowed, which wasn't so rare in Chicago, they'd call and tell her not to come. They would pay her anyway." He had met

Ben-Ami Carter when, tiring of street gang life as a member of the Del Vikings—"yeah," he laughed, "we were named after the doo-bop d'bop singing group"—Carter's Nation of God provided a new identity and vision that filled the vacuum. "The obligation or initiation was 'total commitment' which Carter called 'the freedom concept,'" he explained. "I was 16, and having my own land, language, and prophecy sounded good to me." The test of "total commitment" was an armed robbery of a travel agency. According to Coleman, they got clean away with 3,000 blank airline tickets. In 1971, the only male among 19 black women, Coleman arrived at Ben-Gurion Airport on classy K.L.M. All 20 of the newcomers had availed themselves of the stolen tickets. They were augmenting the Hebrew community of 75 who, after their brief spell in Liberia, had established themselves in unsuspecting, unlikely Dimona.

"How did it feel?," I ventured.

"Just like arriving home. We never once even looked back toward the rear of the plane, else we'd've been like Lot's wife. We all gave Customs people the same address in Dimona. They acted surprised, but there was no hassle."

And in Dimona?

"We were soon overcrowded, but the local people at first were friendly enough. You see, they thought we were just regular Jews like them."

"Overcrowded" meant 35 people sleeping in a normal, single-family apartment. Single men and single women slept on the floor on mats; for privacy, a curtain was drawn down the center of the room. "It improved for a while," Coleman re-marked, "but it's getting that way again. But still," he said re-flectively, "it was in some ways better than the South Side: much less chance of getting into trouble." My eyes met his brown orbs, then looked down at the street map of Dimona that lay between us. "Yeah," he smiled, "I still got my troubles. You know, I was just a kid in 1973 when I renounced my American citizenship. That was a terrible mistake. I've suf-fered for it a lot." I left him poring over the lines on a map of Dimona at table in the quiet of Rabbi Golding's house.

Two weeks later it appeared that Coleman's campaign was making headway. A Likud Knesset member named Shilansky averred that the Black Hebrews of Dimona were a greater menace to Israel's security than the P.L.O. He urged the government to take appropriate action against them. This was soon followed, in spite of the half-heartedness of his disavowal of support from Black Muslim, virulent anti-Semite Louis Farrakhan, by the victory of Rev. Jesse Jackson in the District of Columbia's Democratic primary election. Then an Israeli furor broke out with the revelation that Farrakhan had been carrying on a lively correspondence with one Ben-Ami Carter of Dimona!

Early in May, Amadiah Ben-Yehuda dropped by and, careful to boil the water in a stainless steel pan, prepared himself some herb tea he had brought himself. Yes, things were a bit rough these days, but prophecy declared clearly that "hands will be laid upon the Saints," and these difficult days had been long anticipated. Amadiah had spent three years as a pre-med student at Detroit's Wayne State, the very place where biochemist Bob Johnson, with whom we had comically conspired back in 1967, was now a professor. Detouring from a professional conference in Paris, by chance Johnson was soon to visit with us in Israel. I was tentative: perhaps Amadiah would like to come by when Bob visited? Possibly he could convey a message to Amadiah's family.

There was a pause. "I'm not in close touch with them. But that might be nice," he concluded thoughtfully. "If anyone had told me ten years ago that today I would be pushing a broom, I'd've thought he was crazy," he declared over his glass of unsweetened tea. "But," he hurried on, "it's for the good of the Saints." After his day of work on the Yeroham streets, Amadiah works as one of the Nation of God's twelve "natural-health physicians." "Ben-Ami Carter's taught us all about diet food poisons, and natural medicine," he explained. The touch of dubiety relating to his daily occupation vanished when I asked Amadiah some questions about his physical presence in Israel.

"This is my land according to prophecy and the Law of Return of the Children of Abraham. America is a land of hatred, rape, murder, and trouble. All the brothers who in America were robbers and pimps, who cursed and beat their wives . . .

why, here they don't rob, eat meat, drink, or smoke. We don't even know what a curseword is anymore. Our grandparents and great-grandparents knew that we were really descended from the tribe of Judah, but it was kept a secret. The white men killed anyone who revealed the truth, but there are all sorts of proofs. For example, we blacks say 'ain't' a lot because it comes from the Hebrew word *ein*."

I suppressed even the shadow of a smile. No, I did not have any need for further proofs. It was odd. I could recall only one other person who had sipped his tea from a glass. It had been many, many years since I had last accompanied my father on his monthly Sunday visits to his old father on Foster Avenue in Brooklyn where they would play an hour's worth of gin rummy or casino together. How queer that Amadiah Ben-Yehuda should even fleetingly bring to mind my grandfather Joseph, that fiercely anti-religious engineering graduate of the University of Kiev, dead these many years, who took three lumps in his tea.

I pressed Amadiah, who seemed eager enough to talk, about Coleman's many charges. "Oh man, *sure* there's contact between us and the Muslims, but only because they're black and proud like us." No conspiracy—just communication. Yes, Carter's house was nicer than any of the others " 'cause everyone wants the leader's house to be the nicest." Yes, whites would be able to join the Nation of God in the future: "the tribe of Judah are just the forerunners." And, if asked, the brothers would be happy to serve in the Israeli army, he was sure.

As for Coleman himself, "he just couldn't shake American materialism, the slave mentality. He'd been in trouble about money more than once before. This time when he was caught, his pride wouldn't permit him to take a more menial job. He had reverted." But he was also a proof of the revolution of the heart that the Saints had suffered: "It'd be nothing for some of the brothers to pay him a little visit. In America, if someone stepped on my shoes, I'd fight him. Now all that is out of my heart."

Two former Americans, we laughed together about the comically pushy ways of the "Israelis." Indeed, I easily granted that we two shared more than a little in common. True, I no longer deprecated "Amerika," but had I not like him weighed it in the balance and found it too closely wedded to materialist values? He and I, two "quiet Americans," felt sufficiently at home in Israel where life, even a life sweeping the refuse of Yeroham, was sweeter than in Detroit where it was oh so easy to get over one's head into hot water.

When Lionel, Margaret, and their twin girls took off from California for Albuquerque, my parting jest sounded more ominous than I had really intended: "Stay out of trouble. That's Cowboy Country."

Lionel had grinned broadly: "No way am I gonna find trouble. I'm gonna do nothing but pick off my Ph.D. like an apple off a tree. Gonna find me the straightest, dullest, deadest poet I can find. Then shuffle on out."

A year later, in the summer of 1968, I stopped off at Albuquerque on my way across from New York to California. Lionel was not listed in the phone book. At the university switchboard they had curious orders not to divulge either his phone number or his address.

"But I have his address. I'm a very good, very old friend," I argued. "Just tell me how to get there." The address I had was not current. They were adamant, but I refused to budge from the premises. *I Shall O-ver-come,* I chanted. I threatened a sit-in, and, with the intervention of higher bureaucratic authority (she actually drove me to Lionel's new place), I finally overcame.

The craziness that had occurred had been pure product of America. Lionel had kept his distance from the black groups on campus. He even declined to teach any Black Lit courses. One innocent day—or perhaps not so innocent, who really knows?—he had read aloud a poem containing "fuck" to a freshmen section. A state senator's daughter informed her father. He suffered moral indignation and gastric indigestion from the news. Within a week, there were front-page headlines, editorials, and letters to the editor in the Albuquerque and Santa Fe press about the filthy-worded black English instructor (with the white wife. Had it been known, what would they have made of Margaret's being Jewish?). Threats were de-

livered daily like milk and bread by phone and mail. Fearing
for their twins, Lionel and Margaret moved; Lionel had taken
out a gun permit. There would be no Ph.D. on the straight and the dull from
U.N.M. In the end my friends were trying just to hang on another two weeks before getting away from Albuquerque to save
their black and white skins.

One morning shortly after my lengthy chat with Amadiah,
I encountered Melvyn Coleman on a bus headed north.
He had, he said, an appointment later that same day with
some important officials in Jerusalem. Still, he looked discon-
solate. "Sure enough, the people in Washington turned me
down again," he declared.

The following week *The Jerusalem Post* ran a series of articles "exposing" the Black Hebrews of Dimona. Their major
informant had obviously been my sad-faced busmate. The articles contained little I had not already heard, but the reporter
succeeded in drawing Ben-Ami Carter into making statements
that made him sound mildly deranged: "I have a God-given
job to lead the country [Israel!] spiritually. . . . I would like to
be head of state in Israel; I *do* want to take over because I have
the proper path and plan for today. . . ."

Alarming or alarmist? True, Nation of God ideology does
depict its adherents, tribesmen of Judah, as the true and right-
ful inheritors of the Land; the "European Jews" are described
as "usurpers." This was very nearly the P.L.O. line with a
black twist. It seems to spell a collision course with the usurp-
ing "Jews" of the State of Israel. Coleman in the *Post* had described the 250 Black Hebrew "sabras" as "a time-bomb whose
detonation would topple the present Israeli state." Why, indeed, *should* they be harbored?

Shortly thereafter, Amadiah, looking somewhat abashed,
again dropped by, this time with a special invitation for me and
Marcia to attend some special festivities to accompany the Hebrews' celebration of "New World Passover." There would be
athletic contests, healthy food, and an evening soul concert.
That last sounded like it might be an unusually interesting
Negev attraction. I showed Amadiah my copy of the *Post*'s ex-

posé of his community. Amadiah shook his head ruefully: "There are some true statements here," he admitted, "but it *reads* wrong. Look, Ben-Ami Carter *is* the Messiah. His prophecies *have* come to pass. We expect trouble, but whatever he tells us to do is right." My face must have sagged. "Well, it *is*," he insisted. "We're all coming close now to the End of Days. The great war is coming. Russia will defeat that whore America, and then the Messiah will shine forth." He paused for breath. "We're over 1,500 people who have seen prophecies come true for years. Why should anyone listen to or believe two or three people like Melvyn Coleman?"

After he left, I puzzled for some time over a darkly weird, messianic convergence. Hanging in the Jerusalem office of Rabbi Shmuel Golding, Coleman's Yeroham patron, was, as I had several times noticed, a placard that reads: WE WANT MASHIACH NOW. Large numbers of religious Jews in Israel hold firmly to beliefs quite parallel to those held by Amadiah Ben-Yehuda, Ben-Ami Carter, and the other 1,500 Black Hebrews. Indeed, I had to admit that I myself found it not improbable that the renewal of Jewish sovereignty in the Land of Israel prefigures a new phase in Jewish and possibly global history. (Why, after all, not?) In fact, I *do* believe that this reborn state somehow figures centrally in the intersection of man's history and God's economy. Was that not a central factor in why I chose to come here and choose to remain?

And yet, looking into the eyes of this like-minded, 30-year-old black man, I, like Melvyn Coleman, could see the potential for Jonestown writ all too large. I described for Amadiah the bizarre, climactic interlude of Shabbtai Tsvi in the history of the Jewish people. It was all new to him. He appeared to be mildly interested—or was he merely humoring me? "Be seeing you at the New World Passover," was all he would finally say.

On the very next day, a smiling Melvyn Coleman dropped by with the long-awaited good news: "This looks like the real thing. The Embassy said it's finally been approved in Washington. I should be leaving within a month. And," he hurriedly added, "I'm not gonna drop this business. I plan to expose Ben-Ami Carter as a charlatan as soon as I get to America."

Though it had obviously crossed both our minds simultaneously, neither he nor I made mention of his three oldest sons in Dimona. I hoped that he could somehow pull off his caper, but I suspected that he had reconciled himself to the fact that, under the circumstances, it was not going to be feasible. He would be cutting his losses very close to the bone.

The Cultural Center in Dimona: the Saints in spotless white, knitted turbans, carrying impressive carved shillelaghs, were done up fine in robes of magenta, turquoise, and amber. As guests of Amadiah-the-physician, we were seated just behind a phalanx of five young women, each of whom was balancing a more fantastic headdress, in the fifth row. Save for one other couple, we seemed to be the only whites in the packed auditorium—Harlem's Apollo wondrously transposed to the Negev!

The lights dimmed, and a very tall, very black figure bounded to the stage to lead the audience of 700 in a hymn of praise at the entrance into the hall of Messiah Ben-Ami Carter. Indeed, "New World Passover" is a Black Hebrew enjambment of Passover and Thanksgiving Day, a commemoration of deliverance out of America over the Jordan—and "home." And celebrate they did. The show was a driving display of gaudy, jiving song and dance, a characteristic black mesh of gospel and soul. For one-half hour three bassmen, three guitarists, and the statuesque, long-limbed m.c. bopping on the bongoes that comprised the opening ensemble each took their licks. Then they backed a swinging male foursome who in turn were succeeded by an orange-gowned quartet, Dimona's version of the Pointer Sisters. And on and on. For more than three hours the audience clapped, cheered, and sang along until their throats turned raspy.

It could easily have been Saturday night on 125th Street *and* the morning after at the Zion Apostolic Baptist Church— unless, that is, you attended too closely to the lyrics. The dominant, repeated theme of tune after tune was of thanks and praise for deliverance from the pollution of America and for a safe arrival in the Promised Land. Close to midnight, Marcia and I made our Passover exit, not a single stray matzoh crumb brushed from our laps or teeth.

Near the end of May, just at the time of the bonfire holiday of Lag B'Omer, our old, long-divorced, biochemist friend Bob Johnson landed in Israel and, eschewing for the nonce such well-worn coins as Jerusalem and Tel Aviv, directed his incredulous cabbie to drive him direct to us in Yeroham. What an initiation to Israel! Over morning coffee two days later, Bob, who had not himself taught Amadiah but knew some professors who had, was filling in our amazed streetcleaner (as he drank his glass of water) on the revived fortunes of the unbeatable Tigers. When Amadiah rose to return to work, Bob volunteered to deliver a note or make a call, if Amadiah so desired, to his Detroit family. There ensued a lengthy pause. Amadiah had mentioned that he was virtually cut off from his family in America. I did not even know, I had never asked, what Amadiah's "slave name" had been. Finally deciding what to do, Amadiah wrote a phone number on a scrap of paper and the name "Smalls."

"Just tell them that you saw me and that I'm all right."

Early in the summer I returned from a brief period of reserve duty to discover that Melvyn Coleman, formerly Shamur, had departed from Israel for his former land of promise. Marcia told me that she had given him a battered but usable suitcase for his journey. She reported him as being very grateful.

Later in June we got a phone call from a distraught Rabbi Golding. Coleman had left in his wake unpaid telephone charges that exceeded $5,000! (Two months later a subsequent bill upped that figure to more than $11,000.) For a man in Rabbi Golding's circumstances, it could have been $5,000,000. I confirmed that Coleman had spoken of being in close touch with Washington and Chicago, but I had little solace for the father of five small children at the other end of the line whose *mitzvah* had so badly soured. Almost surely, well-disciplined Coleman would again make sure not to look back. It might prevent what was left of his heart from turning quite to stone.

With the passing weeks and months, with each passing rumor that the City of Dimona, that the Minister of Interior, that the Prime Minister has finally determined what course of action to take with the Black Hebrews of Dimona, I find myself wondering about these hard-working, talented, righteousness-obsessed folks—cultists, to be sure—quite a bit. Lionel, a real-ist who was nonetheless wiped out more than a decade ago on the streets of Santa Rosa in California, that most dangerous of places, would have known just what to make of them. I can imagine his jovial impatience with my sappiness. I would, I think, have granted him his every point; nevertheless, I would in the end have, paradoxically, differed with him.

That sort of paradox is my daily element. I pray three times a day, every day, for the coming of the *mashiach*, but I confess to a perverse indisposition to the forcing of His hand. On my wall you will find no yearning placard. A three-year calendar runs through 1989. We plan to reorder.

One thing that I cannot put to rest, however, is the fractured upshot of events: with a Melvyn Coleman who—albeit without his three waiting sons—seems to have gotten clean away. With Lionel Williams, a good friend, indeed the sole black friend of all my years in America, who did not. And with Amadiah Ben-Yehuda who waits for something he knows will happen to come to pass. I just cannot figure out whether this unbalanced equation speaks most eloquently of America, of Israel, of blacks, or of Jews.

DAYTRIPPING TO

NORTHEAST AFRICA:

CARTER, "GOLBERG," AND

THE PLAIN TRUTH

A month later Amadiah Ben-Yehuda dropped by with a follow-up invitation. The Nation of God was shortly to celebrate "Brotherhood Day."

Brotherhood Day! Instant evocation of a boyish Frank Sina-tra in a rakish hat ambling through the back lots and multi-ethnic corner stores of "The Town I Live In" across the wide-screen of Friday morning School Assembly at P.S. 86 in the

Bronx. Vision of a vast melting pot, like the sorcerer's apprentice overstirred. A brilliant stroke to demonstrate to their Moroccan neighbors that the Hebrews harbored no anti-Semitic malice. That good Hebrews made good neighbors. Pluralism triumphant in the Negev! They should invite Baruch Gold to speak. Why not? And why not go ourselves? I *was* curious to see the Nation in action on its own turf. Leastways, I was certain the music would be great.

I glanced toward Marcia and got an affirmative shrug. "Sure, Marcia and I would be happy to come. Thanks a lot."

Abashed, Amadiah hesitated for a long, clumsy moment. "I suppose she could come too, but you see, this is *Broth*-erhood Day. A day for the brothers. The Sisters have their own day; their role now is just to do all the work for a while so the Brothers can get it on to celebrate. Get it?"

"Heh, heh! Of course! *Broth*-erhood Day!!

Four days later I—unaccompanied—boarded the bus for a 15-minute ride from Yeroham to Dimona. Among the passengers, I noticed four black women, two black men, a handful of black kids all done up very fine. They must have boarded in Mitzpe Ramon. Once in Dimona there was no need for me to follow along with this conspicuous contingent in order to find the festivities. A throbbing beat from a loudspeaker rent the air, penetrated the bus station. I picked up its syncopated thread for ten minutes until I reached a park, where the Negev abruptly reasserted itself, at the very edge of Dimona.

The Hebrews' housing area, an abandoned immigrant absorption center, stood above on a short rise. In the adjacent park below, I gravitated toward the loud music. Perhaps 200 Black Hebrew brothers were rigged out in matching (very sharp) purple capes, white trousers and shoes. Their heads were covered—no, enclosed—by sparkling white, knitted caps. They were moving in a circle, clapping, chanting to the music. In the center played a 10-piece brass band. It was a sort of jivey *hora*. On a raised dais to the front sat the dozen princes of the Nation among whom, I thought, was surely Carter-their-Messiah. I could not, however, pick him out for certain. At the fringes of the snaking circle, picking up the syncopation with their rolling torsos, several dozen Sisters in long red gowns shook in place.

As far as I could tell, I was the only onlooker, the only guest for the occasion, the only white, and the only Jew on the scene. To the driving beat of the priestly master of ceremonies, the men responded TODA RABAH, ABBA / TODA RABAH, ABBA . . . ("Thank you, Father") over and over, all the while shuffling in a shimmying circle. I spotted Amadiah among them, and we gave each other a hi-sign. Some of the Brothers laughed, others punched feathery fists in the air. A Hebrew Sister approached me cautiously. Once identified as an invited guest of Amadiah Ben-Yehuda's, I was escorted to a folding chair and presented a glass of water and a smile. The m.c. took to leading the Brothers in a rousing halftime cheer of what I later learned was the "theme" of the day:

PERFECTION IS OUR CRITERIA! TOTAL
RIGHTEOUSNESS IS OUR GOAL!
PERFECTION IS OUR CRITERIA! TOTAL
RIGHTEOUSNESS IS OUR GOAL!
PERFECTION IS OUR CRITERIA! TOTAL
RIGHTEOUSNESS IS OUR GOAL!

Oh Ye-ah! I suppressed my small-souled grammarian urge to *sic* myself on "criteria." The Brothers were grooving easy. I decided I would enjoy this male chauvinist day of Brotherhood as it served itself up. A priest of the sect flew into a spellbinding oration that was punctuated every few minutes by the refrain "To Finish the Dream." Though only 10:15, it was already hot; these fine-robed guys had been stomping and goofing around since dawn, but the speaker had grabbed them tight with the repeated lilt—"To Finish the Dream." They had journeyed to freedom here in Northeast Africa in order *to finish the dream.* Dreamer Frederick Douglass was invoked. Then martyred Martin. And then Malcolm. The black speaker sailed on home 20 minutes later with a socko climax: "We ain't what we want to be. We ain't what we oughta be. But thank God, we are what we are, where we are."

I heard myself cheering right along with the rest of the queer Zionist assembly. This pack of illegal immigrants might be weirdo "cultists," but among them I was feeling less threat, less anxiety than I had not long before among some messianically attuned American Jews who seemed inclined to display their lethal hardware under the noses of Arabs in the Territories.

The speaker looked past the circle of Brothers. "Sisterhood," he shouted. "SISTERHOOD! Is the Brotherhood lookin' good?"

"YEAH!," returned the high-spirited, high-pitched response from the several dozen voices. The Brothers laughed, did some funky steps, slapped palms. Hot sun or not, I was enjoying the show. The highlight was the Divine Security Unit, a dozen or so solid-looking Brothers who took the stage with a team cheer: "Is everything Se-cure?" (*Yeah!*) "In the North?" (*Yeah!*) "In the South?" (*Yeah!*) "In the East?" (*Yeah!*) "In the West?" (*Yeah!, Yeah!, Yeah!*) They proceeded to convulse their audience with comic parodies, barely appreciated by me, of some of the leading Brothers. I checked my watch: according to my program, the 9:00 A.M. Breakfast at the Nutritional Center was nearly two hours late. On walked a contingent from the Mitzpe Brotherhood to sing "I'm in the Battlefield for My Lord." I surely could not be the only hungry Brother, was I? (I noticed, however, that token I was still the only whitey on the scene. Negev pluralism seemed to be taking a drubbing.)

As the show concluded and the Brothers dispersed, my host Amadiah surfaced from the throng. Breakfast? Not exactly. First a walk around the housing area. Once this complex of 60–70 small, concrete houses (*cottagim*) had been occupied by immigrant Russians and Rumanians. (Was it possible?) They had long since departed them (and, for the most part, Dimona as well), leaving behind, Amadiah informed me, houses that were such wrecks that no contractor would touch them. When he moved the Hebrews here in 1980, Dimona Mayor Jacques Amir had aimed at two birds: to remove the Hebrews from their overcrowded location across from the Egged bus station and to get something done about this abandoned housing eyesore. Thanks to the Nation's hard work, he had scored two hits. The houses seemed generally in good repair and tidy with neat, grassy patches, trees, and vegetable plots planted in the open spaces.

"You wouldn't believe what a dump this was when we first arrived here," Amadiah complained. "Nothing worked—no plumbing, no wiring, no windows—nothing! We had to fix it all ourselves. That is, the Brothers in Divine Building and Maintenance: they deserve most of the credit."

It was not quite model housing, of course, but no one, I think, could fail to be impressed. Save for the growing burden of renewed overcrowdedness (Melvyn Coleman had made reference to this), the Nation had made it livable. How crowded? Each 3-bedroom cottage, Amadiah said, housed a married couple per room; all the children slept in the front room. (Polygamous households exercised variant arrangements.) Lots of children, after all, is the rule. That made, I figured, about 20 persons per *cottage*, a lot but far fewer than the 35 claimed by defector Coleman. Perhaps the truth lay somewhere between those figures.

"Yeah, it does get tight sometimes," Amadiah admitted ruefully. "We grow as much of our own food as we can" (we passed a row of beets, another of radishes), "but there's not much land available for that here." I knew that what the Hebrews still hoped for, what, thanks to the Knesset's Glass Report, for a brief time they expected to get, was land for their own settlement. A black kibbutz in the Arava! Unfortunately for them, with the Camp David Accords and *Tsahal*'s withdrawal from Sinai, they were now in a position similar to the Bedouin. There just was not much Negev land left to parcel out to anyone, anymore.

When Amadiah is not earning a living in Yeroham (most of which goes, of course, into the common fund of what must be Israel's most successful urban collective), he functions, as he had informed me, as a Divine Healer. He indicated the Hebrew "hospital"—half of a small *cottage*. For the first time, I had an opportunity to see him in his other role. "We call it *Bet Hayim*—House of Life—instead of *Bet Holim*" (House of Sick People), he explained. Two people by the front door stopped to ask him questions about their diets. (My own, empty stomach responded with an audible growl. Talk about food seemed almost a provocation. When *did* these folks eat breakfast, anyway?) I was struck with admiration, however, watching this purple-garbed divine healer, our streetsweeper Amadiah, perform his act here in Dimona. "In cases beyond the ability to help with diet," he later admitted, "we do send our people to the *bet holim*. Say, are you getting hungry?"

Heh! Heh! He laughed as well, and soon we arrived at an open plaza that was shaded by sheets beneath which at each table lounged four to six Brothers. Some were already eating! Amadiah led me to a table where we joined two blacks and (what do you know!) another paleface guest. He was an Aussie named Martin, an artist who sold "peacestones" to tourists at his shop in Tel Aviv and who believed in, of all things, brotherhood and peace.

"I like the Hebrews," he said. "Admire them, in fact. I couldn't pass up their Brotherhood Day. Came down for it especially from Tel Aviv."

A Sister appeared bearing a large bowl of tofu and a cannister of sliced peaches to one of us per trip from the kitchen. That, sprinkled with wheat germ, was breakfast. Martin dug in with gusto. In partnership with a black basketball player on Maccabi Tel Aviv—Israel's perennial basketball champions—the Hebrews had recently opened several Tel Aviv "tofuti" parlors "based on a secret Hebrew soy formula." "Man," Amadiah exclaimed, "it's worth a trip there just to taste it. We can't make enough of it for the customers." I assured him that I was most pleased to be sitting behind a bowl of tofu and peaches. Indeed, it was hard not to wolf it down.

I was seated across from Brother Yehiel, one of the Mitzpe Brotherhood. "We get along jes' fine down there," he said. "Most of us sweep the streets. Fact is, I gave Amadiah here some pointers when he first got started, like watchin' out for little air pockets that swirl up the dust that's already been swept. We also have a jewelry-making workshop down there. All of us live in the same apartment building. It gets a little tight, I got to admit."

Amadiah finally was served his breakfast. Another black joined us at the table. He turned out to be 20 years old and Swedish! (His father was an American deserter, Vietnam vintage.) "This is my second visit to Dimona. I've been thinkin' of joinin'. I like it." A Sister offering seconds glided over. Amadiah was ready for another helping: "Heavy on the peaches, Peaches," he bantered.

The Nation of God celebrates all the biblical holidays but with a Hebrew twist. There is the New World Passover whose concert Marcia and I had attended, these Brotherhood and Sisterhood annual specials, and weekly Shabbat as a day of fasting. "We fast so that we and our bodies can rest," Amadiah explained. "We also have got one day a year when we all jes' relax together," my host explained. "We stay up all night listenin' and dancin' to our bands and singers who make the best music in the world right in our own night club that we made in our *miklat*. I'll show you our underground club later on. That's every year on February 28th."

I brightened: "That happens to be my birthday."

"Then you'll just have to make it a point to celebrate with the Brothers and Sisters next time around. You'll never have a sweeter time."

For the next two hours, Amadiah served as my guide through what seemed remarkably elaborate displays for such a dearth of visitors. At the Divine Art Studio and Boutique a gentle craftsman in his 60s, Brother Jacob, and his 11-year-old apprentice showed me paintings (mainly primitives of African life), clothing, quilts, jewelry, even shoes—all made by the Hebrews for their own use and for sale. My eye was caught by a genealogical mural depicting black ancestry. At the top were familiars such as Abraham, Isaac, and Jacob, spiritual ancestors via lines and squiggles to bottom-line Malcolm, Martin, and Hebrew Messiah Ben-Ami Carter. Back there in the nineteenth century, however, the enigmatic name of Abraham Golberg caught my eye.

"Who's Golberg?," I warily inquired.

"Oh," said Brother Jacob, "he's the great German philosopher that prophesied that the black man would return here to Northeast Africa. Haven't you heard of him? A real prophet. There are still societies in Germany that keep up his work. We get letters from them."

"From Germany! Golberg?" I was nakedly incredulous. "I once knew a Richard Golberg."

"Sure enough! You come back any time you want, now."

I promised Brother Jacob that I would try to gain him access to the kiln at Yeroham's Ramat Hanegev College to do some pottery. (It later developed, to my chagrin, that that unbrotherly institution was singularly uninterested in brotherhood or in Brother Jacob's ceramic efforts. Permission denied.)

Amadiah and I next descended on the basement center of the Divine Building and Maintenance Brotherhood. As in the Art Studio, I was the only visitor, but the two divine carpenters on duty did not seem particularly disturbed. The older cheerfully explained how the DB&M Brothers used the tools on display. His oft-repeated refrain: "With a few, basic tools, used properly, nothing is impossible." Indeed, several intricately worked wooden chests, products of DB&M craftsmanship, were proudly offered for sale. "We can make almost anything to order with our few, basic tools. . . ."

When we left, however, Amadiah explained that orders were getting behind because of the pressure on the carpenters to remodel the Tel Aviv tofuti stores. The price of success.

Next the guest house for a water stop. An ill woman called Amadiah away for a consultation, but I wasn't long alone. The guest house was tastefully—expensively, I thought—furnished. Joining me for a shot of water was a middle-aged white woman (Jewish, I conjectured) from Los Angeles with her three black children—two daughters and a son, between 17 and 23. (Eavesdropping shamelessly, I kept my peace.) Apparently the older girl had joined the Nation, and her family had come to Israel to visit her. The Sister was enthusiastically explaining the facts of Hebrew life to her skeptical mother, sister, and brother. (They were particularly dubious about the higher virtues of Brotherhood Day.)

Amadiah returned. It was getting pretty evident that my audience with Carter-the-Messiah (I had armed myself with unbrotherly, Colemanesque questions about Louis Farrakhan as well as the Nation of God's alleged illegal American activities) was not about to materialize. The elegance of the guest house had rearoused my wonder about the gap between Carter's lifestyle and, say, Amadiah's. But then, where was it written that the road to Total Righteousness should run simple and smooth? A flop as an "investigative reporter," I stifled my doubts.

Finally we arrived mid-afternoon at the main exhibition, perhaps a dozen displays spread over what must have been the old absorption center's dining hall. We stopped by the door in front of a display of photos, maps, charts, and a chap named Amadelia, Spokesman for Divine Foreign Affairs (and recent husband to a second wife). Tall, articulate, not yet 30, Amadelia was plainly one of the Nation's bright young comers. With his handy visual aids, he took me on a grand tour of American imperialism, the historic role of Stokely Carmichael, and a clarification of the Nation's understanding attitude toward the other Jews.

For a change of pace, we edged toward the Divine Nutrition Center for a discourse on the medicinal properties of seeds and herbs. Most fascinating was the news that certain diseases responded to fruits and vegetables of similar shape: for example, I learned that for an earache I should try a compress of avocados. Some further steps brought us to the booth manned by some of the Divine Priesthood. The Nation, I was told, had at the time 16 priests: 11 in Dimona, 4 in Mitzpe Ramon (a veritable hotbed of *cohenim*), and just 1 in Arad. On to the Divine Jewelry Makers for their display of earrings and finger rings. Beyond them a man from the Divine College: "We're sort of like a graduate school," a pleasant figure informed me. He was the College Director. "Last year we concentrated on studying the Caribbean. Just now we're studying the black man's role on the islands of Micronesia."

It reminded me of the catch-all, wonderful, funny little museum in Coalinga that had displayed dinosaur bones, oil drilling equipment, 3-row typewriters, campaign buttons, seashells—whatever folks had collected and ultimately disposed of. This Black Hebrew museum, however, was a cornucopia of the present convictions that actually governed the lives of these 1,500 souls. Entering upon it was like descending into a very font of mythopoeia, a collage of disparate elements transformed into a reformed culture. As I had noted earlier, scarcely any outsiders had been invited or had bothered to come. But what a fertile field the social anthropologists from nearby Ben-Gurion University were passing up! All these preparations for no one but me (where was Martin?; the Lady from L.A.?) verged on the bizarre. From Brotherhood Days past, could the organizers not have guessed how few would come? Was their

Messiah trying to demonstrate something on this Brotherhood Day? It was baffling.

A quick descent to the bomb shelter *miklat* the Brothers had converted into a club for the Divine Entertainer units. The floor glittered from the glint of marble. Amadiah described how the Brothers had picked up scraps of discarded marble for the asking, cut and fitted them into this most elegant dance floor. (Ye-ah! This was the place / to cel-e-brate / on Feb-ru-ary / twenty-eight.) A bulletin board featured photos of Nation of God musical groups playing before the Israeli soldiers in Lebanon and several letters of commendation from the Israeli Army for their performances before the troops. I nodded toward stacks of amplifiers, instruments, electronic equipment. "Only the best," Amadiah declared. "Only the best."

The evening, with a gala concert and their Messiah granting merit awards to Brothers of Merit, would bring Brotherhood Week to a grand climax. It was obvious that Amadiah was one of the hopefuls. Could I stay?

I checked my watch; it was already after 3:00. I thought not, but there was one visit more I wanted to make, if possible. Not Ben-Ami Carter or any of the princes. What I wanted to see was the Nation's school. Amadiah brightened: "Let's see what we can do to oblige."

In short order we were entering the Divine Library and talking with the school principal–Divine Librarian. He was about 35 and quite personable. I do not imagine that anyone else came to visit him all that day. I learned that the school's curriculum emphasized Nation religious teachings and foreign languages. "Languages are important to us," he explained. "We have to talk to lots of foreign people." The pedagogic philosophy required much memorization and articulation. Ronald Reagan would have found a great deal here to his taste. The principal struck me, however, as a genuinely caring man, a factor that goes far indeed in any school. Though the Nation had attracted some college-educated blacks (like Wayne Stater Amadiah), the only higher education the graduates of this school could expect would be the studies in the Divine College Graduate School. I had fallen in with a system as encapsulated as that of the Amish—or the *haredim*.

The shelves of the library were stuffed with the obvious culls and gleanings of recruits of the sect. Lots of black consciousness material; nothing patently anti-Semitic caught my eye. I could not suppress a chuckle at a pile of copies of *The Plain Truth*, monthly organ of the Armstrong evangelical empire. "We find material to support the way we see things in lots of places," the principal noted. "Of course, we don't *agree* with all the things it says in there."

After Amadiah arranged with the principal for me to visit the school when classes would be in session, I bade him goodbye. I sincerely hoped that he would win a coveted award that evening. In the park below the housing area I passed an exhibition of tumbling and gymnastics. Brotherhood Day was still in full, energetic swing out there at the edge of Dimona. In short order I arrived at the Egged bus station, a pensive returnee to the Land of Israel.

Neither the Hebrews of Dimona nor even less the Jews seem all that interested in a Brotherhood Day that Frank Sinatra might have crooned about. As far as I could determine, not a single local, bona fide Moroccan showed up to share in the high jinx or to visit the displays put on by the Nation of God on that Brotherhood Day. And this after 15 years of propinquity! The loss is patently mutual, but I think I know who are the greater losers. It is not a pleasant realization.

Later in 1984 about 14,000 Ethiopian Jews were, in a clandestine, then much-publicized operation, flown out of Sudan to Israel. Most Israelis were elated by this dramatic rescue of fellow Jews in distress. The curious and remarkable reaction of Yeroham's Mayor Baruch Elmakias made national news: he informed absorption officials and the Israeli press that he would lay his body down in the center of the highway in order to prevent any Falashas from being transported to Yeroham and settled there. He later clarified his statement with the explanation that his motive had not been racial prejudice; rather it was that Yeroham already bore too heavy a burden of unemployment. This explanation, however, was slow to catch up with his outburst.

At the start of 1986, about 18 months after my daytrip to Northeast Africa, Melvyn Coleman had his first black successors in Yeroham: five young Ethiopian *olim*, their wives and babies moved into an apartment house in Yeroham's Giva neighborhood. They did not, by the way, have to push aside Mayor Elmakias' dead body. They enrolled in the art program at Ramat Hanegev College. Indeed, two of them are highly accomplished artists, perhaps the most skillful of all the Ethiopian ceramicists who have arrived in Israel. Their plans are to remain at the college for at least two years.

Jewish Agency officials have settled Ethiopians in almost all the Negev cities and towns—Kiryat Gat, Ashkelon, Beersheba, Arad, Mitzpe Ramon, and now Yeroham. (Only problematic Dimona, for obvious reasons, has so far not benefited from this latest wave of *aliya*.) Yeroham's new, black arrivals *daven* from time to time at our "American" synagogue—Congregation Afikim Hanegev. In spite of the Mayor's earlier remarks, in spite of doubts that are repeatedly raised by Israel's official Orthodox rabbinate as to the full-fledged Jewishness of the Ethiopian arrivals (a question of admitted complexity), the reception of these five families in Yeroham has been beyond reproach. They are, by all accounts, quite content here and, as far as I am aware, are fully accepted by my fellow townspeople as Jews. As Melvyn Coleman, formerly Shamur, once put it, "the vibes in Yeroham are good." That, I hope and believe, is pretty close to the plainest truth about Zionism and racism in Israel.

In the summer of 1985 came ambivalent word from overseas that the F.B.I. had issued indictments against 25 Nation of God members in America on charges involving stolen airplane tickets and credit cards, forged passports, and bank fraud. At fingering and exposing his former brethren, Melvyn Coleman, I suspect, has been as good as his word. Their conviction, indeed, their guilt, would not come as a surprise. On the other hand, Amadiah Ben-Yehuda and his fellow Saints and streetsweepers of Dimona stoically await the day when there will be "a laying on of hands upon the people of the Lord, and all hell will break loose." I have come to know and like Amadiah better than any black man since Lionel Williams. It is not a pleasant prospect.

Israel is far smaller in reality than most Americans—Jews

or Gentiles—can possibly appreciate. As the Bedouin have learned, there just is not much land available for the asking. Nevertheless, I refuse to accept that Israel is too small for these 1,500 American, health-and-religious, black eccentrics who generally tend to their roses and radishes and have made it over the Jordan to Zion. If it were up to me, I would take the calculated risk that as their end-of-days recedes by inches into the future, they would continue to work, to celebrate, and to make their genuinely unique contribution to this much-chosen, tight little land. In this hope, however, I am not very optimistic.

HEAVYWEIGHT
VISITORS FROM
JERUSALEM

That first week of February proved a time of unlikely configurations. I did not that chilly Thursday evening much want to be outside hefting aloft one-half of a floppy, two-poled picket sign, even one that direly proclaimed (in Hebrew) YOU SHALL NOT INHERIT THE LAND WITH BLOOD ON YOUR HANDS. At 46, surely I was getting a touch old for this uncivil sort of thing. But then, just a few weeks before I had completed my most recent stretch of reserve duty—a mock, four-day exercise during which we elderlies routed "the enemy" who presumably had infiltrated our huge military airport. "Civics" in Israel is not, after all, the exclusive reserve of the young.

I stood among 15 others well back under an arcade between Shekem and Bank Hapoalim in Yeroham's central plaza. Could I already have lived here for seven years! It seemed incredible. The last time I had "demonstrated" on this plaza was four years previously on a Yom Atzmaut—Israel's Independence Day—when I had stood more or less at attention for a two-hour, mid-day stint in front of a ceremonial flame, unloaded M-16 in ceremonial readiness.

It had been hot. Until I was relieved, except for the buzzing flies on that occasion I had stood alone. This time a knot of police clustered some 20 paces away, a barrier between our line of 15 and the crowd that ranged between 60 and 75 persons. Nearly all of them at first confusedly noticed, then pointedly ignored us. They had come to see and hear the man whose

234

banner features a raised, clenched fist: Kach founder and maximum leader, Member of Knesset Rabbi Meir Kahane. Over lunch in our home just two days before, Yehuda Amichai, widely acknowledged as Israel's foremost poet, had commented sardonically that "Judaism, you know, can keep you busy nearly all of the time with things you should be doing." And was not that also one of its prime attractions?, I had offered. Yes . . . and no. It depended, he thought, upon temperament, upon circumstance. Still, this evening it struck me forcibly that it was one sort of thing to have demonstrated in the anonymous, adversary Sixties at New York's Whitehall Street Induction Center or Central Park's Sheep Meadow; it was something else again to "come out" among the 6,500 residents of this mostly Moroccan town. Not all that many "peaceniks" are holed up in these overcrowded apartment blocks—the *shikunim* of Yeroham. I doubt whether more than a handful would grant even an attenuated connection between Torah Judaism and standing among this group of post-adolescents in order to picket Rabbi Meir Kahane. A quick check: yes, by at least a dozen years, I was the oldest among them.

Kahane and Amichai, alternative species of Israeli Jew: radically antithetical embodiments of the country's contours and destiny. Within a space of 48 hours, both had journeyed from Jerusalem to my remote desert town simply to talk to people, to cast their perspective, to project a future—to *move* them. Every poll, every professional observer sees Kahane's vision as the more ascendant. There has been for some time—for all time?—an undeclared contest for the very soul of this people and this country. That Amichai and Kahane are among those who have signed on for the duration, there can be no doubt. I reflected that I was one of a tiny handful of Yerohamites to have attended to them both. For whatever it was worth, I took what wry, little pleasure I could in the private irony it afforded.

Before a crowd, Kahane—his voice rasping across the growing darkness like a dull file—was a better specimen of a demagogue than I had expected. It was the first time I had viewed him in person. Here in the open air, on a raised platform before a crowd of supporters, he was plainly in his most effective element. He filled the plaza with his amplified rant: "At the United Nations, in America, and now here in the Land of Israel, it is we Jews who are the suckers. It's time that we stopped being the world's *freirim*. Give the power to me, and you'll see how it will end soon enough." There is nothing the typical Israeli can bear less well than to discover himself a *freir*. Like a resurrected Joe McCarthy, Meir Kahane is inerrantly on the gutty target. Senator and Rabbi: along with Yassir Arafat, why do so many peddlers of fear and hate seem to wear permanent 5:00 o'clock shadows?

In contrast, Yehuda Amichai, at 60 about a decade Kahane's senior, is soft-spoken, diffident, almost courtly in manner. It would be wildly incongruous to see him on an open-air grandstand. At his Yemin Moshe home in Jerusalem the month before, I had spoken to him briefly about my own life as a writer in isolated Yeroham. "I'd like very much to visit with you to talk to students there," he had surprisingly volunteered. It was soon clear that for Amichai the Negev still exuded an aura of his youthful exploits in battle in the War of Independence. "I like the desert very much," he repeated. I was not sluggish to take up his generous offer.

Since Amichai does not drive, I found myself the Tuesday morning of his arrival striding toward the *sherut* taxi terminal in Beersheba to pick him up. A bit late, I stalked right past my man. Inconspicuous in a workingman's corduroy cap, he sat sipping an espresso at the terminal café and, smiling gently, called out my name while I was apprehensively darting among the tables, looking for his traces. I was relieved but suffered a sudden qualm of misgiving: some years before I had taught part-time in the Yeroham high school. The students can be . . . well . . . cannibals. I feared the worst for the day and for our mild visitor.

The demonstration against Kahane had been organized almost in the last minutes by my indefatigable neighbor Leah Shakdiel, the *datiya*, Ashkenazia, Labor Party member of the Yeroham City Council with whom I had fruitlessly collaborated six months earlier in trying to frustrate the Green Patrol in their wars against the Bedouin.

"I just couldn't live with myself if Kahane had come here and we had done nothing at all," she explained. Nearly all of us standing in a row supporting our verse placards were *datiim*. The young men wore knitted *kippot*, an anomaly Kahane probably had not faced very often. The knitted *kippa* is part of the regulation uniform of the right-wing Gush Emunim settlers among whom Kahane has considerable sympathy and support. Especially in Israel is it a dangerous thing to judge every kook by his cover.

Leah and members of a B'nei Akiva settlement group (*Nahal*), which is doing its military service working in Yeroham (the first such *datiim–nahalnikim* in Israel), had stayed awake most of the night before to fashion these signs and placards. Nearly all the citations were biblical passages. One exception: FORTY YEARS AFTER AUSCHWITZ, FASCISM WILL NOT TRIUMPH IN ISRAEL. Unfortunately, the effect of our religious opposition to Kahaneism was largely nullified by our ethnic composition: save for Samy (a teller at Bank Hapoalim) and a few friendly teenagers, all of us were Ashkenazim.

Leah, an elected public official, after all, had the day before demanded that the local police show her Kahane's official permit to hold a public rally. They had refused point-blank: "Are you serious? He's a Member of the Knesset!" Moreover, the police chief decided that Leah had applied too late to conduct a legal counter-demonstration. (It appeared that the unseriousness of being a mere woman more than counterbalanced the strength of her public office.) All that we protestors were legally entitled to do would be to stand passively, in silence, at a discreet distance from the speaker.

Since Kahane thrives on invective repartee, this seeming setback turned out, I think, to be a disguised advantage and our best tactic. Several times that evening Kahane would turn in our direction and insistently bait us to retort in kind to his ugly sarcasm: "MAPAMNIKIM! PALMACHNIKIM! SHMUTZ-NIKIM! *They* are the same ones who ripped the *kippot* from off the heads of the Yemenites when they first reached the Land of

Israel in the Fifties. *They* purposely settled them on the *kib-butzim* of Hashomer Hatzair where they would have to eat pork. *That* was their idea of absorption to Israel."

Could anyone believe that he was talking about *us!* The charge was so absurd, we were tempted to laugh. And again . . . and again—"MAPAMNIKIM! PALMACHNIKIM! SHMUTZNIKIM!"

*I*n the hushed, expectant classroom sat perhaps 60 students, a dozen teachers, and several visitors. The principal was away on *miluim*, leaving it to Ronit, a nervous, young litera-ture teacher to receive the distinguished guest and to make the brief introduction. Staring out from the blackboard was a multicolored rainbow of a greeting—WELCOME, YEHUDA AMICHAI!—and a poster of the text of one of his short poems.

After Ronit briefly concluded, Amichai strode calmly to the front of the large room and quietly entered upon his talk in a mild but authoritative voice. I covertly watched the students' faces; every word was closely attended. I turned again toward the ex-Palmachnik, poet–teacher. There was, of course, a close resemblance, but his lined face no longer was quite the same as the more youthful one of our first acquaintance: on the dust jacket of his novel from the 1960s—*Not of This Time, Not of This Place*—that had accompanied me to *miluim* just a bit over a year before. Still, with hair a close-cropped gray and strength in his gesticulating hand, Amichai presented in his own way a strong platform figure. I had no real cause for ap-prehension: he had stood before classrooms of students for all of his working life. A practiced hand.

I felt freer to pay closer attention to what he was saying. What, anyway, did he want these high schoolers to hear? His central theme seemed to deal with reality and relativity. "Mythic truth has a power of its own. Rachel, for example, is not really buried at the site in Bethlehem that we call 'Rachel's Tomb.' Nevertheless, that too is the correct site. [What really would these unsophisticated youngsters make of that?, I won-dered.] The fool is the one who insists on his truth to the ex-clusion of others. But after all, truth, the very meaning of words, beauty—all these are relative values." A disarming man, Amichai was utterly charming this audience of local kids—hardly a stronghold of poetry—by declaring most simply what he held to be most true. He was a good strategist. He stood for them as an emissary from a public, larger realm: a name in a book they had studied so as to pass their *bagrut* exam had come in Yeroham to life. It was a kind of magic. Why really had this quiet poet set aside a day to journey to talk to these adolescents? His fee was the ridiculously low standard set by the Hebrew Writers Association, which, a member in good standing, he apologetically, later was obliged to request. That could hardly be *it*. No, as it would be two days later with my friend Leah, the reluctant organizer of counter-demonstrations, this was rather a question of a personal and civic obligation. Amichai, like Noam Cohen and Ezra Kofrey of the Neve Tsedek troupe when they came to play Yeroham almost a year earlier, believed it worth his while that these students become less certain of what they thought they believed, become less dogmatic. He wanted them to ask their teachers and elders the fundamental, perennial questions.

More or less a man of the Left, Amichai is not a political writer in the way of A. B. Yehoshua, Natan Zach, or even Amos Oz. His politics of ambiguity, of equilibrium, of poise are a match for his poetics. He had won over these schoolchildren first by materializing like a miracle from the pages of their texts and then by expressing, seemingly without reserve, what he felt to be important and true.

Amichai is Kahane's egregious *freir*; Kahane is Amichai's perfect fool.

G oaded by Kahane's persistent heckling, a group of smirking teenagers approached us with sneers and threats. Two held a makeshift sign six inches in front of the one held aloft by me and my 19-year-old daughter Jennifer (performing at the time her two years of national service in Yeroham in the framework of Sherut Leumi—a sort of Israeli domestic version of the Peace Corps). I was getting a bit edgy. Often enough Kahane rallies close with violent encounters, and the twin poles that supported our large sign gave threat to act like lightning rods. Jen and I stood our ground; in response to the kids' provocative remarks, we smiled and, mindful of the nearby police, said absolutely nothing.

I again reflected that really I did not at all want to be standing there, that had it not been for Leah's involvement and appeal—and Jen's—I would surely have kept my distance from this visitation by the man from Kach. I might almost have allowed, have persuaded myself, that even Meir Kahane's racist rant deserved its open hearing. (Had I not heard just two days before that truth, meaning, and beauty were relative? Had I not listened approvingly?) Would I really end up that evening bloodied in some stupid melee?

I was suddenly struck by something that made me smile with private pleasure. There was in all of this business something that was so fitting, so appropriate and redemptive that it almost dissipated my forebodings. This occasion marked a full circle, a milestone of sorts—for a "Jew of the Sixties" (one of my firmest imaginative projections of myself). It was *not*, after all, his first father–daughter demonstration. Fully 19 years earlier, Marcia and I had wheeled our 8-month-old baby Jennifer back and forth for three hot hours in front of a Purity supermarket in Fresno, California. And again the next day. And the next. Her carriage supported a placard that boldly portrayed a stylized Aztec eagle and a message. DON'T BUY GALLO! SUPPORT THE N.F.W.A.! Though he said little, I recalled that my father-in-law, a prominent local contractor, had not been terribly enthusiastic about the leisure-time activities of his summertime guests. Jen had been a placid little demonstrator. I smiled; like Yehuda Amichai, essentially she had not much changed.

Burly Chaim Goldberg arrived to join the ranks of our Kahane protest. A Yale grad in linguistics who was now teaching computers in Yeroham's high school, he smiled reassuringly toward me. He held his poster aloft: DO NOT OPPRESS THE STRANGER IN YOUR MIDST! Under the circumstances, it could just as well have been an allusion to us protesting Ashkenazim as to the Arabs of Israel. For frozen minutes, the threatening presence of the two pro-Kahane smirkers seemed to shadow over us.

Leah and Moti (one of the *Nahal* youngsters) had alerted several cops to the provocation. (I waited impatiently to see whether the local fuzz would prove to be "officers" or "pigs." Tell me, which side are you on, boys, so I can get on juggling these oh-so-relative words?) Since my backyard-to-backyard Yeroham neighbor is Yosi, the chief of the local constabulary, I felt reasonably secure. It was a gratifying encounter: after the briefest of scuffles, the police, tearing their offensive sign in the process, moved the harassers to the side. No bruises tonight. Not yet, anyway.

*I*t was time for questions from the audience. An eager, pretty girl in the second row asked Amichai whether he believed in God. The poet stopped wearing a *kippa* in his early teens, but his poems frequently deal with, address, or accuse God or "God." Obviously he had heard this question more than once in the past. "Well, call It God or some Higher Power. The word doesn't much matter, does it? What is important is the manner in which men and women treat their fellow men and women. What is stupid is the nonsense about whether there are ancient bones buried beneath the hotel that the ultra-orthodox are trying to prevent getting built in Tiberias."

Yes, but wasn't there something disingenuous about the way he had treated, had deflected her question? What poet truly believes that "the word doesn't much matter"?

"All abstractions are relative," he continued. "What is 'beautiful'? Today it could be a new Opel or a jet plane. Why should it just be a sunset or a flower? Words inflate like money: the more they're printed, the more value they lose. Consider a serious conversation between you and your boyfriend." The girl was all attention. Old pro Amichai smiled.

"'I love you.' says he.

'Really?,' you reply.

'Really, really?'

'Really, really, really . . .?'"

The bell rang out, but almost everyone stayed seated. All smiles, Ronit announced that the talk could proceed for another twenty minutes. In a subdued, flat intonation, Amichai proceeded to read three of his short poems. The most moving was "God Has Pity on Kindergarten Children" whose ruthless "God" is deficient in pity for His grownup children.

> . . . But perhaps he will watch over true lovers
> and have mercy on them and shelter them
> like a tree over the old man
> sleeping on a public bench.
>
> Perhaps we too will give them
> the last coins of charity
> that Mother handed down to us,
> so that their happiness may protect us
> now and on other days.
>
> (Stephen Mitchell's translation)

Attention in the classroom was exquisite.

Before going to my home for lunch, we briefly strolled around Yeroham. At Ramat Hanegev College, where he was to speak in the afternoon, Amichai was graciously complimentary about a local artist's desertscapes. Ten minutes later he gamely permitted "Tuny," a Yemenite who chairs the Likud in Yeroham, to read his palm. Two charmers! Later Amichai was to praise my wife's cooking and a piece of my writing. (Really? Really, really?)

A poet's tabletalk: "How can someone like Reagan, who's never been under fire, order others to fight and shoot? It's crazy . . . immoral! [For Amichai, there resides in human nature something that is flawed or perverse or cruelly superficial.] What is accepted now is certain to be reacted against by the next generation. Take for example Dylan Thomas, now largely ignored. You may be sure that in a few years some Yale professor will rediscover his genius. [He himself was shortly to travel to the States for a Thomas-pioneered, poetry-reading tour on selected campuses, mainly in California.] Whenever, wherever I travel, I meet ex-Israelis by the dozens. For me, Israel is the only place to be a Jew and not to have continually to think about it. [I demur; he pursues his own point.] Jews are married to Israel. We are past the honeymoon stage, past the romance, but it is a true marriage. Such is my Zionism. I am beyond illusions. [Words made to be eaten? What greater illusion than that?] In America, people without the slightest intention of doing so every year repeat 'Next year in Jerusalem.' Now *that* is what I call 'cynicism.'"

"*This* is the land of the Jewish people. Whoever is unclear about that, whoever does not *know* that is the enemy of the Jewish people. *My* enemy. The Arabs have dozens of lands. GIVE ME THE POWER AND I SHALL SEND THEM THERE. [Pause] Now really, I am not an Arab-hater. Not at all. I admire them. The fact is that the Arabs still know how to defend the honor of the tribe, of their people. WHAT HAS HAPPENED TO *JEWISH* TRIBAL HONOR? WHERE IS IT? Go to Tel Aviv, and you will find out: all of the prostitutes are our own Jewish women; all of the pimps are Arabs!"

A soldier on reserve duty sidled up to me. "*Kol hakavod!,*" he muttered rapidly. "More power to you! A lot of people here really agree with you about Kahane, but they're afraid to say anything." (Really?)

I grimaced agreeably and looked around for other bashful supporters. Actually, there were fewer people on the plaza than I had feared. An encouraging sign? Sixty people was not all that much of a turnout. In the last election, the Kach slate had received fewer than 20 Yeroham ballots, about the same as for peace candidate Lova Eliav on whom I had expended my vote. (Since Eliav had not garnered even one per cent of the total vote, his votes, under Israel's proportional representation system, were of no account.)

I was distantly acquainted with one of Kahane's Yeroham balloters: Bob, an unstable American musician in his 30s. He was unmarried and had, for a time anyway, been ambiguously "hip." Shortly after his bizarre engagement to a Yeroham girl had fallen through, he disappeared from town only to turn up on Election Day to cast his ballot. Hip Bob was resplendent in colorful *kippa* and ritual fringe *tsitsiot* dangling from the four corners of his shirt. A *ba'al tshuva*, one of the newly "religious," Bob was one of the reborn pioneers of the Land of Israel. Though he now lived in a Gush Emunim settlement in the Territories, his name was still to be found on the voter registration rolls of Yeroham. His was one franchise that had swollen the local ranks of cranks for Kach.

"Just give me the power, my friends, and those Mapam-nikim, Palmachnikim, and Shmutznikim will get the message soon enough. [Kahane really loved to lay into those rotten . . . *nikim*. Wasn't that also a conscious takeoff on that Goldwater slogan of 1964—Send a Message to Washington!—I wondered?] Those people dare to call *me* a fascist! Those people back there with those signs"—*us*—"now they, THEY are the real fascists."

I fully expected that whatever the evil that Amichai thinks is fundamentally defective in human nature would rise to the surface, reveal its ugly face and shape, and make its running entrance on that unmistakable cue. But except for a slight turning of heads, absolutely nothing happened! Perhaps, after all, demonstrating on one's own turf had its compensations. I had not been particularly happy to see among the faces surrounding Kahane the Assistant Principal at my 7-year-old's elementary school, the more amiable co-owner of the hardware store, or several students I had once taught in the high school. On the other hand, I *knew* them, and they *knew* me. That made head-bashing a much harder proposition. Leah, Chaim, Samy, I, Jen, the others were, after all, Yeroham townspeople: like that fat soldier who clearly enjoyed harassing Yeroham area Bedouin, Meir Kahane was the greater outsider.

At the college after lunch, Amichai suggested to the 30 or so students in attendance that, set in a display case under a spotlight at the Louvre, even a glass of tea would make visitors gape and gasp in aesthetic wonder. Yes, he felt a current of cynicism about human beings, but perhaps man's inherent flaw or superficiality—perhaps it was childishness—could yet be redeemed by the manner in which he related to others. There were still, he thought, concrete grounds for legitimate hope.

Later, a religious woman who is an enthusiastic admirer of Amichai's poetry volunteered to chauffeur us back to the taxi terminal in Beersheba. When we arrived, the poet automatically (or was it that inner, impish perversity, in which he believed, rising to the surface?) reached out for her hand in order to bid her his farewell. I just barely suppressed smiling at her in her fluster. Religious women just don't go around taking the hands of men into their own. Confused, she proved unable to withdraw her hand from his. Yes—a genuine poet, a powerful charmer! Was there a connection?

"I had a wonderful time here," Amichai concluded. "If we can arrange it, I'd like to come down again next year, even for a few days." How many American poets of the first rank would be willing to spend "even a few days" talking to young people in Twin Falls, Yuma, or Mankato? It does give one pause.

"*T*onight was my first time in Yeroham, my friends, but I promise you it will not be my last. Spread the word to your friends. GIVE ME THE POWER, and things here will change." The rally closed with gravel-throated Kahane leading all of us in a wearisome version of the Israeli national anthem—*Hatikvah*—The Hope. Both his supporters and we demonstrators joined in. What could be the nature of the hope that this man was offering those people clustered around his podium?

Later, Leah told me that many of those who approached her during the demonstration had scanned her placard only to ask, "Are you for Kahane or against him?" Not a very encouraging response. Still later I learned something that further mitigated my pleasure at the meagerness of the turnout: that same Thursday evening yet a third heavyweight had been present and speaking in Yeroham: Aharon Abuhatzeira, leader of the ethnic-Moroccan Tami Party and nephew of a much-revered Moroccan wonder rabbi. There was no way to tell—until the next time?—how much greater Kahane's crowd would have been had there been fewer evening diversions.

Some parting words from a middle-aged woman to my daughter: "Just you wait! I hope you get raped by an Arab. Then you'll change your mind." Save for that low verbal thrust, there was that night no violence in Yeroham.

*S*uccessful in sending but a single representative to the Knesset (Kahane himself) in the 1984 general elections, Kach, everyone grants, feeding on a growing, often unacknowledged fund of fear and anxiety, will do better in the future. There is little doubt that it will attract many more votes in Israel's many Yerohams.

There have been times when I have harbored an indulgent image of my life and self in this small, Moroccan-flavored town in the Negev: a kind of very minor-scale Lawrence Durrell or Robert Graves literary expatriate sort in a Mediterranean clime. It is a literary conceit as well as a personal one; it has sometimes helped me to maintain working psychic distance from some of the absurdity that comes and goes with the territory, with this Land of Israel. It is fun, it is consoling, but it is essentially a fiction. The forces that drew me here in no way resemble whatever propelled a Graves or a Durrell. Even could I better immure myself, my first- and third-graders in the local schools, my daughter (now at university) behind a picket line, my son studying some of each year in a *yeshiva* (and for the rest in military uniform on the Lebanese border), and my daily commuter, wage-earning wife comprise an undertow, an irresistible tide of reality, a splash in the face of too-private, romanticized musings.

Yehuda Amichai plans to return next year: Yeroham is a legitimate fruit of his true marriage. The sometime cynical charmer is also a loving parent. Nor dare I doubt that Meir Kahane will also return. He is in it for Jewish honor, for the duration—and for blood.

I knew exactly what I thought I meant when once I flashed DON'T BUY GALLO! signs toward shoppers' faces: Don't be a fink! Buy Christian Brothers instead! However, the alternatives, the consequences, the muzzy upshot of YOU SHALL NOT INHERIT THE LAND WITH BLOOD ON YOUR HANDS are more elusive, more complex, more *personal* by far. Only a fool would be naïvely optimistic about the outcome of these daily skirmishes, of the long-term encounters between *hatikva* and despondency that are occurring all over Israel. History may well decide that the biggest *freirim* are those who have already discounted the result.

SUPPER MUSIC
AND ZIONIST
JAZZ

Summer is when those on-the-move move. Seattle, Phoenix, Israel—it's the same all over. Or nearly so. Who could have imagined that within weeks of each other, from a single small, North Negev outback, three families would be moving to the same suburban, largely American-Jewish enclave? As might be conjectured, it wasn't all that coincidental. First the couple I'll call the Arenbergs flew off on an academic sabbatical. Then there are those I'll call the Hechts, close neighbors for these five years. As long as Yair Hecht was going abroad for graduate training anyway, why not choose the area where his old friends, the Arenbergs, would be touching down?

Finally, there were the Barzulais who were selected as official government overseas emissaries—*shlichim*. What could be more natural than that they should select from the list of all possible destinations, instead of, say, Buenos Aires or Vancouver, the same locale as that of their old neighbors? Still, I confess that it did seem queer: whereas many native Israelis nonchalantly toss off Hebrish inelegancies like "slowly, slowly," in the six years that we have known them, never once had we heard either Moshe or Simi Barzulai utter even a stray syllable of English.

The Arenbergs declared they would be away for at least one year or, as is often the case with Israeli academics, even possibly two. Moshe and Simi, as is normal for *shlichim*, intended to be gone for three years. But it was only when we invited Yair and Marge Hecht for a sendoff dinner that it broke with painful clarity that their sojourn in America-the-Golden for "an indefinite period" would probably be for keeps. For the first time in our five years of lively interaction, sentences froze in mid-air, words shivered and dropped with a soft, voiceless thud.

Not, to be fair, that they had been secretive, exactly. Like us all, they had voiced their full quota of gripes over inflation, reserve duty, banks, schooling, etc. True, they had sold their house, which was, we surmised, safer than subleasing it. There were, I suppose, other, clear enough signals that we must have tuned out and suppressed, for it was only when sharing a farewell meal, with Yair exhaling the air of a knight–pilgrim who had slain dentists and overcome dragons, whose quest was in view, that I fully realized that the Hechts were not any longer like the rest of us at all. Yair, at least, had made his peace, was cutting his losses, and bidding goodbyes to all that Zionist jazz.

In his late 20s, he was born in Israel, grew up in the States, and in his mid-teens was returned with his parents to Israel. In spirit, however, he had never returned. Ordained as a rabbi, he never since we knew him had pretended interest in a rabbinic or even a religiously observant life. It was as if his ordination had "put paid" to the force of some pressing, prior obligation. In Israel he had worked with delinquent teenagers as part of his army service, and later did some teaching.

Marge had come to Israel in her teens on her own to study in a women's *yeshiva* in Jerusalem. Unlike her husband, she preferred a religiously observant life. Frequently she would appear alone with the children on Shabbat at our local synagogue. She remained, we were aware, a Zionist. It was all too apparent that she was resigned but deeply uneasy in planning her latest new life. The United States had never been her goal when she left her parents—British colonials—behind to come to Israel, but plainly she saw no present alternative.

They have two children: a daughter and an infant son. As she wryly put it to my wife the next morning when bringing us a box of leftover coat hangers and spices, "I've kept him in this country nine years against his will. Now we'll just have to see what happens."

When a few years ago Israeli writer Amos Oz came to the end of his melancholic, base-touching tour, *In the Land of Israel*, he summed up with characteristic understatement: "The situation is not good." Oz was, of course, referring mainly to the chronic, gnawing, manifold abrasions of contact and distance between the Sephardim and the Ashkenazim, the Religious and the Secular, the Arab and the Jew, the Us and the Them. His touchstones then were Lebanon and Begin, both of which have since moved to the margins of Israeli public consciousness. Terror and an adversary economy now preoccupy us. "Us" includes nearly everyone; "Them"—the banks, the phone disservice, the government, the Arabs, the system, the guy who just pushed in front of me in line—is, alas, Israel Herself far too much of the time. A few hopeful signs have appeared, but "the situation" since Oz has written has not substantially altered.

Over cookies and coffee Yair described in vivid detail their recent close call at the American Embassy in Tel Aviv. His rendition already had the flavor of a twice-told tale, which would bear the refinements of many future tellings in America. They had already held their tickets for their flight two weeks thereafter. Leaving with their two little kids on the 5:30 A.M. bus, they had arrived at the Embassy at 8:30 to take their distant places in the waiting throng who stood outside in order to obtain their precious visas. Yair is a dual citizen, but ex-Brit Commonwealth Marge needed those special forms.

An anxious hour passed before they learned that they had surely made the trip in vain. Where was their proof of home ownership? Where was their bank account? On every hand were those who knew the score, who would surely make it big in America, who patronizingly informed them that their chances of being processed that day were ridiculously slim. As for obtaining their precious documents, well, the Hechts were positive greenhorns. It was hopeless.

Still, fatalistically, with scarce time for a return trip before their scheduled flight, they handed in what documentation they had . . . and waited. The kids fussed, fretted, cried. They held on. In the dank, afternoon heat of Tel Aviv, the crowd gradually melted. Yair likened themselves, the hundreds in the larger scene, to Jews in desperate Frankfurt, in despondent Vienna, waiting, waiting, waiting for their proper stamps and papers in the 1930s. (I winced at his grotesque similitude; he seemed not to notice.) With less than an hour to closing, the melodrama in Tel Aviv dissolved into comedy. Thirty inexplicable numbers in a row—including a lucky one held by Marge Hecht—were granted visas. *Deus ex machina.* Goodbye! Good luck! Time to lock up for the day!

Marge sat silently through Yair's recounting of their tale of good fortune. Their daughter chattered in Hebrew with our four-year-old. "Yael's English will surely improve. She'll even pick up an American accent."

"No doubt," we all agreed.

Our intercourse stumbled lamely. (Will her Hebrew survive at all?, I wondered.) Waves lapped at the edges, threatened to engulf the island of neutral terrain we had left to banter over. It was the meal after a return from the cemetery; we ate in silence.

The month before, while Marge had been visiting her parents, Yair had flown to the States and purchased for them a two-family house. Oh, oh, oh was he eager to put Israel behind! Just a tangle of thorns to be tweased, a mistake to be rectified.

A toast, of sorts, over *kiddush* wine: "Gather your degrees where you may, and come back as soon as you can!" We all winced, then laughed at the wan formality.

"We'll do our best," Yair murmured. Earlier they had told of one of Marge's relations. A well-known figure in the rabbinic world in his own country, he had for two desultory years after making *aliya* sold computers. Six months before he had begun to answer advertisements listed in *The Jerusalem Post*: congregations in Ireland, in California, in South Africa all sent him tickets for interviews, all wanted to hire him. The future was rosy. Only Israel appears to suffer from a glut of rabbis.

Yair had had resort to a harmless subterfuge. He felt amply justified. His departure was just three days off, a week ahead of that of Marge and the children. Three weeks before, however, he had received a call-up notice for military reserve duty. He had had his troubles with the Israeli army. He had served as a medic in Lebanon—once. Medics in the Israeli army have considerably more reserve duty to perform than the normal citizen. Next tour of duty, he refused to go to Lebanon. There followed a month in a military jail. Finally, promises as to where he would be asked to serve were extended. On some of them, he felt, the army had reneged. What Yair had to look forward to was nearly half-a-lifetime of military hassle—not an easy prospect.

No Israeli over 17, however, may depart from the country without permission from the army. Yair applied for and received his "postponement." Nevertheless, just in case of any unforeseen military roadblocks at Ben-Gurion Airport, the Hechts were taking no chances. They would be traveling separately.

Ben-Gurion! *Ben-Gurion!* The intent was surely that the very first place that immigrants felt the firmness of the Land beneath their feet would uplift them with his name and vision. No, the current situation is not so very good.

A few days later it took me five trips to carry home our last gift from the Hechts: their 30-volume *Encyclopaedia Americana*. It was too heavy to ship, too dated to be of any use upon their return, whenever . . .

A recent May, nearly a year later, I was visiting with my sister who lives on Manhattan's West Side. It was midway through my month's stay when she invited to dinner a child-free couple in their early 30s whom I'll call Tamar and Dale Berger. Dale, I was cued beforehand, was just completing his doctorate in a specialized branch of public administration. After all the years of graduate school penury, he was obviously inhaling the first, heady draughts of the debutant: he was being ardently wooed. The last my sister had heard, his professional choice had narrowed between lucrative Atlanta and a cozy academic seat. I was introduced, "in for a while from Israel."

"Oh, we've heard all about you," said Tamar.

She was dark-haired, attractive, exuded an air of subdued intelligence, but her eyes betrayed a flicker of anxiety. I accidentally caught them several times glancing over the rim of her glass with an edge of apprehension. I'd been told that she had come to New York alone, knowing no one, and had scrambled from teaching part-time in a Jewish day-school to a tenured track at a major university. For over a year she had been giving private, classy Hebrew lessons to my brother-in-law, and the couples had become friendly. The dinner was by way of a career sendoff and Manhattan farewell.

"I plan to keep on with a solid investment program right from the start," Dale was relating to my brother-in-law. No time to waste on the peripheral. Both held drinks; they were going over familiar ground. "It'll cost us at the start to get established, but after that, if I do it right, I could reach a million in equity in six to eight years." He seemed to wait for confirmation.

"Well, if it's to be Atlanta, look up Manny Perlman when you're settled. If I ask him, he'll take you on even if you're a small account at first. I'll call him about you."

Dale was hardly nostalgic about graduate school pleasures-on-the-cheap. Evidently, my brother-in-law had assumed the avuncular role of financial mentor. I played with my drink. At my sister's call, we drifted into the dining room.

"A college town has, of course, an atmosphere where we'd find our niche right away," Dale pursued, "and the set-up, the facilities, the immediate responsibilities are attractive . . ."

"Right away—or never," Tamar countered, "and the Jewish community is so . . . uh . . . insubstantial."

"True." It was clear, however, that they had actually reached their decision, even concurred, but threatened nevertheless to lead us over their feints and skirmishes anyway. "When we looked over the college town, we really enjoyed ourselves and got pretty enthusiastic—until we considered what it would be like after a few years."

"So it will be Atlanta," my sister, a trifle impatiently, concluded for him.

"How, really, can we turn it down?," he shrugged. "Sixty-five thou to start and a clear road for moving into the top spot before I'm forty. But next week will be the first time I'll be taking Tamar out to look Atlanta over. We don't know a soul there. It might give her hives."

Tamar looked up toward me. "What do you think, Haim? Would you choose Atlanta?"

"Well, from my point of view, of course, the two places are not really all that different." But that was tactless. I pressed restart. "I've never lived in either place. I have friends in both. The couple in Atlanta is two Americans, about your ages, who met and married in Israel. He was the head of the original group, the *garin* that Marcia and I had joined before making *aliya* to Israel in '76. They returned to the States four or five years ago to get higher degrees and make a bundle to afford an Israeli mortgage. But instead they bought a house and boat about two years ago, so who knows? I know they use Hebrew at home so their little girl won't forget how to speak it. You'd like them, I think. I'll ring them that you're coming if you like."

"Yes, thank you," Tamar said eagerly. She seemed really to mean it. Perhaps Atlanta was more terrifying for her than I could imagine. "You know, it's taken nearly ten years for me to feel at home in New York. The idea of moving around in America make me very nervous."

"I can understand that," I concurred.

"I've worked very hard to make a place for myself. There's lots of competition, lots," she was smiling, "of Israeli academics who can teach Hebrew. I am really very good, but I made it on hard, hard work."

"That she did," my brother-in-law confirmed, "even if you can't tell much from my Hebrew chit-chat."

"And I've succeeded! In another two or three years, I'd have tenure. For me Atlanta, Denver, you name it—all would mean starting over from scratch. It's really very painful."

"Atlanta is, I think, where we'd want to be living," said Dale, "and it'd be nice to have some friendly contacts."

"My friend works with some Israel government trade office. His wife is a social worker."

My sister served up salmon steaks while my brother-in-law refilled our glasses.

"You know," Dale pursued a bit hesitantly, "we did look into the prospects in Israel. We both miss the country dreadfully. I could get work in my field, but what I was offered was a bad joke. I would have to take my place in line; if I were lucky, in twenty years those in front would have retired or moved to the States, all of which would give me a shot at a job with the responsibilities I'm being offered now by some of the topnotch units with the most up-to-date facilities here in the States. And the money!" He started to laugh, then to cough when a piece of fish stuck momentarily in his throat. It was so mirthful, we all joined in. "We'd be scrimping all of our lives, and we'd end up with nothing. What kind of sense would that make?"

There was a pause. It seemed to be my part to speak.

"Nonsense, I suppose," I said softly. "Unless you line your life up with it, no sense at all."

"Exactly," Dale agreed. "No sense at all."

The young couple began to edge toward departure immediately after the chocolate mousse and coffee. They had to pack for their trip.

"Terrific meal. Thank you," said Dale to his host and hostess.

Tamar assented, then turned to me. "It was really a pleasure meeting the brother we'd heard so much about. Also," she added, "it was nice that you didn't make us feel uncomfortable about not living anymore in Israel. It will," she added rapidly, "always be my real home." Her voice trailed off. "Maybe, some day . . ."

It certainly had proved less daunting dining with them than it had been with the Hechts. There were several obvious reasons for that, but in addition to these, maybe I'm just getting more accustomed to dealing with the varieties of *yordim*. They're not, I have to grant, all that different, after all, from you and me.

*L*ater that week I met Mordecai Arenberg at a coffee shop near the Frick Museum. He and Lucille were doing wonderfully. Yes, they missed Israel, our little town in particular, terribly, but Lucille just had one more year to finish off her M.A. in ceramics. Things there were really tough in Israel, weren't they?

Well, yes, I acknowledged, in many ways, but why dwell on it? And Yair and Marge? How were they all doing as suburban worthies?

"Absolutely terrific," he exclaimed. "You couldn't believe how well they're doing. They're both enrolled in graduate programs. Their kids are in Jewish day-schools and love it. And Yair spent nearly all of last year completely refurbishing the other half of the two-family house they'd bought. Can you believe that he sold it for about as much as they paid for the whole thing?"

"That's just great," I said perhaps too brusquely. I knew that they had not come to America primarily to make some killing in real estate, and I knew that Yair's conscientious-objector position, invoking a principle not well understood or even recognized in Israel, would, had they remained, have sentenced him to chronic, grinding conflict with military authority for years to come. "Give them my regards. We think of them whenever we pass their old house or look up something in their *Americana*."

No, the present prospects, the muddle, "the situation" in Israel are not good. It is only fools, deceivers, and stark blue believers—as well as, perhaps, the favored few who actually benefit by the skewed system—who would claim that the very notion of bugging out of Israel never, ever crosses their minds.

For the foreseeable future, the crowds will continue to converge each morning on Rehov Hayarkon in front of the American Embassy in Tel Aviv. Neither the Hechts nor the Bergers will be the last nice couple we will discover ourselves willy-nilly entertaining at a last supper. I wish all these people their success, but how could they not fill me with profound sadness? I believe in the law of averages and can extrapolate with ridiculous ease from the lives of distant cousins, of old friends and classmates, and from the early warning signals emitted by the lives of their painfully few children.

It is helpful, it is healthy, under the present circumstances it is a virtual necessity to adopt a long, broad perspective: historically, the situation for the Jewish people in the Jewish land has often, even usually been dire. For thousands of years, Jews have cocked their heads and tapped their fingers to the siren-chant of some version of America. A fraction have held; others, later on, return.

Our ear may, it must be granted, prove flat, our hearing grossly defective, a taste for this stuff passé, but we find that we have wagered merely our lives that, in the last analysis, it is the refrain of Zion that corresponds most closely to the urgent, vital beat of Jewish selfhood and our destiny as a people.

I have heard the variations on this theme that people abroad whistle and hum. Who truly cannot descry it as kitsch? Yet people are moved! Indeed, *they move.*

However, I think I know a great deal about what prospects the future holds for Marge and Yair's sunflower-blond kids in America. The situation is not good.

CODA.

STEALING HOME

I wanted to see the Statue of Liberty, which I hadn't seen since I was a boy, and I wanted to see simply the water itself, which Melville, I remembered, had come to stare at, pulled away from home toward the blankness he finally knew as God because he couldn't ever locate what he was supposed to love.

Frederick Busch
(*Invisible Mending*)

Nearly ten years had slipped past since I last visited this dream-lined place. Coalinga, population 6,500, is a neat, isolated town of parallel lines (presidents, colleges, trees) and overlapping circles (Rotary, Elks, Lions, Mormons). It is inset on a wedge of plateau before the highway noodles west to rolling country between California's elongated Central Valley and the Steinbeck-tinted, green salad tracts over toward the cold Pacific. During the time of our early-to-middle 30s, of the two kids' approaching their teens, it had for seven years been our home.

I had been aware from the start that choosing Coalinga meant playing out an insular version of the myth that that boy from the Bronx, who at Penn had tiptoed to a graduate degree in "American Civilization," had, along with generations of other Jewish-American kid fantasists, abducted and appropriated as his own. As dreams went (and it has), it did not seem illicit—or even especially fanciful. On the contrary, I saw few impediments to running with it as far as I pleased.

Just about as Far West as Marcia and I could push, Coalinga had also been about as deep into America as we could squirrel. The seven good years there were a descent into the pond, into the great Heidelberg tun, into the black, continental forest— an incursion, an exploration, a self-conscious performance that always, I knew, verged on parody. Only after five rapid years had passed, when we suddenly began to sense that Coalinga threatened engulfment, when I began to tingle at the specter of our bones' ultimate disposition into those soft, alluring, dull-brown hills, did we surprise Coalinga and startle ourselves by bolting farther from the morphinic bargain American Civilization painlessly exacts than we or anyone could have anticipated. It had suddenly become clear that crafty America had been playing for keeps.

For the past ten years we have made our place in Israel's Negev, once again, by design, in a town containing around 6,500 souls. Siren America still fitfully touches both raw imagination and black spleen. Like our "Moroccan," "Russian," and "British" neighbors, never before have we been so irremediably—and justly—marked by our native hue. But even when seething with the knowledge that our nearby branch of

Bank Leumi is our implacable foe, that "Israeli Civilization" daily threatens to transform itself into a higher kind of racket, still have we felt less than earlier in America the gutty tremors of self-betrayal. Until, that is, one recent spring . . .

I landed alone in Fresno on a Thursday to visit briefly with Marcia's family after having spent some weeks with my sister in Manhattan. After many seasons apart, Central Park, the Metropolitan Museum, Barnes & Noble and the Strand, new films, simply traversing 57th Street had been heady.

What had produced the deepest agitation, however, was a counter-current my eye collided with on the milk container each morning over corn flakes: a haunting photo of Nicole Byrner, age 6, of Pittsburgh, last seen 3/11/82. And smiling Kristopher Siegal, 8, La Grande, Ore., 8/12/82. In fact, every corner lamppost between 34th and 59th Sts. displayed photos, a grotesque Midtown Review updating itself monthly, of dozens of missing kids from all over the continent! A plague! I heard several mollifying explanations of the nature and extent of the situation, but Nicole, Kristopher, Cheryl Mahan (8, Saxonburg, Pa., 2/26/85—just 3 months before!), seemingly countless more, had bracketed, had tainted my reimmersion into Manhattan.

What sort of profound deceit had this place America practiced on its children? Formerly a student of its civilization, of late disowned, I had, I was forced to admit, lost vital touch.

Friday morning I borrowed my mother-in-law's Volkswagen and pointed it toward Coalinga. Several colleagues at the smalltown college, in the past companions and confederates with whom we had shared causes, losses, laughter, and foes, were there still. Two years before, Coalinga had intruded on my consciousness in totally unexpected fashion. The 7:00 A.M., Israeli English-language news reported that in the foothills of western Fresno County, very close to the town of Coalinga, a major earthquake had struck. *Coalinga!* The quake had rumbled down most of the turn-of-the-century brick downtown and caused extensive general damage. The oddest thing, however, was that the notorious fault was not that of subterranean San Andreas—sly, bandito menacer of fog-gold coast from San Francisco to L.A.—which ran about 20 miles west of town. No, the perpetrator was a heretofore unknown earth-breach, an altogether new cleft that ran eight miles to the east. American Civilization had been enclosed by fiercely contending, parallel flaws. Had not our decampment been mightily endorsed by signal events?

Coalinga and its earthquake turned out to be an unexpected boon, speculative capital, my writer's grubstake. In a ruminative article, I described how it felt to hear about California calamity on the Israeli news. The piece was accepted, and thus I closed out my nearly two-decade career as teacher. If I was ever to be "a writer"—a celebration of self that oddly, perversely never had flourished in America—this was the time. Now, two years after the event, I felt the urge to see rebuilt downtown, turn the corner of our old two-chimney house with the French doors, Dutch door, sliding doors, talk changes and stabilities with on-hold friends, track my old self—the Bronx-born English instructor—rounding the corner of Yale Avenue on a bicycle. Time enough had silted up. To Coalinga I was a debtor fallen in arrears. Surely there lurked no further danger.

I asked no directions, had no urge to consult the county roadmap in the glove compartment: the 60 miles southwest from Fresno are a stretch I had driven at least once a week for seven years. Shaking loose of Fresno, however, proved a queer self-embarrassment. Veering to skirt a block-long length of traffic held in tow by a crawling string of Santa Fe stock, I turned up what seemed a short hypotenuse cut abutting an irrigation canal, swerved again, and ten minutes later discovered myself heading north. *North!* I had stood Huck & Jim on their innocent heads. What demon of adversity, or silliness, was conspiring to thorn my decade's daytrip back?

Ten minutes later, however, sailing west on Whitesbridge Road, I found that things had righted themselves. Out in the country, nothing appeared to have changed. Golden Oldie KYNO exorcised my soul with Sam Cooke and Creedance Clearwater Revival, great shiny snatches of the Socking, Mocking Sixties as grapes yielded to cotton on either side of the highway. Fingers flicking the beat on the wheel, minutes miled the years into an ebony root beer float I could sweetly suck through the heavy white foam. The generator at Helm (whose lounging ten-galloned "wise men" still slumped on the bench outside the store and Chevron Station), then the turn after the country market at Five Points—*nothing had changed!*—and my heart was weightless as music in the night.

Could it have been that just a week before I had been so anguished because Bank Tefahot's Beersheba branch had two months running automatically billed our Bank Leumi account for mortgage payments I had already made *and then charged me interest*; so overwrought over Bank Leumi whose computerized teller had just swallowed our bank card ("a technical problem," the manager drawled over the phone), whose financial advisers had stuck us with thousands of their own bank's shares shortly before the October '83 crash froze our diminishing assets, who thereafter dallied over cashing a large banker's check for four days causing us to lose nearly $100 due to the fall in the exchange rate; so disgusted over Yeroham's home branch of Bank Hapoalim in whose lines I measured the teaspoons of my hours and months? These institutional termites, stalking relentlessly at my spirit and heels, have nibbled blindly at my Zionist vitals, eroded my Israeli well-being more than Arafat, Khomeini, or Assad could ever dream or hope. How really could Americans comprehend how gangrenous to the wounded Zionist corps it is every day to feel compelled to jig the best, new, sad strategy for safeguarding the value of salary and melting capital?

A few miles past the West Side Aqueduct, where the overpass of the interstate begins its rise, the sweet stench of 50,000 dozy steers at the Harris feedlot elicited an audible chuckle. More infallible than eye or ear is the nose's sidewise dive into the past. And then began the last twelve miles of rises, turns, and dips over the first range of hills before Coalinga would spread herself invitingly out. Muscles negotiated each satisfying twist in the road on their own recognizance; I merely watched the performance with shy pleasure.

There bobbed "the clown," the first of several dozen roadside oil rigs gaudily done up as rabbits, Poohs, and kangaroos to beguile the traveler. I was uncommonly pleased that no new ones had been added in my absence. There were, it seemed, things that held.

A short distance from the highway plied hundreds of these

perpetual teeter-totters, "grasshoppers" undisguised by finery, pumping steam into the earth's creases day after night after night to draw up the black, oozy stuff. These self-same hills are richly larded with dinosaurs and mollusks, fossils—bedded and boned. Marcia, the kids, and I used to stride eons and sort eras on a simple hike in the hills. This was California's first oil field, the strike which built the turn-of-the-century brick downtown that the turning earth had recently reclaimed. This earth is alive, produces, bargains, and, latterly precise as a Latter-day Saint, exacts its full tithe. Coalinga was bound to it still.

The final long arc, and the town affords a quick glimpse of its surprising sprawl before ducking coyly behind some final folds of the highway. The straightaway reveals all. Because of the lights and riggery of Standard, Shell, and Texaco in the surrounding hills, Coalinga, especially at night, looks larger than it really is. It is an innocent deceit, but suddenly recalling the partially camouflaged State Police station just over the bridge, I shifted down to make my entrance. I was guilty of an uncommon excitation.

JESUS IS LORD OF COALINGA loudly declaimed a billboard just after the motel.

Now *that* was a new one. True, this particular board had always welcomed the new arrival to the 17?, 20?, 23? churches of Coalinga. There was no "Jewish Church" listed among them; in our time, our family had comprised one-quarter of the local Jewish community. Obviously not Roman Catholic, vaguely considered by some of our less-sophisticated neighbors as "kinda Protestant" (variants, perhaps, of the locally very active Seventh Dayers?), we were generally undismayed by the Lord of Coalinga. Oh, once we were conned into attending a slide show demonstration of the truths of Mormonism at the home of our son's den mother. (We had thought we were in for an evening devoted to the Archaeology of Mexico.) There were the comic Sunday morning visitations from the suits and ties and white pleated skirts periodically sent around by the Jehovah's Witnesses. And of course the crèche and caroling in school at Christmastime. In short, nothing more than mildly nettling.

And yet, *and yet*, how far from the historical, the psychological mark were our neighbors? Heedless newcomers to the territory, we were less acutely aware than many of them that hereabouts the firm line between "kinda Protestant" and "somekinda Jew" tended with time to slacken, wiggle, slide, and wane into some stray dots and dashes on the floor that kids or grandkids one day finally would sweep out with the trash. Pleasantly disoriented by Coalinga's charm and remoteness, we had overlooked that in time we would fall liable to make good our good fortune.

The campus of West Hills College, a struggling institution with no pretentions to excellence, spread out in a great grassy square on my right. In my seven years here, I had encountered some highly intelligent, effective instructors and a small but nourishing number of bright students. Coming here in 1969 meant I had declined to jog on the academic career track I had set out upon at Fordham, Penn, and Brown. It was a proper decision, a premonition (had I eyes to foresee) of the later choice of *aliya*, of emigration to Israel. Indeed, like Israel, West Hills was a place that broadcast the scent of being needed, a gift I have always found headier than career. It had not disappointed.

A marquee announced Graduation Ceremonies and an Earthquake Conference for the following week. I realized that I had arrived during final exam week. A billboard proclaimed that Horned Toad Derby, the major local celebration, would be that very weekend, before the college students had dispersed. I drove straight through to Fifth St., the business district. To be sure, the red brick rubble had vanished; it had been replaced by shopping mall modern. Coalinga was less distinctive but plainly declared itself to be distinctly classier.

Two downtown stops: the Bank of America for cash and the new Western Auto for chatter with the purchasers of our former home. American banking: only Israel could have brought me to gawk at its plastic woody lines and smiles, to loll in its shadowless efficiency. There was only one other customer in the entire place.

"I used to live here," I heard myself volunteering to the young woman teller. "Used to teach in the college. Live in Israel now."

"Really," she gaped. "It must be dangerous over there."

She took my passport and VISA card to a man seated behind a desk. He looked toward me briefly, scrawled something, and two minutes later I had my money. Oh B! O America!

The Olivers' new Western Auto is the largest appliance store in town. Its old pleasant jumble had been replaced by what must be double the textured floor space. A young clerk ushered me to see Jerry and Norine in an interior office. The young couple was now energetically middle-aged, but the earthquake had been good to them.

"Your house stood up beautifully. Only the chimney in the living room had to be replaced," said Jerry.

"Yes, we really liked that house," was my wistful retort.

"We do, too."

"You should visit us in Israel. The climate where we are is almost the same as here. We even have an earthquake fault not far to the east."

The college where I had taught for seven years was wondrously familiar. I found jovial Jim Hicks still blasting the Administration "sodbusters" from his chem lab fortress and Terry Corcoran with his quick intelligence and easy laughter over in Physics. Some of the same campaigns with the Administration and with the *other* organization of instructors were still being fought by the outmanned battlers of the A.F.T. But we "good guys" were still Avis Number Twos; the sodbusters still rented their tractors from Hertz.

"We have some good new people both in the Administration and on faculty," Terry declared. "Someone you should meet in your old division is Mrs. Zwang." My ears perked. "She teaches part-time. Her husband was a professor at Cal, but they've retired down here."

In my article on earthquaked Coalinga, I dwelt significantly on the matriarch of a family I had called the Zwangs, an original settler family of Coalinga area ranchers who several generations back had been Jewish. The old woman, I had been given to understand, was the last Jew of her line. She died toward the end of our sojourn in Coalinga. The fate of the Zwangs had seemed to me an emblem, American Jewish life formulated on a pin, a dead-end pursuit, and the last Jewish funeral of the clan had in fact been instrumental in spiraling us toward Israel out of the maw of America.

"I'd never heard about leftover Zwangs who were still Jews," I lamely confessed.

"As far as I know," Terry said, "they're rather observant."

It was for me a tantalizing morsel. What might, in fact, these relatively observant footnotes, this Zwangish return from the grave to mock my literary myth-making, this odd portent possibly signify?

Outside I passed the main lecture hall, now labeled "Wakefield Everett Hall" after my officemate for four years, a friend, campus iconoclast who boomingly held forth here on Socrates, Hamlet, and Babbitry semester after semester after semester. He died two years after I left of complications from a chronically bloody nose that refused to clot. Mary Forth was walking toward me. It was to her and her husband Don I'd written that I thought I would visit Coalinga this time around in California. Smiling, she looked as trim and lovely as ever.

"Let's go to the cafeteria. You can usually get some salad and cottage cheese, a glass of milk there." She hadn't forgotten how broad a dietary swath the Chertoks cut in their final years in Coalinga. After three paces we were intercepted by the Fowlers and paused to glance at wallet photos of their boys. Not all American kids had been misplaced: these two strapping youngsters now attended different campuses of the University of California.

"We read your article about Coalinga," John Fowler said. "Liked it very much."

"Any trouble figuring out the pseudonyms?"

"Who was the Jewish lawyer?" Mary asked.

"Oh Mary," John answered for me, "didn't you recognize . . .?"

It suddenly struck me that these old friends and colleagues—stouter, more lined, a bit grayed—who astonishingly had stayed put with props and lives intact in this small-town stage-set that Marcia and I had outworn nearly a decade before, were an invaluable and irreplaceable cast of witnesses. Children are proofs against our most harbored illusions, but we change only at the margins for the survivors of our earlier dreams. Israel was our ampler shaping myth, a movement and returning to a stony earthpatch that defined personal points on a reflexive arc traversing millennia. But John, Norine, Terry, Mary, even departed Wakefield were innocently scripting a counter-assertion, a narrower but intensely valid claim I recognized in the quiet, diffuse surge of feeling that settled in my throat. The sentiment declared a legitimacy I was not then— *not ever?*—prepared fully to gainsay. There was here a special circle of self and past that was still dear. Against all odds and preconception, was not this place too still somehow *home?*

Together with people I did not know—an assistant dean, a new English teacher, a jabbering aeronautics instructor—Don Forth joined us at lunch. He was now a half-time administrator heading up Humanities programming. Tall, bearded, still a careful speaker and an unusually attentive listener, Don had remained in place as one of the truly fine people at West Hills. He was curious about the state of things in Israel, not a matter easy to relate even superficially between salad-bites in a California cafeteria. I fell back on a few stock episodes—I even had some "war stories" in my pack—and generalizations. He realized that the slippery tenor of my report reflected the difficult times Israel was currently undergoing.

"Things are tough," I concluded, "and in some ways living in Israel sometimes is not merely a disappointment but almost verges on a con. Still, no place else could Marcia and I be leading the satisfyingly full lives we live as Jews. The question whether we like it is usually beside the point: it's the place we feel we have to be. We're wedded to the place. That isn't re-negotiable." But had I not just been feeling that Coalinga also had a claim on our affections? Wherein really lay the vital difference?

"The Chertoks were our local political activists when they lived here," Mary was explaining to the assistant dean. "Marcia started an ecological awareness group, Earth Friends, that organized conferences on pesticide problems. I wonder whether we could do something like that again? Later, she won election to the school board. And Harvey ran the McGovern campaign."

"I'd rather not be reminded of that one," I chimed in.

"Yeah, but McGovern actually won in Coalinga," Don recalled.

"And he got over 49% in Fresno County," I foolishly (still

proudly!) added. I suffered then the subversive realization that
my life in Israel was in many ways far more borderland, more
privatized than the one I had abandoned so precipitously in
America. I would never run anyone's political campaign in
Yeroham or Tel Aviv, care much about the doings of Maccabi
Tel Aviv or Betar Jerusalem, or half-consciously sing the popular songs.

Mary turned to me almost shyly. "You know," she said
quietly, "I really didn't agree with the ending of your article on
Coalinga. I almost wrote to you about it."

I knew by heart what she was referring to. It had taken me a
dozen tries to get it concluded on just the flatted off-note that
would cause it to be rejected on ideological grounds by any
Jewish monthly committed to the viability of American-style
Judaism: "Coalinga, its downtown a ruin, its college in serious
disrepair, will surely pull itself together and rebuild. Letters
from old friends make this clear. It really doesn't need any Jews
at all." Only "neo-conservative" Commentary had been liberal
enough to accommodate such outright heresy.

Half-an-hour later I turned down College Street. The Norris driveway, which I remembered always being cluttered with
bicycles, now was clogged with cars. Their five children had
outgrown two-wheelers. Had erstwhile Earth Friend Maxine
wholly abandoned ideology before the onslaughts of her family? Chatting with neighbors across the street as I approached,
she and Hal spotted me first.

"HARVEY CHERTOK! The long-lost one! We were just talking about you the other day. Come in!"

Hal was as gangling, garrulous, and genial as ever, though,
like me, a bit grayer. Their two youngest boys, now in their
late teens, declared that they recognized me—more, of course,
than I could claim for them. They settled down comfortably to
listen in on how things went for a former resident in the big
world beyond the valley. There had been a recent wedding:
their Joline had married into the Lacey family. Our daughter
Jennifer had had Mrs. Lacey for her third-grade teacher, and
Annie Lacey had been her babysitter. Had we stayed put, dug
in, kept at it as we might, would Jennifer and Ted not also
likely be going with, involved with, engaged to locals? Could I

truly dare question how urgent really had been the impetus to leapfrog the fate of the Zwangs?

Originally from Minnesota, the Norrises were Humphrey–McCarthy, Farm Labor–Democrats; Maxine had been perhaps our closest ally in past political undertakings. A small group of us had for the first time established a local working liberal–Chicano coalition, monitored school board and hospital board meetings, promoted ecological projects, worked for McGovern, gotten Marcia elected to the school board, and established the first Central California chapter of Amnesty International. Then we Chertoks had decamped, vamoosed, utterly vanished into the earth. What was there now to show for all that grassrootsing?

"Does the Amnesty International group still meet?," I queried.

"We kept on for a few months after you left," Maxine replied reflectively, but they finally wrote us that we were too small to function effectively." Her voiced turned somber. "Almost all the political high-jinks fizzled after you and Marcia left."

After burrowing into a pile of things on a bookshelf, Hal, a high school English teacher, triumphantly surfaced with a copy of a college creative writing annual I had, as faculty moderator, helped to turn out.

"Look at the names," Hal pointed excitedly. "Nan, Penny . . . these were mainly my old students as well."

"Well, you must have taught them something in high school. They were my best."

"Sure, but the sad thing is that this was the last issue. After you left, no one at the college took the thing up."

An hour later I headed down Elm Street and out of this corner of my past. It was Friday afternoon; I had to get back to Fresno and get myself ready for Shabbat. I stopped for a milkshake at an unfamiliar drive-in, then found that I couldn't turn the key in the ignition of the Volkswagen. Apparently I had jostled an automatic locking device on the steering wheel with my knee—that much I remembered—but I could not recall how to unfreeze it. First bewitching me in Fresno, then trapping me in Coalinga, what gremlin was pursuing me this day?

Inside the drive-in, working the pinball, I found the two Norris boys. The Volkswagen's mysterious mechanism yielded almost at once before their concerted efforts, and I was soon again gently rising into the hills that, ceaselessly jollied by rabbits, Mickeys, and clowns, issued forth its black, seminal ooze. No one knew when or even where the earth's accumulation of resentment might next shake the rebuilt foundations of cautious Coalinga, my ultimate emblem of America. All that was certain was that, in time, it would.

The next morning I walked the two miles to attend Shabbat services at Fresno's conservative synagogue. (In all of California's Central Valley, only Sacramento supports an orthodox congregation.) I knew what to expect; achingly, I was not disappointed. Perhaps fifteen men and one woman slumped scattered throughout the room. I nodded at three who were former acquaintances. Most there were Social Security recipients. I was called up to the Torah for *shishi*, but in my uneasy haste to return to my seat, I muffed the second blessing.

The rabbi, new since my departure, a hulking figure in his 30s, sermonized broadly about Judaism and ecology—the earth itself had rights under Judaism. (A rabbinic Earth Friend: why, alas, was I so little pleased?) This tack drew no response whatever from his audience of pensioners, so he goaded "Ol' Willy." Promptly rising to his foil's role, he changed the subject to the Jewish maltreatment of slaves in the Bible. The rabbi made some capital of this, then threw in a joke or two of his own. After a truncated *kiddush*, I walked back the two desultory miles. Such remained the stuff of organized Jewish life in the sidepockets of my old America.

On Sunday morning Don Forth telephoned. Might I possibly be interested in doing a turn as Writer-in-Residence for a semester in a year or so at West Hills? He couldn't make a definite commitment, but perhaps I had enough time to drive out that evening so that I could meet with the new college president at a cocktail party.

For a seductive season, stilling both surface tremors and deeper perturbation, could I not accept the narrow accuracy of Mary Forth's disclaimer? That unstable stretch between the parallel faults and the great shining seas was secret, active counterweight; sharer of all my turns toward final abnegation. It I may covertly relish or disdain to the end of my days, but its current of power and affection could now be acknowledged. It would stand beyond further challenge or remorse. Affirmed and firmly fixed in duality and otherness, I could conceive no further cause or occasion to flee. A limited tour on the American stage could now be entertained.

Is it, I wonder, despite or rather because I have departed that America now projects less its old threat than an intimacy as compelling as an old catcher's mitt long left at the bottom of a carton in the back of the closet?

GLOSSARY

This Glossary is intended primarily to explain Jewish or Israeli terms to persons with a limited acquaintance with them but additionally to be instructive and/or entertaining for those with greater background in these areas.*

A.A.C.I.: Association of Americans and Canadians in Israel, a self-help lobby and social organization of ex-North Americans.

Abba: Father.

Abuhatzeira, Aharon: Former cabinet minister. A jail-stretch for illegally siphoning revenues to favorite causes and cronies seems not to have dampened the ardor of his Tami Party supporters. He was re-elected.

Adon Olam: "Master of the Universe," a hymn affirming faith in God that traditionally closes Shabbat morning services.

Afikim Hanegev: Streams in the Negev. Its source is biblical.

A.F.T.: American Federation of Teachers (A.F.L.–C.I.O.). It tries harder but is perennially Number Two to the more conservative National Education Association.

Afula: Regional agricultural center in the North of Israel with mixed Jewish and Arab population. Sister city to Fresno, California.

Agrexco: Israel's overseas marketing cooperative for fresh fruits and vegetables.

Akiva (Akiba): Revered rabbinic scholar, martyr to the Romans in 135 C.E.

Al Azazma: Largest of Negev Bedouin tribes.

Aleph (Alef): First letter of the Hebrew alphabet.

Note: The Hebrew sound for the English combination "ch" is a guttural "h."

* Unless otherwise indicated, all translations are masculine singular forms from the Hebrew.

Alignment, The: Long-time electoral coalition—now defunct—between the Labor Party and Mapam.

Aliya(h): Ascent. More generally, immigration to Israel; a *mitzvah* honored more in the breach than in the observance.

Altneuland: "Oldnewland." The title of the 1898 utopian novel of the Jewish State by Theodore Herzl. (Hebrew translation was "Tel Aviv.")

Americai: American (masc.).

Amichai, Yehuda: Major contemporary Israeli poet and short-story writer, born 1924 in Germany.

Amidar: Israeli government construction and housing agency. In development towns, it acts (usually slowly) as major landlord.

Amir, Jacques: Labor Party Knesset Member; until defeated in 1984, long-time Mayor of Dimona.

Anglos, Anglo-Saxim: Generic term for immigrants to Israel from English-speaking countries.

Arad: Bland Negev city of around 13,000, east of Beersheba.

Arava: Israel's hot, open spaces. Laura Ingalls Wilder's prairie melodrama was TV-rendered "Little House on the *Arava*."

Army Radio: Most popular and trusted of Israel's four official radio stations.

Artza Alinu: "Our Land," a catchy *hora* tune.

Ashkelon: One-time Philistine center, now sprawling city on Mediterranean.

Ashkenazi, -a (fem.): Generally, a Jew of Northern and Eastern European (or North American) background.

Association for Civil Rights: Israeli equivalent of (but far less successful than) American Civil Liberties Union.

Avdat: Nabataean city, now remarkable archaeological site in the Negev.

Avraham Avinu: Our Father Abraham.

Ba'al T'shuva: "Repentant," newly-religious Jewish male. There are *yeshivot* that specialize in this breed of Jew.

Ba'alat T'shuva: Ditto for Jewish female.

Ba'al Shem Tov: "Master of the Good Name." Popular name

for Rabbi Israel ben Eliezer, charismatic founder of modern Hasidism.

Babi Yar: Site outside of Kiev where in 1941 the Nazis shot hundreds of thousands of Jews and others and buried them in mass graves.

Bagrut: National high school matriculation examinations. It produces university entrance, anxiety, and eczema.

Bar-Ilan: Only Israeli university under religious auspices, located in Ramat Gan.

Bar Mitzva(h): At 13, coming of age of Jewish boy with his public reading of a portion of Torah scroll in synagogue. Food, celebration, food, gifts, and food ensue.

B.C.E.: Before the Common Era. Jewish gloss on B.C.

Bedouin (Beduin): Nomads, indigenous Moslem tribespeople living mainly in the Negev. Young Bedouin frequently volunteer as scouts for *Tsahal*.

Beersheba: Literally "seven wells"; city of 120,000, capital of the Negev region.

Begin, Menachem: Gentlemanly former Prime Minister and maximum leader of the Likud whose war hastened his withdrawal to silence.

Beirut: Fireworks capital of Lebanon. Once a delight, now a running sore.

Bench Licht (Yiddish): Kindling of the candles, usually by women, that initiates Shabbat.

Ben-Gurion, David: Israel's first Prime Minister and last prophet.

Bensalem College: Fordham University foray into experimental education. Conceived in a poet's dream, its successes nettled its foes and exhausted its friends. R.I.P. 1967–1972.

Bet (Beth): Second letter of the Hebrew alphabet. (Also "house.")

Bet Hamidrash: Center for Jewish learning. Study hall.

Bet Holim: Hospital.

Bet Knesset: Synagogue.

Betar Jerusalem: Israeli soccer's Brooklyn Dodgers.

Beth-el: Biblical site where Jacob had a vision of God. Now a Gush Emunim settlement and Israeli army post on the West Bank.

Bialik, Haymin Nachman: Foremost Hebrew poet of the pre-State period for whom the awaited signs of Jewish "normalcy" would come when Jewish crooks and Jewish prostitutes walked the streets of Tel Aviv. Were he alive, he couldn't complain.

Black-Coat: Garb of ultra-orthodox adherent, hence metonomy for such person or political party, most of whom are non-Zionist or even anti-Zionist.

Black Hebrews: Popular name for the "Nation of God."

Blue & White: Israeli flag's colors. Consumers are often exhorted to buy b & w as a matter of patriotism.

B'nei Akiva: Sons (and Daughters) of Akiva, the Israeli mainstream orthodox youth organization.

B'nei Brak: Large, nearly 100% religiously orthodox suburb of Tel Aviv. A bit of Old Brooklyn.

Boker Tov: Good morning. (Also a sugary Israeli breakfast food.)

Bornstein, Zvi: Son of President of Tempo Bottles (largest industry in Yeroham) who was killed in an air crash.

Bourg-al-Bourajneh: Largest of the P.L.O. refugee camps on outskirts of Beirut.

B'reshit: "In the beginning . . . ," the opening words of the Book of Genesis and the title generally ascribed to the entire book.

Brit: Covenant, like the rainbow for Noah.

Brit Milah: Ritual circumcision (literally, "covenant of circumcision"). A patriarchal business of, by, and for sons and fathers.

Burg, Yosef: Noted for canniness, veteran political leader of the National Religious Party. He's served in every Israeli government since 1948.

Carter, Ben-Ami: Black leader, Messiah for his Nation of God adherents.

C.C.C.: Civilian Conservation Corps, a swing-that-ax expedient to counter the American Depression of the 1930s.

Chabad: See *Habad*.

Chaver (Haver): Comrade.

Chutzpah (Hutzpah), *-im* (pl.): Fabled Jewish nerve (a boast and failing). Classic example: the man who kills his parents, then pleads before the judge for mercy as an orphan.

City Island: The Bronx in spite of itself.

Coalinga, California: Glocca Morra.

Cohen, *-im* (pl.): Jewish priest (not to be confused with a rabbi).

Cottage, *-im* (pl.): Semi-detached, ground-level residence.

Cous-Cous: Meat and meal dish of North African origin. The best Israeli cuisine is generally considered to be North African.

Dati, *-im* (pl.), *-ya* (fem.): Orthodox, religious.

Daven (Yiddish): Pray, but it sounds more soulful.

Derech Hevron: Hebron Road, the hilly, scenic, most direct route between Beersheba, Hebron, and Jerusalem. Egged buses do not take this route after dark.

Development Town: Urban settlement in outlying areas established after War of Independence. Israeli rule of thumb: the more outlying, the less development.

Dimona: Site of Israel's atomic reactor, city of around 27,000, 30 kilometers south of Beersheba.

Dizengoff: Tel Aviv's Piccadilly and Broadway. (Mr. D. was the city's first mayor.)

Eastern Parkway: World center (in Brooklyn) of the Lubavitch Movement.

East Jerusalem: Arab Jerusalem. Terra incognita for Jerusalem's Jews.

Egged: Israel's largest intercity bus cooperative. Its *muy macho* drivers are Israel's symbolic equivalents of America's long-haul truckers.

Eilat: On the Red Sea, Israel's southern extremity, a port & resort for sun-yearning Scandinavians and blonde-yearning Israelis.

Ein: A Hebrew negative function word.

Ein Breira: No alternative, a frequently heard, sometime true, Israeli plaint. The name of a fringe American-Jewish organization, now defunct, that was highly critical of

Israel's policy vis-à-vis the Arabs was "Breira" (Choice).

Eitan, Rafael ("*Raful*"): Army chief of staff during Lebanese War; now ultra-nationalist Knesset member.

El Al: Israel's safety-first, national air carrier. Literally, to the heavens.

Eliav, Lova: Town planner, educator, politician, idealist author of *Land of the Heart*.

Emden, Jacob: German rabbinic authority of eighteenth century; enemy of followers of Shabbtai Tsvi.

Eruv: Symbolic, ritual boundary defining a community for the purposes of activity on Shabbat.

Esau: Elder son of Isaac and Rebekah, a traditional Jewish type for Romans and Christians.

Eurovision: Upbeat annual contest among European countries for best new song. When Israel won two years running, it withdrew the year thereafter because (*ein breira!*) it couldn't afford again to host the proceedings.

Falashas: Black, Ethiopian Jews, most of whom have now made it to Israel. Of late the term has picked up a negative connotation.

Federation: Fund-raising and allocating organ of American Jewish communities. In most U.S. cities, the power-brokering local Jewish organization.

Freirim: Suckers (Israeli popsicles & momsicles).

Galut: Exile. A concept and state of Jewish soul.

Garin: A seed. The core group of a new settlement or organization.

Gazit, Shlomo: President of Ben-Gurion University, formerly in charge of Israel's intelligence services.

Gemara: Rabbinic commentary on the *Mishnah*.

Gematria: Mystical, sometimes tendentious cryptographic system whereby the hidden meaning of words is revealed through a numerical value of letters. Especially used in study of *Kabbalah*.

Gemayel, Bashir: President of Lebanon, Israel's only trumps, whose assassination spelled *finis* to its inflated designs in Lebanon.

Geva, Eli: Israeli ex-Colonel, tank commander whose resignation during Lebanese War was a *cause célèbre*. He refused to lead his troops on to Beirut.

Giva: Hill.

Givati: Closest *Tsahal* equivalent to the U.S. Marines.

Golan: Heights of Northern Israel captured from Syria in 1967 and since annexed into Israel proper. Local Druse residents are ambivalent about their new nationality.

Golberg, Abraham: A puzzlement.

Gonovim: Thieves.

Goyim, -ish (adj.): Nations. Generally, non-Jews; often (but not always) derogatory.

Great Panjandrum Himself, The: Nursery jingle and a sweet, frustrating activist year. The way it was in 1968–69.

Green Line: Line on map designating border of Israel before the 1967 War expanded the area of Israeli suzerainty to include the West Bank, the Gaza Strip, East Jerusalem, the Golan Heights, and Sinai. East Jerusalem and the Golan have been annexed; Sinai, of course, has reverted to Egypt.

Green Patrol: Para-police organization that keeps tabs on ecological developments in the countryside. Also known for Bedouin-baiting.

Gruzini: Immigrant from Soviet Georgia. Usually an individualist.

Gush Emunim: Band of Believers. The right-wing, religio-nationalist movement that has made settlement of the Territories captured by Israel in 1967 (historic Judea and Samaria) its raison d'être.

Gush Etzion: The bloc of religious settlements south of Jerusalem that was overrun by the Arabs in 1948; recaptured by Israel and re-established after 1967.

Ha'aretz: The Land. Also, Israel's *Le Monde, Guardian,* and *Christian Science Monitor.*

Habad: Acryonym of first letters of Hebrew words for wisdom, understanding, and knowledge. The outreach arm of the Lubavitch Movement, much concerned with enhancing

Jewish observance of *mitzvot,* especially on American college campuses and among Israeli soldiers.

Hadash: New. See *Rakah.*

Haddad, Major Sa'ed: Organizer, first leader of the Israel-supported South Lebanese Army.

Haga: Home guard defense force whose most conspicuous activity is checking suspicious parcels for explosives at public places like bus stations and *souks.*

Haganah: The pre-State Jewish defense force from which *Tsahal* sprang.

Hagim: Holidays.

Halacha: Normative Jewish religious practice and law.

Halil: A shepherd's flute.

Halutz (Chalutz), -im (pl.): Pioneer. A secular *tsadik.*

Hanukkah: Minor Jewish festival commemorating rededication of the Second Temple in 165 B.C.E. by Judah the Maccabee. Its exaggerated prominence among Diaspora Jews is signaled by the calendar: it falls in December.

Hapoalim: The workers. Name of Histadrut-owned, largest bank in Israel.

Har: Mount, mountain.

Haredi: See Black-coat.

Har Etzion: Hesder yeshiva at Gush Etzion.

Hasbarah: Public relations, propaganda, an Israeli preoccupation.

Hashomer Hatzair: Young watchmen. Left-wing of the kibbutz movement.

Hasid (Chasid): Member of a hasidic sect.

Hasidism: Jewish mystical pietism with many sects and branches. Its modern roots go back to medieval Poland and the Ba'al Shem Tov. Its colorful adherents wear distinctive black caftans and chapeaux that hearken back three centuries.

Hatikvah: The Hope. Israeli national tune, as of yet unperformed at Olympic Game anthem-fests. A tough hurdle for Arab Israelis.

Havdalah: Division. A brief, sensual ceremony performed with wine, candle, and spices to mark the close of Shabbat.

Hayim (Haim, Chaim): Life.
Hebrew Writers Association: Outside of the Iron Curtain, probably only Israel has unionized its major writers.
Hebron (Hevron): Arab-populated city, former Jewish center in Judea. Jews there were massacred in a pogrom in 1929. A few Gush Emunim stalwarts have returned.
Helm (Chelm): Legendary town of saintly Jewish fools.
Hermonit: A jumpsuit, named after Mount Hermon, site of Israel's only (most modest) ski-slope.
Herzog, Chaim: Current President of Israel.
Hesder: An arrangement. The program whereby young religious men combine military service with *yeshiva* studies.
Hesdernik: Part-time soldier, part-time *yeshiva* student: 5-year schizophrenia.
Hevra (Chevra): Comrades, companions.
Hevramen: Good team players.
High Holidays: A 10-day period from Rosh Hashanah through Yom Kippur, sometimes called the "Days of Awe," when many assimilated American Jews find their way back to synagogues.
Hillel: First-century B.C.E. rabbinic authority noted for his modesty, patience, and leniency. The full citation which is referred to reads "If I am not for myself, who will be for me? And if I am only for myself, what am I? And if not now, when?"
Hirsch, Baron Maurice de: Late-nineteenth-century Jewish philanthropist who, after colonization of Palestine seemed to him hopeless, funded Jewish settlements in Argentina.
Histadrut: Organization. The Israeli Labor Federation. Also Israel's major entrepreneur.
Holim: Sick people, patients.
Hora: Israeli circle dance, kitschy indoors.
Horned Toad Derby Day: Annual day of hop, hops, and hope in Coalinga, Calif.
Hough: Black Cleveland.
¡Huelga! (Spanish): Strike!
Hummus: Bean dip made of chickpeas, a staple in Middle Eastern salads.

I.D.F.: Israel Defense Forces (*Tsahal*).
Ishmael: Son of Abraham and Hagar, traditionally for Jews a type for the Arab people.

Jerusalem Post: Influential, English-language daily newspaper.
Jewish Agency: *Sochnut*, one of several official (often competing) bodies responsible for immigrant absorption.
Judea: Hilly, southern half of the West Bank; biblical Jewish heartland (alloted portion of the tribes of Judah and Benjamin).

Kabbalah (*Cabbalah*): Jewish mystical interpretation of the Bible.
Kach: Political movement, led by Rabbi Meir Kahane, advocating expulsion of Israel's Arabs and/or apartheid.
Kaddish: Jewish doxology, most frequently recited Jewish prayer at public worship, often associated with mourners who are obliged to recite it thrice daily for an 11-month period.
Kaddosh: Holy.
Kahane, Meir: American-born, rabble-rousing rabbi, Member of the Knesset, who espouses expulsion of Israel's Arabs.
Kahaneism: Born of desperation, the spirit of vengeance.
Kakha: Because. Fallback position of parents and teachers.
Kashrut: Quirky system of Jewish dietary law.
Katif: A zone of Jewish settlement in the Gaza Strip which the Jewish Agency prefers to consider "in the Negev."
Keren Hayesod: Foundation Fund, originally founded in 1920 to buy land for Jewish colonization of Palestine.
Kibbutz, -im (pl.): Rural communal settlement, usually socialist and prosperous, sometimes prosperous and socialist.
Kiddush: A ceremony over wine that sanctifies Shabbat (and other holy days).
Kineret: Sea of Galilee.
Kinus: A meeting or convention.
Kippa, -ot (pl.): Often colorful skullcap worn by observant Jewish men.
Kiryat Malachi: Development town in the North Negev.

Kitah: School grade.
Kittel (Yiddish): White robe (usually linen) worn on Rosh Hashanah, Yom Kippur, Passover. Also used as a burial shroud.
Knesset: Israel's Parliament of 120 chosen on principle of proportional representation. As in England, it is the single font of government. Symbolically, it comprises a *minyan* from each of the twelve tribes.
Kol: Voice.
Kol Hakavod!: More power to you!
Kol Yisrael: Voice of Israel radio broadcasts originating in Jerusalem.
Korah: Jewish rebel against the authority of Moses (Book of Numbers).
Kosher: Ritually clean or acceptable. In America, U's and some K's on food packages vouch for their being kosher.
Kotel: Western Wall of the Temple of Jerusalem, most venerated site of Judaism.
Kotler, Oded: Prize-winning, experimental-theater director.

Laban: Jacob's father-in-law (and uncle).
Lachish: Reclaimed region of intensively irrigated agriculture in the Northern Negev.
Lag B'Omer: Minor, somewhat obscure festival occurring during 40-day period of semi-mourning between Passover and Pentecost.
Lama?: Why? The response to which is generally *kakha* (because).
Land of Israel: Nationalist movement and philosophy, associated with Gush Emunim, holding that Jews must settle all of the Land of Israel and cede none of it in any negotiations with the Arabs.
Lashon Ha'ra: Evil tongue. Speaking ill of others, even if truthfully, is forbidden according to *halacha*. Perhaps the toughest of all commandments to keep.
Latrun: On Tel Aviv–Jerusalem highway, the site of major attempts (and failures) to break the siege of Jerusalem during the War of Independence (1948).
Law of Return: Law granting Israeli citizenship to any Jew

who immigrates. Perennial focus of "Who is a Jew?" controversy.

Likud: Union. An alliance of three right-of-center political parties that came to power under Menachem Begin in 1977 and shares it with the Labor Party under the National Unity Government agreement of 1984.

Little Triangle: Hilly region of Galilee where Arabs far outnumber Jews.

Lod: Ancient, now proletarian Israeli city close to Ben-Gurion Airport.

Lubavitch: A hasidic sect, whose world center is in Brooklyn. Its head is the charismatic Rabbi Menachem Schneerson whose strongest emphasis is that Jews should keep the ritualistic *mitzvot* because the time for the coming of the Messiah is close at hand. (Indeed, adherents hint that Schneerson himself is the Messiah.)

Ma'ale Adumim: "Ruddy Heights." New suburb of Jerusalem located in the Territories.

Ma'arach: Alignment. The electoral coalition, now defunct, between the Labor Party and Mapam.

Ma'arbara, -ot (pl.): Temporary transit camp that received homeless immigrants to Israel, mostly from Arab countries, in the early 1950s. In some cases, "temporary" endured for more than a decade.

Ma'ariv: Evening. Designation for one of the three daily occasions of Jewish public prayer. Also, name of Labor Party–affiliated afternoon newspaper.

Maccabi Tel Aviv: Israel's Boston Celtics.

Machtesh Hagodol: Grand Canyon. Yeroham's is not Israel's deepest but it is its grandest.

Mafdal: Acronym for National Religious Party.

Mahane Yehuda: Crowded outdoor produce market of Jerusalem.

Maharati: Written language of India.

Makolet: Small grocery store. These still account for largest share of Israel's food marketing.

Mapam: Leftist party whose political base is its own kibbutz movement.

Masada: Dramatic site of last resistance of Jewish Zealots against Romans. Contemporary symbol of Israeli determination to survive. It overlooks the Dead Sea.

Mashiach: Messiah.

Mashmia Shalom: Proclaim Peace, an intentional community of religious *olim* families that settled under the aegis of the National Religious Party in Yeroham in 1977. Now dormant.

Masuot Yitzhak: An attractive *moshav shitufi* at which reside some warm, intelligent people. Between Ashkelon and Kiryat Malachi. ("Beacons of Isaac," this Yitzhak being not the son of Abraham the Prophet but Isaac [Yitzhak] Herzog, former chief rabbi of Ireland and father of Chaim Herzog, Israel's current President.)

Matzoh: Unleavened "bread of affliction" eaten at Passover. Terrific scrambled with eggs (just ask for *matzoh brei*).

Mazal Tov!: Congratulations!

Megilla: Scroll, a story.

Megillat Esther: Scroll of the Book of Esther.

Mehablim: Terrorists; by their own lights, "freedom fighters."

Melamed: A simple, proverbially poverty-stricken, Hebrew teacher.

Menorah: Ritual candelabra, a resonant Jewish symbol.

Merkava: Israeli-manufactured tank.

Meshuge: Crazy.

Mezuzah: Doorpost. A small parchment containing the first two paragraphs of the *Shema* that is placed in a small case and affixed to the doorposts of Jewish homes.

Middle East Airlines: National air carrier (generally grounded) of Lebanon.

Midrash, -im (pl.): Legend. Non-literal but often authoritative interpretation of the Bible.

Midresha, Midreshet: Institute.

Miklat, -im (pl.): Underground shelters, often used as well for clubhouses and other purposes.

Mikveh: Ritual bath or immersion. Jewish communities are traditionally obligated to construct a *mikveh* even prior to a synagogue.

Miluim: Army reserve duty.

Miluimniks, -ikim: Reservists.

Mincha: Offering. The afternoon public prayer.

Minyan, -im (pl.): Ten men, the minimum required for public Jewish worship.

Miriam: Moses' sister whose leprosy is traditionally attributed to *lashon ha'ra*.

Mishna(h): The oral law, codified in the third century C.E. by Rabbi Judah ha-Nasi.

Mitzpe Ramon: Remote, scenic Negev settlement of 3,000 people.

Mitzva(h), -ot (pl.): A religious obligation. A Jew has 613 *mitzvot* to perform, but many, in the absence of the Temple, have long been suspended.

Mizbaiach: Ritual altar.

Mizrachi: Eastern. Also Religious Zionist Movement.

Modern Orthodoxy: The Jewish tendency that attempts to harmonize Torah Judaism with contemporary life. "Young Israel" congregations are its American community bulwarks.

Moroccait: Arabic dialect spoken by Jews in and from Morocco.

Moshavnik: Member of a *moshav*.

Moshav Shitufi: Communal agricultural settlement that differs from a kibbutz mainly in that children sleep together with their families, which here eat together in their own homes (rather than in communal dining halls). In contrast to a more private form of *moshav, moshav shitufi* forms a unified economic unit.

Nabateans: People who flourished in the Negev from the fourth century B.C.E. till they were conquered by the Romans. Past masters at water utilization.

Nablus: Arab city in Samaria. Biblical Shechem.

Nachal: (*a*) River bed, arroyo; (*b*) Acronym for Pioneering, Fighting Youth, an army option for men and women soldiers—*nachalnikim*—to pioneer new settlements or live and work in development areas.

Nachman, Rabbi of Bratzlav: Late-eighteenth-century, hasidic descendant of the Ba'al Shem Tov; a master of the parable.

Nation of God: Cult of American blacks living precariously in Israel, most of them in Dimona.

National Religious Party: Israeli political arm of Mizrachi.

Negev: The arid region that comprises most of Israel's land mass.

Neot Midbar: Oasis in the Desert. Confusingly, both a hotel in Beersheba and a defunct *garin*.

Netivot Shalom: Paths of Peace. Successor to *Oz V'Shalom* and just about as effective.

Neve Tsedek: Oasis of Justice. A politically committed, Tel Aviv theater company.

New World Passover: Celebration of Black Hebrews' arrival in the Promised Land from the American Egyptland.

Next Year in Jerusalem!: For hundreds of years, the concluding words to every Jew's Passover meal (*seder*) as well as to Yom Kippur worship.

N.F.W.A.: National Farm Workers Association (led since inception by Cesar Chavez).

Nisan: First month of the religious year (month of the feast of Passover).

Normalcy: Jews are Jews like Swiss are Swiss. A chimera.

N.R.P.: National Religious Party (*Mafdal*). Outflanked by more rightist religious parties, it's been long in the doldrums.

Nusach: Style or version of worship. Three major forms in contemporary Israel are Ashkenazi, Sephardi, and an official compromise form called Sfard.

Olam Ha-Ba: The World to Come. Jewish Heaven where, tradition has it, men will spend all their time studying Torah. (And women . . .?)

Oleh: One who ascends. Immigrant to Israel.

Olim: Ascendents. Immigrants.

Olim Hadashim: New Immigrants. Among the first protagonists in the elementary language dialogues designed to teach new arrivals rudimentary Hebrew.

Omanut La'am: Art for the People. Israel's most successful cultural supermarket.

Operation Peace for Galilee: Disingenuous official tag to the Israeli strike into Lebanon in 1982.

Or Etzion: A *yeshiva* near Ashkelon.

Oseh Shalom Bimromav: "May He who creates peace in
His high heavens . . . ." Passage said at close of silent,
standing devotions three times a day. Also a popular peace
refrain.

Oz, Amos: Foremost contemporary Israel writer and social
critic. Much-translated and traveled.

Oz V'Shalom: Strength and Peace. Ineffectual grouping of
well-intentioned religious doves.

Pagis, Dan: Israeli poet and medieval scholar, born 1930 in
Transylvania, died 1986.

Pale of Settlement: In Czarist Russia, outlying areas in which
Jews from annexed areas of Poland and Baltic states were
permitted to live.

Palmachnikim: Members of the fabled, pre-State Jewish army,
which was the core of Israel Defense Forces (*Tsahal*).

Patio: An Israeli version of a detached private house. It often
has a patio.

Peres, Shimon: Labor Party Prime Minister and Foreign
Minister; a patient, competent man.

Pesach: Passover.

Phalangist: Member of the Lebanese Christian movement
or militia, the Phalange (inspired by its fascist Spanish
version).

Pilots: Contemporary Israeli morality drama of war and
conscience.

Pisher (Yiddish): A little squirt.

Pita: Flat, round Arabic bread.

P.L.O.: Palestine Liberation Organization. A violent umbrella
organization that claims credit for numerous murders of
Arabs and Jews.

P.L.P.: Progressive List for Peace. New joint Arab–Jewish
Party which won two seats in the 1984 Knesset elections.

Pluralism: An American ideology; an Israeli slow starter.

Pogrom (Yiddish, from the Russian for "riot"): An
unspontaneous massacre.

Preil, Gabriel: Last of a line of Hebrew-language poets living
in the Diaspora; born in Estonia, 1922.

Project Interchange: Program that brings American young leadership groups for study tours of Israel "to win their hearts and minds" and pledges.

Project Renewal: Five-year program of economic linkage between locales in the Diaspora and specific hard-pressed towns or city neighborhoods in Israel.

Purim: "Lots" as in "lottery." Spring festival commemorating Jewish deliverance from extermination at hands of the Persians (an event of doubtful historicity).

Rabin, Yitzhak: Israeli Defense Minister, former Labor Party Prime Minister who resigned in 1977 over the affair of his wife's modest (but, alas, illegal) American bank account.

Rachel: Jacob's preferred and more lovely wife. She died giving birth to Benjamin.

Raful: Popular nickname for Rafael Eitan.

Rakah (also *Hadash*): Communist Party (pro-Moscow). It won four seats in the Knesset in 1984 elections (no change from 1981).

Ramat Aviv: Well-to-do suburb of Tel Aviv.

Ramat Gan: Large suburb of Tel Aviv.

Ramat Hanegev: Negev Highlands. An unlikely college founded in Yeroham by American academics in 1978. Still surviving, it has outlived Bensalem.

Rambam: Acronym for Rabbi Moses ben Maimon (Maimonides), the pre-eminent twelfth-century Jewish philosopher and codifier.

Ratner's: Famous Jewish dairy restaurant on New York's Lower East Side.

Rebbe: Rabbi. A special honorific.

Rebbetzen: Wife of a rabbi.

Rehov: Street.

R.I.S.D.: Rhode Island School of Design.

Rosh Hashana(h): The Jewish New Year, an occasion for introspection and repentance.

R.P.G.: Rocket-propelled grenade.

Rubin, Samuel: American philanthropist who designated funds principally for Cultural Centers in development towns.

Sabra, Sabrit (fem.): A spiny, cactus fruit. A native Israeli.

Safad: City in Galilean hills with lengthy tradition of mysticism, light, and art.

Saints, The: "When Black Hebrews, Come Marchin' In . . ."

Sapir, Shoshana: Wife of former Finance Minister Pinchas Sapir. For why she is also the name of a high school in Yeroham, see Golberg.

Savidor, Menachem: Former Liberal Party Speaker of the Knesset.

Savyon: Very posh suburb of Tel Aviv.

Schneerson, Menachem: "The Rebbe"; see Lubavitch.

Sde Boker: "Cowboy Field." A kibbutz in the Negev. Close by academic center (of same name) for desert studies and David Ben-Gurion's burial plot and archive.

Second Israel: Underprivileged segment of Israeli society, predominantly Sephardim, living in depressed city neighborhoods and in development areas.

Seder: Order. The Passover ritual meal—Jewish opera. Two performances are held annually for Diasporites, just one for Israelis.

Selichot: Special Jewish penitential prayers.

Sephardim: Most Jews of Mediterranean background. A minority world wide, they are a clear majority of Jews within Israel.

Sfard: Contemporary Israeli compromise *nusach* used in army *siddurim*.

Shabbat: Jewish Sabbath extending from sundown Friday to sundown Saturday.

Shabbtai Tsvi: False Jewish messiah whom more than half the Jewish seventeenth-century world followed until he converted to Islam. He still had disciples into the twentieth century!

Shachrit: Morning. Term for first occasion for prayer of the day.

Shaked: Almond.

Shaliach: See *shlichim*.

Shalom: Peace, Hello, Goodbye.

Shana Tova!: Happy New Year!

Sharett, Moshe: See Shertok, Moshe.

Sharon, Ariel (Arik): Likud Minister in several national governments. A cross between John Wayne and Andy Devine among the crowd of ambitious, nationalist, politician former generals.

Shas: Political party of Sephardi *haredim* that emerged and did surprisingly well in the 1984 elections.

Shavuah Tov: Have a good week!

Shavuot: Pentecost. Springtime festival celebrating both first fruits and the giving of the Torah at Mount Sinai.

Shekel: Israeli coin of constantly uncertain value.

Shekem: Retail chain with reduced prices for army personnel. It is patronized as well by residents of remote areas.

Shertok, Marcia: Absent-minded photographer.

Shertok, Moshe: Later Moshe Sharett. Suave first Foreign Minister, second Prime Minister of Israel. Overshadowed by Ben-Gurion. Nephew of Joseph Chertok (my grandfather).

Sherut: Pack 'em into a Mercedes and cowboy drivers head 'em out. Inexpensive, speedy taxi transport between major cities. Not door-to-door.

Sherut Leumi: National Service. Full-time, 1- or 2-year work in education, health, or the like as an alternative to bearing arms for religious, 18-year-old girls.

Sheshbesh: Backgammon, more popular than chess or checkers as an Israeli pastime.

Sh'huna(t): Neighborhood.

Shikun, -im (pl.): Neighborhood(s); usually lower-middle-class.

Shishi: Sixth of seven who are honored by being called to say the Torah blessings on Shabbat.

Shlichim (Shaliach sing.): Official overseas emissaries responsible for encouraging *aliya* and fund-giving but sometimes less responsible for their word.

Shm'a (Shema): Hear! The first word of the central Jewish affirmation of God's unity: "Hear, O Israel, the Lord is our God, the Lord is One." It is spoken by Jews on their deathbed.

Shmalz (Yiddish): Chicken fat. Metonomy for Jewish sentimentality.

Shmutz (Yiddish pejorative): Dirt.

Shohat, Avraham: Perennial Labor Party Mayor of Arad.

Shtetl (Yiddish): Small Jewish town in Eastern Europe. Extinct.

Shul (Yiddish): Synagogue.

Shvili: Son of. Equivalent name-ending in Soviet Georgia for ". . . son" in English. Ya'acob Yacobshvili = Jacob Jacobson.

Siddur, -im (pl.): Jewish prayerbook.

Skokie: Brookline West.

Slowly, Slowly: Hebrish for "take it easy." A shade less ear-offending than "feefty-feefty" (a fair compromise).

Smicha: Rabbinic ordination (literally "support").

Sochnut: See "Jewish Agency."

Sofer: Writer. In the Torah world, a scribe of sacred texts and religious documents.

Sofrut: The study and practice of the skills of the *sofer*.

Soloveitchik, Rabbi Joseph: The most influential Orthodox thinker in America. *Lonely Man of Faith* is his most accessible text.

Souk (Pronounced "Shuk"): Outdoor department store. An adventure.

Strand, The: Labyrinthine used book store in Manhattan.

Sukkot(h): Festival of Booths, a harvest holiday week that follows shortly after Yom Kippur.

Sylvester: A partying impulse that accosts secular Israelis at the turn of the Gregorian year.

Talat: The *haredi* community in Yeroham; an acronym for "Spreading Torah throughout the Land."

Tami: Ethnic Moroccan political party.

Tammuz, Benjamin: Israeli novelist, born in Russia in 1919.

Tanach: The Bible, acronym for Torah, Prophets, Writings.

Tel: Prominent, flat-topped mound indicating prior habitation in an earlier period. Archaeologist's turf.

Temple: Twice-destroyed center of Jewish sacrificial cult. Also, oddly enough, most Reform synagogues.

Territories, The: Difficult to conceive that a patch the extent of 1½ Rhode Islands could be so called. Yet another rubric for the historic Jewish heartland with its conspicuous Arab majority. It borders on Jordan. (See West Bank.)

Tevach: Massacre.

Tiberias: Resort city on the Sea of Galilee. Traditionally, one of the four sacred Jewish cities of the Holy Land. It still boasts hot springs and hot controversies over building and burial sites.

Toda Raba(h): Thank you very much.

Tora(h): Bible. Jewish learning.

Torat Moshe: Torah of Moshe (an ultra-orthodox grammar school in Yeroham).

Tsadik: A saintly man.

Tsahal: Acronym for the Israel Defense Forces.

Tsedaka: *Mitzva* of giving alms or assistance to the poor. Unlike "charity," the word's root is not "love" but "justice," the point being that *tsedaka* depends less upon feeling than on duty.

T'shuva: Repentance, turning.

Tsin: Distinguished. Name of a dramatic gorge in the Negev.

Tsitsit, -ot (pl.): Ritual fringe at four corners of undergarment worn by Jewish men.

U.I.A.: United Israel Appeal; Canada's financial funnel to Israel.

U.J.A.: United Jewish Appeal; American Jewish $-raising.

Ulpan: School for intensive training, most popularly, of Hebrew.

U/U's: Unitarian/Universalists good-doing folks. Emerson Lives.

Vayetze: "And he went . . ." The opening word and title assigned to the weekly reading of the Torah that features Jacob's ladder.

Via Dolorosa: In Jerusalem's Old City, the traditional route of Jesus carrying the cross.

Villa, -ot (pl.): A detached residence with a garden. Much more modest in Israel than on the northern shore of the Mediterranean.

Wadi (Arabic): A dry riverbed.

Weizmann, Chaim: Distinguished scientist, life-long Zionist, outflanked politician, and first President of Israel.

Weizmann, Ezer: Centrist Member of Knesset noted for good rapport with Arabs.

Wences, Señor: "How do you feel?" "All right." "All right?" "ALL RIGHT!"

West Bank: Area captured by Israel in 1967 adjacent to Jordan. Historical Judea and Samaria, it contains 600,000 Arabs and scattered Jewish settlements.

Who is a Jew?: According to *halacha*, someone born of a Jewish mother who has not formally converted to another faith. Most non-orthodox offer more flexible replies.

W.I.Z.O.: Women's International Zionist Organization. Women who donate much time and money for good Israeli causes.

W.U.J.S.: World Union of Jewish Students, a cultural institute for young, professional prospective immigrants. In Arad.

Ya'akov: Jacob, one of the three patriarchs. Literally, "follow."

Yad Vashem: Memorial and Museum of Holocaust in Jerusalem.

Yahad: Together. New, centrist political party headed by Ezer Weizmann that won three seats in the 1984 Knesset elections.

Yankel (Yiddish): Affectionate nickname for Ya'akov (Jacob).

Yarkon: Tel Aviv's Mississippi.

Yediot Aharonot: Latest News. Israel's major circulation tabloid.

Yehoshua, A. B.: Much-translated, outstanding contemporary Israeli novelist.

Yemin Moshe: Begun by Sir Moses (Moshe) Montefiore in 1860, it was the first Jewish district in the bandit-ridden area beyond the old walls of Jerusalem. Intended for bold-hearted artisans, it now calls for more cash than courage.

Yerida: Emigration from Israel. Painful symptom of Zionism's chronic crisis.

Yeroham (Yeruham): "Given mercy." A town of 6,500 in the Negev.

Yerushalayim: Jerusalem. City of Peace, the capital of Israel and traditionally the focus of Jewish historical consciousness. In various ways, a San Francisco to Tel Aviv's Los Angeles.

Yeshiva, -ot (pl.): Traditional center for Jewish religious study.

Yeshivat Hesder: A *yeshiva* that hosts a *hesder* program.

Yishuv: The pre-State, permanent Jewish settlements in Palestine. A term that today overbrims with Ashkenazi nostalgia.

Yom Atzmaut: Israeli Independence Day. Fireworks and old Palmach campfire ditties every year in May.

Yom Kippur: Day of Atonement. Most solemn day in the Jewish year.

Yom Kippur War: Initiated by Egypt and Syria on Yom Kippur 1973, it succeeded in expelling surprised Israeli forces from the Nile basin, thus scoring a limited military but major psychological victory for the Egyptians.

Yordim: Those who descend. Derisive term for emigrants from Israel.

Yored: Singular of *yordim*.

Zach, Natan: Prominent Israeli poet.

Zevel: Garbage.

Zionism: Ideology of Jewish nationalism. Sometimes confused with capitalism, communism, racism, Judaism, and philanthropy.

Zionist: Supporter of Israel as a Jewish State. That one can choose to reside in the Diaspora and remain a genuine Zionist is a curious proposition, subject to ongoing controversy.

M.A.
Penn 1959